Heroic Parenting

Heroic Parenting

An Essential Guide to Raising Safe, Savvy, Confident Kids

For Parents of Children 0 to 9

CJ Scarlet

© 2020 CJ Scarlet

Every effort has been made by the author and publisher to ensure that the information contained in this book was correct as of press time. The author and publisher hereby disclaim and do not assume liability for any injury, loss, damage, or disruption caused by errors or omissions, regardless of whether any errors or omissions result from negligence, accident, or any other cause. Readers are encouraged to verify any information contained in this book prior to taking any action on the information.

For rights and permissions, please contact:
CJ Scarlet
cj@cjscarlet.com

Table of Contents

Intro: If You Skip This Section, a Baby Llama Will Cry 1

Part I: The People in Your Child's Circle **15**
Chapter 1 The Skinny on Predators 17
Chapter 2 Stranger Danger... Not So Fast! 21
Chapter 3 Siblings, Peers & Older Kids 25
Chapter 4 Adults Closest to You and Your Child 30
Chapter 5 Child Caregivers 37
Chapter 6 Other Adults & Authority Figures 46

Part II: Where Danger Lurks **53**
Chapter 7 Bullying 55
Chapter 8 Digital Dangers 80
Chapter 9 Sexual Molestation and Assault 104
Chapter 10 Child Abductions 113

Part III: How to Talk to Kids at Their Level **127**
Chapter 11 Infants up to 24 Months 131
Chapter 12 Young Children 2 to 5 137
Chapter 13 Children 6 to 9 170
Chapter 14 Children with Disabilities 205

Part IV: Essential Life Lessons to Keep Your Child Safe **229**
Chapter 15 Fostering Your Child's Confidence & Self-Esteem 231
Chapter 16 Your Child's Three Superpowers 240

Chapter 17 Fighting Like a Rabid Tasmanian Devil · 246
Chapter 18 Daily Sharing & Family Meetings · 251
Chapter 19 Badass Grandma's Final Thoughts · 260

About the Author · 263
Acknowledgements · 265
Appendix: If Your Child Has Been Sexually Abused · 267
End Notes · 287

INTRO

If You Skip This Section, a Baby Llama Will Cry

All right, all right. No baby llamas will actually *cry* if you don't read this section. But they may get their feelings deeply hurt, so for heaven's sake, please read this section. Seriously, it sets the groundwork for all the chapters that follow.

I want to begin by complimenting you on your incredible intelligence and taste in books. *Heroic Parenting: An Essential Guide to Raising Safe, Savvy, Confident Kids* is the most comprehensive manual available to parents who want to empower their kids ages 0 through 9 to avoid danger and teach them to protect and defend themselves from predators and bullies.

This Isn't Your Momma's Parenting Book Because You Ain't Your Momma

Dr. Spock is rolling over in his grave, I'm sure, over the mere existence of this book.[1] Put flatly, it's as irreverent as it gets. This "gallows humor" is my way of dealing with distressing topics so that I—and you—don't get lost in the darkness.

I did remove the swearing that I used liberally in the other version of this book—*Badass Parenting: An Irreverent Guide to Raising Safe, Savvy, Confident Kids*. However, know that while the swearing has been redacted in this version, the wisdom has most certainly not!

I wrote the book to be snarky very intentionally; it's mainly for GenXers and Millennials (and the generations that follow) and, well, it's hard as the dickens to get your attention. Your world

---

[1] Dr. Benjamin Spock, not to be confused with Mr. Spock from Star Trek, was a pediatrician who wrote a mega bestselling book in 1946 entitled *The Common Sense Book of Baby and Child Care* that encouraged parents to pick up their kids once in a while. The book radically advised parents to see their kids as individuals, not just tiny slaves, and to be affectionate towards them.

(today) isn't even remotely close to the world I lived in when I was parenting back in the 80s and 90s.

I'm not saying there weren't school shootings and bullies to deal with, but it wasn't, like, IN YOUR FACE EVERY SINGLE SECOND OF THE DAY NO MATTER WHERE YOU LOOKED! AAAAAHHHHHH!

I watch my daughter-in-law Bekki struggle every day—not so much with parenting; she's got a solid handle on that—but with the immense pressure she feels bearing down on her to compete with the (alleged) super moms on social media, and in the media in general, who appear to be, do, and have it all.

Yeah, the Interweb is great and all, but it also makes it appear that every other mother (but you) is a pro at whipping out over-the-top cupcake designs and drives a minivan so sparkling it looks like it was cleaned by a serial killer trying to cover a crime scene. As parents, you're constantly reminded how badly you're failing because you're bringing (gasp!) store-bought cupcakes to the kindergarten Valentine's Day party and your car looks like the crime scene *before* the serial killer broke out the Shop-Vac®.

And the nastiness online! Goodness, people! What happened to common courtesy? Every photo, video, opinion, or frustration shared by a parent online is taken out of context, dissected, distorted, and then harshly judged by a jury of their peers. Doesn't matter which side you're on, half the people not only disagree with it, they're going to insist that you're Hitler and should be summarily shot.

It doesn't stop with the media, though. There are the older generations of parents, many of whom are now grandparents, who feel like it's their job to hand out advice to every young mom and dad they encounter about how they handled kids "back in the day."[2] Sure, back in the day that kind of behavior may have been perfectly fine, but if you tried that now, it could land you in the headlights of Child Protective Services or the "popo."[3] Almost as bad, it could make you the newest "bad mom" meme on Instagram, guaranteeing you'll be harassed by trolls into infinity.

---

[2] Just so you know, when your toddler's pitching a fit in the grocery store and that sweet old man sidles up and says, "Back in my day, I used to slap the silly out of my kids when they did that" or some other such nonsense, you'll feel better about yourself if you just let it slide instead of unleashing the hounds of Hades upon his ignorant, unsuspecting butt. Back in his day, that really WAS how it was done.

[3] Popo = The police.

Heroic Parenting

Never have so many judged so many others so often based on so little evidence and aforethought. No wonder Bekki and every other young mom I've talked with feels like they can't possibly win this rigged parenting game.

Well, I'll let you in on a little secret: It's all an elaborate hoax. There are no perfect moms (or dads) and no one, not one single parent out there, knows with certainty what they're doing. We're all just winging it and praying we don't raise a serial killer (although on the plus side, his car would be very, very clean. Just sayin').

Know that *I see you*. I see you doing the very best you can under tremendous pressure, and I think you're doing one heck of a job. So stop comparing your hot messy insides to other people's seemingly-together outsides.

Just like a Horror Movie, Only with a Happier Ending

When writing this book, I struggled mightily with how to present the facts about childhood danger without scaring you so badly that you'd put the book down and never touch it again.

It's hard to discuss subjects as harrowing as sexual abuse, bullying, and abduction without dragging you and your child into a dark place that can lead to hopelessness and helplessness, which then morph into apathy and paralysis. Definitely not a productive place to be when you're trying to protect your little one. I don't believe terrifying you will spur you to action, as most experts and authors on these topics appear to believe.

After reading this book, I want you to feel confident in your new-found ability to talk candidly with your child without scaring her to death. So, I chose to take a different tack in *Heroic Parenting*. I chose to focus on what this book is really about—*love* and *empowerment*. Your love and desire to protect your child are more powerful than fear and they're your best "weapons" for protecting her.

Yes, I'm going to let you know what you're up against but in a way that's enlightening and not designed to sensationalize the information and scare the daylights out of you.

Speaking of which, I am going to scare you initially because I want to juxtapose[4] the petrifying facts you'll find on the Internet and evening news with the more realistic data based on actual studies. So, let's begin.

---

[4] My darling niece pointed out that I tend to use a lot of "fancy" words and advised me to dumb it down. I LOVE using just the right word to make a point and know you're an intelligent person open to learning new terms, so I'll

The Awful, Horrible, Terrifying Facts

Did you know?

- Half of all children in the world experience some form of emotional, physical, or sexual abuse by the time they're 18.[i]

- Survivors of child sexual abuse are 10 to 13 times more likely to attempt suicide.[ii]

- Abusive experiences in childhood create fresh victims and predators, who often pass these experiences down from generation to generation.

- Over half of the human trafficking cases active in the US in 2018 involved children.[iii]

- This is the one that used to keep me up at night: There are hundreds of thousands of predators on the streets and online at any given moment trolling for victims.[iv]

- While kids today participate in regular active shooter drills at school, only the tiniest fraction get body safety training.[5] When they do, the focus is often on "stranger danger" when, in fact, over 90 percent of molestations and assaults are committed by people they know.[v]

Quivering with fear yet? You're not alone. Most parents feel anxious when confronted with these jaw-dropping facts. They feel overwhelmed by the enormity of the problem and by their own lack of knowledge about how to prepare their kids to live in a world that's often hostile to them.

Parents are doing the very best they can, but in an effort to not scare their kids, they aren't being honest about the dangers they face. As such, they're making their children more vulnerable to predators. It's time to change this self-defeating, no-win situation and give your children what they need to live safe, confident, happy lives.

And Now for Something Completely Different

Okay, you can stop hyperventilating and take a deep breath. The world isn't as bad as the media makes it sound and you and your child actually have the power to keep her safe.

---

be adding footnotes to explain the meaning of words and acronyms that might not be clear to every reader. Oh, and "juxtapose" means to compare two objects to identify the differences.

5 Body safety training generally focuses on basic skills, like saying "no" to adults, what to do to get away from predators, and who to tell if something bad happens.

Heroic Parenting

Let's balance the terrifying statistics listed above with a bit of perspective:

- Of the 424,066 children reported as missing or exploited in 2018, about 94 percent simply misunderstood directions or miscommunicated their plans, were lost, or ran away.[vi]

- 4 percent were kidnapped by family members involved in a custody dispute.[vii]

- 1 percent were abducted by non-family members, usually during the commission of a crime, such as robbery or sexual assault. The kidnapper was often someone the child knew.[viii]

- Only around 105 children are kidnapped each year in the stereotypical stranger abductions that are sensationalized on the evening news.[ix] *(Of course, that's 105 too many!)* Of these, just 65 were complete strangers to the children (the rest were "slight acquaintances," meaning the victim had known them for only a short time or didn't know them well).[x]

- A whopping 99.8 percent of the children who go missing (whether abducted or runaways) make it back home![xi]

- The number of identified incidents of child sexual abuse decreased by at least 47 percent from 1993 to 2006.[xii]

- Rates of sexual assault and domestic violence have been declining for decades and are now a quarter or less of their past peaks.[xiii]

- Since the early 1990s, the rate for all crimes—violent and non-violent against both children and adults—has plummeted by up to 77 percent.[xiv]

- According to cognitive psychologist and author Steven Pinker, "Violence has been in decline for thousands of years, and today we may be living in the most peaceable era *in the existence of our species.*"[6] (Italics mine.)

We've Got It All Wrong

Despite these encouraging facts, nearly 90 percent of adults say they feel *less* safe than when they were growing up, even though today's crime rates are at a level not seen since the 1960s![xv]

So if crime rates in the US and the world in general have gone down so dramatically, why do we remain convinced that our kids are in grave peril if we let them out of our sight? I think it's

---

6 From *The Better Angels of Our Nature: Why Violence Has Declined.*

because the teasers for the evening news assure us that if we don't watch their programs, we'll miss details of the latest ghastly shooting spree or never learn critical things like the three ways our toaster oven is plotting to murder our entire family while we sleep. It could also be that we binge-watch too many horrific crime dramas and shows filled with apocalyptic images of dead people who want to eat our brains.[7]

We also worry because we're genetically hardwired to pay more attention to things that *appear* to pose an imminent threat than to stuff that seems unlikely to happen, say, being killed by a vending machine or a falling coconut (which happens more often than you'd think). Parents are terrified of terrorist attacks and serial killers, when in fact their child is far more likely to be killed by a rogue champagne cork. I mean sure, it *could* happen, but are you really going to wrap your child in bubble wrap and make him waddle to school like a drunken troll every day?

Bubble Wrap? Hmmm…

Clearly, you love and want to protect your child from harm or you wouldn't be reading this book. You may worry about her safety and want to arm her with information, but you don't want to leave her feeling petrified. You may have no idea what to say or how to say it so she'll actually listen to and apply your cautionary advice.

Face it, you're not your child's BFF[8] and you shouldn't be. You're meant to be her protector, role model, gatekeeper, boundary teacher, motivator, sounding board, comforter, and yes, accountability holder when needed.

You may want to wrap your child in a protective bubble and defend her from every harm but doing so could emotionally cripple her and make her more, not less, vulnerable to predators. Teaching your child to fear every stranger and new situation actually inhibits her own intuitive wisdom that tells her when she's in danger.

Don't be afraid your sweetums will lose her innocence if you teach her about body safety. Won't happen. This is a cold, cruel world we live in and your kid knows more than you realize. In fact, she'll be empowered and far safer when she knows what the dangers are and how to meet them head-on. It's waaaay better to teach your child about sexual abuse, for example, than to pick up the pieces later because she didn't know how to protect herself.

---

7 My biggest problem with being turned into a zombie would be all that walking! I'm frankly exhausted just thinking about it.
8 BFF = Best friends forever.

And don't think she's too young either. The most likely age for a child to be sexually abused is between the ages of 3 and 8. That means you need to begin the body safety conversation as soon as she's verbal and keep it up until she leaves your care as a young adult.

A Word about Worry

I'm going to stop for a minute to talk about worry and how to release it because, frankly, it's freaking you and your child out and making the situation worse. While it's important to be informed about the dangers your child faces, such knowledge is destructive when it spirals into worry and obsession over his safety.

Worrying is not a sustainable state; a normal person simply can't maintain that anxious state of mind and remain sane. Plus, it's shrinking your brain mass, making you age faster, and lowering your IQ. Look it up; it's science.[9]

As I wrote earlier, worrying leads to feelings of helplessness and hopelessness, which are paralyzing. So to escape these awful feelings, many people dive into denial and avoid the subject altogether. But denial of danger doesn't enhance your child's safety; it compromises it.

Author and personal protection expert Gavin de Becker notes that "Worry fights off that dreadful feeling that there's nothing we can do, because worrying feels like we're doing something…" Just reading that observation helped me kick most of my worry to the curb!

De Becker goes on, "When faced with some worry or uncertain fear, ask yourself: 'Am I responding to something in my environment or to something in my imagination?'" He advises that the best antidote to worry is *action*, which he addresses in his outstanding book *Protecting the Gift*.

Here's what I do when my mind starts wigging out at 3 a.m. as I envision something horrible happening to my grandbabies. As soon as I catch my thoughts spinning out of control, I blink my eyes closed and say to myself *"Control-Alt-Delete"* and then open my eyes. Those of you who aren't complete Luddites[10] know that pressing "Control-Alt-Delete" on your keyboard will enable you

---

[9] Seriously, a guy named Don Joseph Goewey wrote a whole book about it called *The End of Stress: Four Steps to Rewire Your Brain*.

[10] A Luddite is a person who fears new technology. The term "Luddite" comes from an Industrial Revolution-era group, of which Ned Ludd was a member. He believed machines would cause workers' wages to be decreased. The mob ended up burning a number of factories in protest. Luddites are not to be confused with thrifty people who don't buy the newest iPhone the second it's released, choosing instead to withstand the mockery of their peers, who in turn would rather spend $1000 on a new phone and ditch their perfectly good older phone rather than pay down their student loan debt.

to reboot your computer. Do this blinking exercise as many times as it takes until the boogeyman in your head goes away.

Okay, you think it sounds stupid or too simple, but I'm telling you there's something about mentally thinking "Control-Alt-Delete" and blinking your eyes that takes the needle off that murdery broken record playing in your head.

Stress expert Don Joseph Goewey[11] uses a different technique called "The Clear Button" to stop worry in its tracks. He notes that, "Nature gave us a 90-second window to bust stressful thinking before it takes a long walk off a short pier." The more you use techniques that divert stressful thoughts (like "The Clear Button" or my clever little blink mantra), the stronger the synapses that end worry become.

I love the way Goewey explains how this works: "The part of the brain that causes stress reactions literally has the intelligence of a toddler. And every parent knows you don't stop a tantrum by appealing to a child's logic. You distract the child. This tool [The Clear Button] distracts the terrible 2-year-old in your brain from casting you off the deep end."

So next time you can't sleep because you have visions of predatory sugarplums dancing in your head, try using the "Control-Alt-Delete" maneuver or "The Clear Button" and get some sleep!

Because I Said So! Or, Why You Should Listen to Me

Who on earth am I to hand out advice to parents on how to keep their kids safe? Well, I'm a victim advocate, danger expert, and author of two books on personal safety. I'm also the survivor of childhood molestations and sexual assault as a college freshman, offering me the unenviable perspective of a crime victim.

I served as executive director of a child advocacy center for abused children and as Director of Victims Issues for the NC Attorney General's Office. I hold an interdisciplinary master's degree in human violence. I volunteer for SafeChild's "Funny Tummy" program, which teaches first graders about how to say "no" and tell if they encounter dangerous people. I also continue my work with survivors of child abuse, domestic violence, and sexual assault, so when it comes to discussing abuse and danger, I'm considered an expert.

Finally (and most importantly), I raised two sons and am the doting Grandma to three precocious toddlers. I've helped thousands of crime victims, but when confronted with the simple

---

11 Author of *The End of Stress: Four Steps to Rewire Your Brain*.

innocence of my grandchildren, I felt utterly helpless. How to protect them? More importantly, how to teach them to protect themselves?

Heroic Parenting is my way of doing just that and, in the process, helping YOU protect your loved ones too.

Why You Should Read This Book

Throughout your darling's childhood, he's going to encounter tons of people, most of whom you both know fairly well—at daycare and pre-school, on playdates, at events, in your own home—and any one of them could be a predator. I don't care how alert you think you are; you can't keep him in your sight every second. It's not possible and it's not even remotely healthy.

Your child's best bet to stay safe is for you to teach him how to protect and defend himself when you're not around. Forewarned is forearmed, as they say. By reading this book and following my advice, you're doing the one, most important thing you can do to protect your child from harm—*taking action*.

Research shows that children who are taught to protect and defend themselves—by doing things like yelling, running away, saying "no," or by fighting—are less attractive to predators and stand a significantly greater chance of escaping an abusive situation or potential abduction.

Educating yourself and your child is super liberating and the positive seeds you plant in his mind today will blossom into positive behaviors that will serve him throughout his life. Rather than worrying about nebulous[12] dangers, you'll know the facts, and once you teach your child what I share in this book, you'll sleep better at night knowing you've taught him to be a little baby hero who can take care of himself.

As former slave and abolitionist Frederick Douglass observed, and I'm paraphrasing here—"It's far easier to raise strong children than to repair broken adults." I'm convinced that if I'd been taught that it was okay to say "no" in situations where I felt uncomfortable, 99 percent of the crummy things that happened to me as a kid and teenager would never have occurred and I wouldn't have had to grapple with PTS[13] for most of my life.

---

12 I use the word nebulous instead of "unclear" because I like the way it refers to a whole cloud of uncertainty. AND it's a prettier word.
13 PTS = Post-traumatic stress, once called post-traumatic stress disorder.

BTW,[14] if you yourself are the survivor of child abuse, absolutely incorporate what you learn in this book to your own parenting repertoire.[15] It's your best chance to break the cycle! Be excited about having this opportunity to learn how to step up and protect your child in a way you weren't.

What *Heroic Parenting* Will Teach You

Before I began writing this book, I surveyed parents, grandparents, and caregivers about their top concerns for their children's safety and the same questions kept cropping up. Here are the top five:

1. How do I teach my children about danger without scaring them to death?
2. *What* do I teach them to empower them to protect and defend themselves?
3. What are the signs my child is being bullied or abused?
4. How do I get my kids to come to me if something happens to them?
5. How do I make them actually listen to me and apply what I teach them?

Heroic Parenting will answer these questions and more so parents can confidently empower their children from birth up to age 9. (I'll publish a second book in the *Heroic Parenting* series in 2021 for parents of kids 10 to 18.)

Here's how the book is laid out:

First, I go deep and dark by addressing the dangers your child faces head-on. In Part I on *The People in Your Child's Circle*, I talk about the categories of predators that might have access to your child. In Part II on *Where Danger Lurks*, I discuss bullying, digital dangers, sexual abuse, and kidnapping, including who the perps and victims tend to be and what to look out for. Stick with me through the heavy parts because it's essential information. The book gets MUCH lighter from there on out.

Then I move you into the more fun and empowering action sections, beginning with Part III on *How to Talk to Kids at Their Level*. This is where I tell you exactly what body safety skills your kid needs to know. Regardless of the age of your child, please be sure to read both Chapters 12 and 13 because much of what I share in the chapter for children 2 to 5 is also relevant for kids 6 to 9.[16]

---

14 BTW = By the way.
15 Repertoire = A stock of skills of behaviors a person habitually relies on.
16 Sorry; that was a confusing sentence, I know. Just trust me and read both Chapters 12 and 13. K?

In Part IV, *Essential Life Lessons to Keep Your Child Safe*, I share ways to foster your child's confidence and self-esteem and teach her some serious verbal and physical moves she can use to escape dangerous situations. I also tell you how to actually break down all this critical information through manageable, ongoing conversations and family meetings.

Finally, to ensure you know what to do if your child *is* victimized, in the Appendix on *If Your Child Has Been Sexually Abused* I cover the practical and legal steps to take once you learn something has occurred.

You'll notice that throughout the book I refer you to my website for free bonus content that'll take you deeper into the topics I cover. I'm constantly adding cool freebies and parenting hacks to my site, so visit often to see what's new and interesting.

What this book doesn't cover:

- Drug and alcohol abuse
- Hazing
- Gang violence
- Auto safety
- Firearm safety
- School shootings

I couldn't do it all, folks. There simply wasn't enough room to cover *every* danger your kid may encounter. There are literally thousands of great books on these topics that you can buy online or in any bookstore.

10 Things You'll Get from Reading This Book

I love Top 10 lists, so here's one about the benefits you'll get from this book:

1. Clarity—knowing what's true and what's not and what you need to focus on.
2. A greater ability to spot people and situations that might pose threats to your child.
3. Clear instructions on how to have crucial conversations with your child.
4. Ideas for injecting body safety advice into everyday conversations.
5. Confidence in your child's ability to protect and defend himself.

6. Information that will help you be safer too.

7. A sense of relief from knowing things are going to be okay.

8. Less worry and more sleeeeep.

9. Peace of mind.

10. Freebies! As I said, I'm going to slather you with free materials and content you can find on my website.

For the Heroic Grandparents Who Are Reading This Book

Grandparents play a special role in the life of their grandchildren and can be a major source of wisdom and support. There are currently more than 2.4 million grandparents who are now raising their grandchildren.[xvi] If you're one of them, good on you! You're the one who's responsible for teaching your little charge the information I share in this book.

Some grandparents refuse to believe their grandchildren's claims of abuse, especially if it happened at the hands of a parent, aunt, or uncle. No one wants to believe their own grown-up child could do such a thing, but it happens every day all over the world and you need to believe your grandchild.

Believing and supporting her doesn't mean you don't love your own child who was the offender. It means you love them enough to get them the help they need to stop hurting children and, yes, hold them accountable. If the abuser was a family member, you're in a unique position to put a stop to the abuse, protect and support the victim, and ensure the perp never again has free access to the victim.

Be there for your family. You are the matriarch/patriarch and can set the tone for how all this goes down.

Another great way to help your grandkids is to buy this book for your children who are parents and ask them to read it and apply what they learn.

A Few Disclaimers

Every single chapter of this book could be a book unto itself. I've tried to give you the basics and I encourage you to dive more deeply into whatever topics you're especially interested in. Under the Resources tab on my website,[17] I list a number of excellent books, websites, and advocacy

---

17 www.cjscarlet.com/resources

Heroic Parenting

organizations, but the list is hardly comprehensive, so do your own homework to find other good books on the topics I cover here.

Throughout *Heroic Parenting*, I mainly use the male pronoun to refer to predators because about 95 percent of the time the perps are male. Women can and do perpetrate some sex crimes against children, but the numbers are very low. (Although, when it comes to physical child abuse and neglect, women are even more likely than men to be the abusers. A pox on them all!)

I alternately use "she" and "he" when talking about your child, although I try not to switch the pronouns within sections, which would give you whiplash.

To be clear, when I talk about victim dynamics in this book, I'm in no way suggesting that being victimized is a failure on the part of the survivor. While some children make better targets because they're vulnerable and/or unprepared or unable to protect themselves, it's NEVER their fault. It's always the offenders' wrong actions that are to blame. Period.

Be sure to read the footnotes, which are fun and provide extra details you need to know.

The names and other details of people featured in this book have been changed to protect their identities.

One final disclaimer: this book was written to help you teach your child to protect and defend herself. If you faithfully use the techniques contained within these pages, you'll help her minimize dangerous encounters and she'll likely be safer. However, the advice found in *Heroic Parenting* cannot protect every child in every situation. Use the ideas found here when you can, and your common sense and best judgment always. You know your child better than anyone and are the authority on what information she needs and can handle.

BE the parent your child deserves!

Love,

Badass Grandma

PART I

The People in Your Child's Circle

In this section I talk about the general categories of people your child will likely interact with as he grows up and the threats they may pose.

CHAPTER 1

The Skinny on Predators[18]

Who *Are* These People?

Some people like to comfort themselves by believing that predators are complete monsters who lurk in the shadows. But in reality, predators look like ordinary people and come from all walks of life. They're shared ride drivers, they're teachers, they're religious figures, they're high school jocks, they're grandmas, they're ballerinas and firemen and even our partners.

Let's look at what we know about predators:

- Up to 95 percent of child sexual abusers are male and virtually all of them are heterosexual.[19][xvii]

- The younger the victim, the more likely their abuser is a family member.

- On average, sex offenders begin molesting others by age 15 and will go on to molest an average of 117 children.[xviii]

- The abuser may be in an adult sexual relationship and still have a predilection[20] for children.

- Predators often have a strong sense of entitlement, believing life owes them something and that people exist for them to use and abuse.

---

18 Skinny = Inside knowledge.
19 Virtually all sexual predators are heterosexual, meaning they're not gay. In fact, 98 percent of male sexual abusers identify as heterosexual. Sexual preference has nothing to do with pedophilia. Straight men who are pedophiles may molest girls as well as boys.
20 Predilection = A preference for something.

- They may have difficulty forming intimate relationships with adults and choose to create relationships with children because they can control them and feel powerful.

- They often lack empathy and don't care how their actions make their victims feel.

- They may have experienced a troubled childhood and/or sexual abuse themselves.

How Predators Groom Their Victims

Predators use grooming tactics to manipulate their targets and gain their trust. They're pros at quickly assessing the strengths and weaknesses of their chosen targets to decide which tactics will work best on each child.

According to author Steve Kovacs, the child may crave attention, acceptance, love, or friendship. He may have material needs, like the need for money, food, or clothes. Or the child may covet luxury items, such as digital or electronic games and movies.[21]

Kovacs notes that pedophiles work hard to learn the names of popular rock or rap stars, the latest fashions, and who stars in kids' favorite television shows or movies so they can be seen as "cool" and relatable. The perp will try to meet as many of her needs as he can, patiently plotting to assault her in the future. When a predator showers a child with attention and gifts, she naturally feels grateful. She may also feel guilty if she doesn't reciprocate with affection or doesn't want to keep a secret for the predator.

What Grooming Looks Like

According to ChildLuresPrevention.com, "Early grooming efforts by sexual predators seek to determine if the child has a stable home life or one where the family is facing challenges like poverty, divorce, illness, drugs, homelessness, etc. Children lacking stability at home are at higher risk for sexual abuse, as there is usually more access to the child and opportunities to abuse the child."[xix]

Some child molesters prefer to target kids on the brink of puberty because it's easy for them to prey on their sexual ignorance and curiosity. ChildLuresPrevention.com quotes one sex offender, who said: "Give me a kid who knows nothing about sex, and you've given me my next victim." The website adds that "Child molesters have admitted they are less likely to abuse children who have a basic understanding of sex education, including knowledge of the proper names for private parts."[xx]

---

[21] From *Protect Your Kids! The Simple Keys to Children's Safety and Survival.*

Here are some grooming behaviors predators use that you should watch for:[22]

- Seeking out children who lack self-confidence and have low self-esteem.
- Targeting kids who aren't adequately supervised by their parents or other caregivers.
- Spending time alone with the child, just hanging out or attending outings with him.
- Giving gifts, favors, or special privileges.
- Asking the child to keep secrets.
- Touching, tickling, patting, stroking, or wrestling with the child to desensitize him to the predator's touch.
- Hugging, kissing, and sharing other physical affection as a prelude to sexual contact.
- Telling sexual jokes, showing pornography, or asking sexual questions.
- Making the child feel responsible for any sexual misconduct that occurs.

You're His Target Too

Know this—predators don't just groom their victims. No, they can also groom the child's parents and other family members and friends to gain their trust and greater access to the child. A predator does this by charming the adults in order to convince them he's a stand-up guy and role model. Many a perp have befriended a child's parents, particularly single moms, just to gain access to their children. In many cases, pedophiles marry women to be their "beards"—their cover stories—so people will think they're solid, upstanding citizens who can be trusted around kids.

Keeping Grooming in Check

Don't be afraid to ask your child if anyone has asked her to keep secrets, which the predator may use to test and control her. For example, the perp may give your child ice cream when she comes to visit and warn her not to tell you or she'll get in trouble. This secret creates a bond between them and acts as a "feeler," meaning he's testing her willingness to keep a secret so he can escalate his behavior at a later time.

Some perps skip over the charm offensive and jump right into threatening your child that if she doesn't keep his assaults a secret, he'll hurt her, her siblings, her friends, her pets, or even you,

---
22 From www.ChildLuresPrevention.com.

the parent. He may also use shame and guilt to keep your child from talking, telling her that she'll get in trouble or be blamed for what happened.[23]

Sadly, some predators manipulate their targets so thoroughly that the victims may come to believe the predator genuinely loves them. In return, they develop strong, loving feelings and come to depend on their abusers. This is especially common in cases such as child sexual abuse involving a parent. If the child is emotionally and physically dependent on the predator, it's easy to fall into his trap and it becomes more difficult to resist or report him.

What Predators Really Want

Bottom line: Predators have only one interest—to satisfy their own need for power, control, or sexual satisfaction. They enjoy their victims' response to the acts as much as the acts themselves. They seek children who respond as they desire—either by fighting, which allows the predators to overpower them, or by complying, which enables the predators to complete their crimes with no resistance.

When a perp[24] assaults a child, it's usually about control—of the child's behavior, body, emotions, or boundaries. Predators will usually begin by taking control of little things, such as running the conversation or telling inappropriate jokes to gauge the child's reaction and, if he doesn't object, the perp will move on to increasingly invasive behavior.

Predators are also on the lookout for the means to commit their crimes. They may watch a child closely for a period of time, from minutes to months. They're always looking for the best locations to commit their assaults that offer the greatest secrecy and ability to flee quickly and easily. They're counting on the child to be terrified and compliant.

Above all, predators want victims who won't report the crime.

Badass Grandma's Two Cents

In the remaining chapters in Part I, I go into greater depth on the exact types of predators there are out there so you can be more aware and vigilant when your child is exposed to people in these categories.

You're doing great! Keep reading.

---

23 Dirtbag move, I know, but VERY effective.
24 Perp = Perpetrator.

CHAPTER 2

Stranger Danger... Not So Fast!

The 99.999+ Percent

I'm going to blow a few minds here by saying that teaching your child to fear strangers by harping about "stranger danger" is, well, downright dangerous.

Virtually 100 percent of the world is made up of people your child doesn't know, and nearly every one of those gazillion people *pose absolutely no threat to her.*

Kids often believe strangers look "different" (in a strange way) from people they know. For example, in the HBO special "How to Raise a Street-Smart Child,"[25] the children featured thought a stranger was someone who appeared threatening and evil, and looked "mean and ugly."

Teaching her that strangers shouldn't be trusted can cause her to feel anxious and afraid when she encounters people she hasn't met before.

Your Very Worst Nightmare

So what is that we *really* afraid of when we warn our kids not to talk to strangers? I don't know about you, but I'm quite frankly terrified that a stranger will molest or abuse my grandchildren, and maybe even abduct and murder them.

But consider this: According to the US Department of Justice, of all children under age 5 murdered in the 30 years from 1976-2005:[xxi]

- 31 percent were killed by fathers.
- 29 percent were killed by mothers.

---

25 This movie is a bit dated, having been released in 1987, but more recent research shows that kids react just as recklessly today.

- 7 percent were killed by other relatives.
- 23 percent were killed by male acquaintances (people known to them).
- Just 3 percent were killed by strangers.

The moral of the story according to the report? *Your safest bet is to leave your child with a stranger.*

Seriously though, it's every parent's worst nightmare—a faceless, nameless monster snatches your child from you and escapes with her into the mist, forcing her into a sex trafficking ring, and you never see or hear from her again.

Whew! That was terrifying just writing it down. Probably as much as it was for you to read it. My gut clenches like a fist even thinking about it and I'm flooded with fear and panic for the safety of my sweet grandbabies.

Let's all take a deep breath and look again at those reassuring facts:

- Reports of missing children are down 40 percent since 1997.[xxii]
- Only about 65 children are kidnapped each year in the US by total strangers.[xxiii]
- 99.8 percent of the children who go missing *do* come home.[xxiv]

Okay, I'm breathing a little easier and hope you are too. So now that we're being more realistic about the infinitesimally small possibility that someone will abuse your darling child, let's explore why it's important to teach her how to interact with strangers.

Everyone Is a Stranger Until They're Not

Literally every single person we've ever met was once a stranger—even our parents. Your kid will meet thousands, or even tens of thousands, of people in her lifetime. A few of them will be truly bad, but most of them will be good.

And guess what? Most of the time, you won't be there to help her figure out who to trust and who to avoid. It's way better to teach your child from the time she's small how to use her intuition to assess whether that stranger (or even those she knows well) feels and acts like a safe person.

If what you really want is for your child not to go anywhere with anyone—stranger or otherwise—without your express permission, then teach her THAT, rather than scaring her into believing all strangers are dangerous.

Again, everyone's a stranger at first and your child needs to learn how to use her intuition to put people into the "safe" or "unsafe" categories so she knows who to be on guard around or avoid completely.

Teaching her how to discern who to trust takes time and ongoing conversations, which I cover next.

Playing the "Stranger Adventure" Game

One fun way to teach your child how to differentiate between safe and unsafe people is to play the "Stranger Adventure" game. You can play this with your child anytime, anywhere.

Simply watch the people around you and talk about them. (C'mon, you know you do it anyway! Just tweak your comments a bit from being catty to being open and observant about the clues they're sending out through their appearance and behavior.)

This game helps you teach your child how to critically observe people for signs that they appear safe. As you and your child watch people and talk about your impressions of them, make it clear that she should mainly focus on their actions and body language, looking for clues that a particular person deserves extra scrutiny and caution. For example, help her note when someone looks angry or aggressive, which may indicate a controlling or volatile personality, or if she feels weirded out by someone who leers at women or children as they walk by.

By closely watching people's behavior, your child will learn that just because someone's wearing a suit doesn't automatically mean he's trustworthy, any more than a person wearing a hoodie and sporting multiple body piercings means she's dangerous. Put simply, it's how a person makes your child *feel* that counts the most, and you should validate those feelings when she shares them. Talk about the clues she picked up on that prompted those feelings.

Use roleplaying to help her think through how she would react if she was approached by one of those people. Depending on your child's age, you can say, "I can see why that person makes you feel uncomfortable. I sense that too. If he tried to talk to you and you felt uncomfortable, you could say something like, 'My mom's waiting for me. I have to go.' Or, if he was making you feel afraid, you could even yell for me and run away as fast as you can to a safe person."[26]

---

26 I'll talk about safe people in Part III.

Let your child think through what she would do in each situation. Listen to her full answer and validate her impressions. If necessary, help her tweak her responses to ensure they're on target and effective.

Playing the "Stranger Adventure" game with your child will enable her to feel greater confidence when encountering strangers, knowing she can trust herself to know when someone or something doesn't feel right, and that she has the right and power to take steps to avoid or get away from them.

Who *Should* Your Child Trust?

If your child got lost in a park or at the mall, would she know whom to approach for help? Many parents tell their children to find a police officer, but the chances of one being close by at that exact moment are slim. You can also encourage your child to look for a store clerk who's wearing a badge or vest, but these people may be hard for her to spot.

If your child doesn't immediately see a police officer or store clerk, teach her to look for a woman, preferably with children or one who's older, and ask her for help. Women, as we have learned, are far less likely to be predators and are more likely to stay with the child until she's reunited with you.

Remind your child that before approaching anyone, woman, police officer, or clerk, she should watch them carefully for a moment and check in with her intuition about whether they feel "safe."

Badass Grandma's Two Cents

Now that we're clear on the fallacy of "stranger danger," in the next chapter I'll focus on people your child knows and interacts with on regular basis who are more likely to pose a threat.

CHAPTER 3

Siblings, Peers & Older Kids

You Show Me Yours and I'll Show You Mine

When I was 5, I got caught by my mom with Jerry Sechanek's[27] ear smashed up against my bare chest as he listened to my heartbeat. My mom scolded us and sent Jerry running home, propelled, I'm sure, by sheer terror that my mom would call his and report our little dalliance.[28] I felt horribly guilty, but the incident didn't squelch my sexual curiosity in the least little bit.

Over the next few years, I played "doctor" so much I could have opened my own private practice. Most of it was innocent, lighthearted, and mutual. Just two incidents weren't, and although they were slightly traumatizing, I didn't say a word for decades.

At some point in their childhood, most kids engage in sexual exploration with other children—a "you show me yours and I'll show you mine" kinda thing. Half of adults can remember engaging in "child's play" when they were kids. It's normal and to be expected since kids are insatiably curious, particularly when it comes to their bodies and those of their peers. In most cases, parents are oblivious to these activities, but sometimes the kids are caught in the act or one of the children tells on the other.

This is an awkward and unsettling situation for a parent to stumble upon, and adults are all over the board in how they react. Some brush it off or ignore it, others scold or punish the kids and warn them never to do it again. I know of one case where an 8-year-old victim of sexual abuse was actually punished after she was caught having oral sex (and by having, I mean being coerced) with her uncle who was 13. That incident stands out as starkly in her mind as the ongoing assaults did (which lasted for *10 years!*) because it was just so unfair.

---

27 Jerry, it's been, like, 55 years. Are you ghosting me? Call me, boo!
28 Dalliance = Amorous hijinks.

CJ Scarlet

When Child's Play Becomes a Crime

The general rule is if the kids are within three years of age of each other, are similar in size and emotional development, *and* it's mutually acceptable to both children, it's considered normal, innocent child's play. But when the behavior involves kids who are farther apart in age, size, or emotional maturity, or when one child is being forced to participate or is being sexually assaulted, it's considered to be abuse and may even constitute a criminal offense.

And that can be far more egregious[29] than most people imagine. While statutes vary by state, the national Sex Offender Registration and Notification Act requires juveniles of at least 14 years of age who've been convicted of aggravated sexual abuse crimes or rape to register as sex offenders. In at least one case, a 10-year-old child was convicted of sexually assaulting five younger boys and had to register as a sex offender for the rest of his life! This is serious stuff, people.

Who the Juvenile Offenders Are

People don't morph into predators the minute they turn 18. Many of them start abusing others when they're kids themselves. Shockingly, more than one-third of reported offenses against children are committed by other adolescents.[xxv] 23 percent of these young offenders are just 10 to 12 years old and 70 percent are under 16.[xxvi] Most target other kids who are younger than they are.

Juveniles who commit child-on-child sexual abuse are more likely than adults to do the following:[xxvii]

- Offend in groups with one or more co-offenders (24 percent for juveniles versus 14 percent for adults).

- Offend at a school (12 percent versus 2 percent).

- Commit sodomy[30] (13 percent versus 7 percent) and fondling (49 percent versus 42 percent).

- Target younger children under the age of 12 (59 percent of juvenile offenders versus 39 of adult offenders).

- Victimize males (25 percent versus 13 percent).

---

29 Egregious = Extraordinary, in a bad way.
30 Sodomy generally refers to oral and anal sex acts.

Children who sexually abuse are FAR more likely than the general population to have been physically, sexually, or emotionally abused or neglected themselves. Studies show that between 40 to 80 percent of youths who sexually abuse other kids have themselves been sexually abused, and that 20 to 50 percent have been physically abused.[xxviii]

Regardless of the reason young people sexually molest or assault other kids, abuse and assault by a peer or sibling can be just as frightening and traumatizing as abuse by an adult.

Who the Victims Are

- 18 percent of girls and 3 percent of boys say that by age 17 they had been victims of sexual assault or abuse at the hands of another adolescent. 15 percent of these incidents involved penetration.[xxix]
- In 43 percent of cases involving assaults on children under 6 the offenders were juveniles.[xxx]
- 84 percent of the victims of other adolescents were 6 to 11 years old.[xxxi]
- 94 percent of victims knew the juvenile offender.[xxxii]

The Dirty Little Secret No One Wants to Talk About—Abuse between Siblings

The majority (69 percent) of sex offenses committed by juveniles occur in the home.[xxxiii] When the offender is a sibling, the child victim is at greater risk of repeat abuse because he's constantly exposed to his perpetrator. In fact, sibling sexual abuse is significantly more common than parental sexual abuse and is often more intrusive and occurs over longer periods of time.[xxxiv]

That's worth repeating to make sure you heard me—*sibling sexual abuse is significantly more common than parental sexual abuse.* Got it? Good.

Sexual abuse by a sibling, which is a form of incest, can be traumatic and emotionally devastating for a child and haunt him throughout his life. Victims are known for blaming themselves and for feeling they somehow brought it on themselves or "asked for it"—by not saying "no," by being too pretty, by not resisting, by initially enjoying it, etc.

The buried trauma can cause survivors to experience long-term mental health problems, trouble forming healthy relationships, sexual dysfunction, and other symptoms of post-traumatic stress.

When child victims tell on their abusive sibling—which isn't often—some parents are supportive and proactive, working to stop the abuse and get counseling for both children. Others may react with shock, disbelief, or denial, which can further enable the abuse. It's very rare for parents to report their abusive child to authorities.

I get it. Really, I do. There aren't many things worse than learning one of your children is molesting or even sexually assaulting one of your other children. But if you think or know that one child is being abused by another, you *must* act as quickly to ensure the victim's safety in the home, and get immediate help from a professional counselor for both kids (who will have separate appointments, obviously).

Signs That a Juvenile May Be at Risk of Harming Another Child

In many cases, especially those involving sexual activity between younger children, the "offender" may not recognize his actions are harmful. And for the parent, it can be tough to know when the line between innocent child play's and sexual harm has been crossed.

According to StopItNow.org, here are some behaviors to watch for that may indicate a child is at risk of sexually harming another child:[xxxv]

He's confused about social rules and interactions:

- Experiences typical gestures of friendliness or affection as sexual.
- Explores his own natural sexual curiosity with younger children or those of differing size, status, ability, or power.
- Seeks out the company of younger children and spends an unusual amount of time with them rather than with peers.
- Takes younger children to "secret" places or hideaways or plays "special" games with them (e.g. playing doctor or engaging in undressing or touching games).
- Insists on physical contact with a child even when they resist the attention.

He's anxious, depressed, or seeming to need help:

- Doesn't want to be alone with another child, or group of children, or becomes anxious about being with a particular young person.
- Was physically, sexually, or emotionally abused and has not been offered adequate resources and support for recovery.

- Seems to be crying out for help or behaves as if he wants to be caught. He leaves "clues" or acts in ways that seem likely to provoke a discussion about sexual issues.

He's impulsively sexual or aggressive:

- Links sexuality and aggression in language or behavior (e.g. makes sexual threats or insults).

- Is unable to control inappropriate sexual behaviors involving another child after being told to stop.

- Engages in sexually harassing behavior.

- Shares alcohol, drugs, or sexual material with younger children.

- Views sexual images of children on the Internet or elsewhere.

- Forces sexual interaction, including direct contact and non-contact (like exposing his genitals) on another adolescent or child.

If Your Child Is the Juvenile Offender

On my website, I offer a special handout on what to do if your child is the juvenile offender. Visit www.cjscarlet.com/freebies to find this handout and many more helpful freebies.

CHAPTER 4

Adults Closest to You and Your Child

Incest.

Blech! The word is universally reviled and so far "out there" that some people literally shudder when they hear it.

Incest is defined as sexual relations or abuse perpetrated by someone who's considered a family member of the victim—whether they're biologically related or not. Incestuous behavior includes:

- Having a child pose or perform in a sexual fashion.
- Peeping or spying on the child.
- Having the child view sexual acts in person, in movies, or in magazines.
- Having explicit sexual conversations with the child.
- Sexual touching.
- Sexual assault (which can include sodomy or rape).

There are disagreements between sociologists about whether the prohibition against incest is innate or socialized; regardless, it's perceived by virtually every culture on the planet as unnatural and emotionally traumatizing behavior.

Of course, any form of abuse or assault can be traumatic to the victims, but incest is worse because the perpetrators are people the victims love most and may rely on for their very survival and welfare. They're the people the children should be able to trust the most. When that trust is violated, it creates a deep moral wound that can cause lasting psychological harm, impairing the child's ability to lead a normal, healthy life.

I'll talk about the short- and long-term effects of sexual abuse in Chapter 9. Now let's look at who the familial offenders are.

The Call Is Coming from *Inside the House!* When the Abuser Is Your Partner

For many parents, learning their child has been sexually molested or assaulted is about as bad as it gets. But it can get even worse if the abuser is someone the parent is in an intimate relationship with.

Children who live with their married biological parents experience the lowest rates of abuse and neglect, while those living with a single parent who has a live-in partner (about a third of all children) are *20 times more likely to be sexually abused.*[xxxvi]

You read that right. Children living with a single parent and their non-related live-in partner are 20 times more likely to be sexually abused than their peers in two-parent families.[31]

What on earth is *that* all about?

It may be because people who aren't biologically related to the children don't feel an emotional connection to them. Also, surrogate parents may be less able to convince the children to obey them and so resort to psychological control or physical force to exert control over them.

Sociologists argue (they do that a LOT, apparently) about the causes behind this "Cinderella Effect." The solutions they propose basically involve completely altering societal realities and family dynamics. Their suggestions are well-meaning but unrealistic because people are people and some people just suck!

Seriously, there will always be buttheads in our world who are driven, for whatever reason, to hurt other people. The purpose of *this* book is to prepare you and your child to live in a world with those kinds of people and still come out unscathed because you both learned to protect and defend yourself from said buttheads.

Things That Make You Go Hmmm

Some sexual predators marry women either to use them as their "beard"—meaning they use the marriage in order to appear normal and respectable while they're actually busy molesting

---

[31] They're also 100 times more likely to be killed by a stepfather than by a biological parent, according to Gavin de Becker.

kids—or to gain access to children (theirs through the marriage or their partner's) whom they can victimize.

My former brother-in-law, who was a classic pedophile, used my sister as his beard. He married her and they had four children, but my sister always sensed that he barely tolerated her from the get-go. He was a great dad in some ways—he spent time with his kids, helped with their homework, cooked most of their meals, and did all the usual dad stuff. But he also spent an inordinate amount of time alone with teenage boys.

Other men enter into relationships with women who already have children just to gain access to their kids. They can be extremely charming to both the women and their children—grooming the whole family—all while they're plotting to molest the kids as soon as they can.

I urge everyone who's thinking about dating, moving in with, or marrying another person—man or woman—to do a background check on them first. Maybe even hire a private investigator to ensure they're everything they claim to be.

Wha??? "*But that's... so... so... underhanded!*" you argue. "*I couldn't possibly spy on my boyfriend!*" you cry. "*I don't want him to think I don't trust him!*" you bleat.

Get over yourself. This is about your kids (or future kids if you don't have any yet). You should do at least as much research on someone who may become your child's caregiver as you do, say, figuring out which streaming TV service to buy.

I can't tell you how many women I've helped over the years whose partners turned out to be terrible, abusive jerks whose backgrounds were a total lie—something they would have discovered in minutes if they'd invested any time looking into their backgrounds. A good background check service only costs around $20 and will tell you if the person you're researching has any criminal convictions, is on the National Sex Offender Registry, has declared bankruptcy, and so on.[32]

But don't rely just on a background search. After all, the person may never have been caught and convicted so there won't be a record. An intuitive hit is your most important clue; *trust it*.

---

[32] Please be sure you're looking up the right person. Use the correct spelling of their full name and any aliases they use (as well as name variations they may use—e.g., "Tammie" and "Tammy"), and their address and birthdate to help you narrow the search to the right individual. And don't forget to check the National Sex Offender Registry (www.nsopw.gov) and your state's sex offender registry for their name. You don't want to base your decisions on information about the wrong person!

Heroic Parenting

Soooo so many people have nagging feelings they can't quite silence, no matter how hard they try, that whisper to them something's not right about the person they're dating or living with or have already married. They tell themselves it's nothing; that they're imagining things or being overly sensitive when their partner does something that makes them uncomfortable. They squelch that sick feeling in the pit of their stomach when they see the creepy way their partner smiles when he looks at their children.

But they *know*, deep in their heart and in their gut, that something's wrong. They just don't want to consciously admit it because it would mean they'd have to end the relationship. *And that's SO hard!*

My advice? Suck it up, buttercup. If your gut is sending you distress signals (no matter how miniscule) that something's off with a person you're seeing, stop seeing them.

Yes, it's that simple.

Your gut knows things your mind hasn't noticed yet and it'll never steer you wrong. Trust it and you'll avoid months or years of torment, regret, and therapy bills for both you and your sweet baboo.

Even if everything seems hunky-dory with your new love, spring for the 20 bucks and do a background check anyway. To quote Forest Gump quoting his mother: "Life is like a box of chocolates; you never know what you're gonna get." Could be nothing, could be something. Either way, you'll feel better knowing you took action.

The Call Is Coming from *Outside the House* and It's Your Ex on the Line

It never ceases to amaze me how much people can come to absolutely *loathe* the partner they used to think hung the moon once they believe that person is no longer meeting their needs or has thwarted[33] them in some way.

Think about it. If you're honest, look back over your old relationships and you'll find that your feelings toward your mate changed only after they DIDN'T DO something you WANTED or they DID something you DIDN'T WANT. Do you see it yet? C'mon, you have to be really honest here!

Whatever the reason you broke up with a past partner, if you have a kid together, you're bound to each other until the child is at least 18. Hopefully, for the child's sake, you both play nice.

---

33 To thwart someone is to do something they believe blocks their happiness or goals.

But what do you do when your former partner is abusing your child? *You do whatever it takes to protect your child*, short of breaking the law or kidnapping her.

If you think your child has been physically or sexually abused by your ex (or anyone else, for that matter), there are several things you should do:

- If your child returns from a visit to your ex-partner with injuries, take her to a hospital right away. Her immediate safety and wellbeing are your most pressing concern.

- Next, call your local Child Protective or Social Services agency and report the abuse. They'll investigate the case and arrange professional help for your child.

- If there's a court visitation order in place, contact the court right away and ask for an immediate hearing to temporarily revoke visitation or provide for visitation with supervision until the investigation is over.

- Contact your local child advocacy center, which can help you navigate the social services and criminal justice systems and provide counseling for your child.[34]

- Sit down and thoroughly document what you know and/or have witnessed [e.g., bruises or other injuries on the child after a visit to your ex-partner, symptoms of sexual abuse (which I detail in Chapter 9), statements she's made about being fearful or hurt by your ex, etc.]. Include as much detail as you can, including dates, times, and locations. This will bolster your claims and provide social workers and the courts with a timeline of events.

A Cautionary Note on Using Children as Pawns

When I was the executive director of a child advocacy center in the mid-90s, I witnessed some of the most horrible child abuse cases imaginable. Some of the worst *never actually happened.* You see, they were cases in which separated or divorced parents worked to punish and/or manipulate each other by using their children as pawns, claiming the other parent was abusing them.

Whether it involves a contentious custody case or "just" a vindictive act of revenge to get back at one's ex, this is *despicable* behavior. Don't play that game. If it's being done to you, lawyer up[35] (the best you can) and fight it! But whatever you do, don't retaliate in kind. Your soul and your child's happiness and mental health are on the line here.

---

34 ChildHelp.org's National Child Abuse Hotline number is 800-422-4453.
35 Lawyer up means to get an attorney to represent your interests.

Heroic Parenting

Other Relatives as Threats

There's such a thing as too much family closeness. Relatives tend to have more access to kids than other people, and access is the most obvious thing someone needs to abuse a child. I myself was molested by a brother-in-law and, in one particularly horrific incident, by a drunken uncle *within hours of my aunt's funeral.* True story.

Many parents who are suspicious of other adults are often oblivious and even careless when their children are around relatives. Most families have a handsy, slightly rapey "funny uncle" that everyone knows to avoid. But, just as with teenagers who WILL find a time and place to canoodle[36] despite all your efforts to chaperone them, sure as shootin' that funny uncle will find a way to be alone with your child.

If you're one of those families and you have any inkling that one of your relatives poses a threat to your child (or any child), the only way to ensure your son or daughter's safety is to prevent them from being in that person's presence. *Cut off the access and you eliminate the threat.*

Now, what about the ones who aren't so overtly pervy? Well, most of the time when we tell ourselves we had no idea Uncle Teddy was "like that," there were actually glaring clues that he was. Read some of the telling signs below. When you observe any of these signs, take my advice and cut off all access to that person who makes you or your child go "ick."

Be especially wary of someone who:[37]

- Spends a suspiciously large amount of time with children or a particular child.

- Makes sexual jokes or comments or talks about sexual activities with or around children.

- Calls kids names with a sexual overtone (e.g., slut, whore, stud, etc.).

- Is overly complimentary about a child's appearance.

- Looks at or talks about child pornography. (Some studies estimate that around 35 percent of people who view child porn sexually abuse children.[xxxvii])

- Tells children to keep secrets and to not tell anyone of certain activities.

---

36 Canoodle = Fool around.
37 From *Protect Your Kids! The Simple Keys to Children's Safety and Survival* by Steve Kovacs, who warns parents to watch out for relatives who do the certain things *(I added some too).*

- Is overly affectionate with children, including too much hugging, kissing, tickling, wrestling, holding them on their lap, or other touching, especially if they continue even when the child tells them to stop.

- Walks in on children in the bathroom or bedroom more often than could be chalked up to an "accident."

- Becomes defensive when asked about a child's health or gives conflicting stories about injuries on the child.

Badass Grandma's Two Cents

If your child tells you he's been molested or assaulted by someone in your family, or even that he's just uncomfortable around them, you *must* take action to protect him from further harm. Yes, that may mean reporting the perp to the police and Social Services and, yes, it may tear your family apart, but would you prefer to live a life of complete denial and face the roaring flames of eternal damnation or do the adult thing and protect your child and family? Hmm?

This particular scenario happens more often than not: A child (or grown adult who was molested as a child) summons the courage to tell his parents that a relative abused him *and the parent doesn't believe him and does NOTHING about it!*

I'm serious, I've heard this story from way too many adult survivors whose parents simply didn't want to believe that Aunt Lulu would do such a thing.

Don't be that parent. Just… don't.

CHAPTER 5
Child Caregivers

You're Gonna Let Me Do What?

I'm still shaking my head today.

I could hardly wait for my birthday to arrive! The year was 1972 and I counted down the days until I would be eligible to get my babysitting certificate through the Girl Scouts, which meant I could start earning money to go to the movies with my friends. I signed up for the Babysitting 101 class the day after my birthday and attended all two hours of the training (I don't remember child CPR[38] being one of the lessons, btw). Within days I had my first babysitting gig—for an *actual* baby—and thus began my working career.

I was 11.

You read that right—11! I wouldn't trust an 11-year-old with a hamster, let alone a real human child, but many parents have and still do. Heck, my oldest sister was looking after the *four* of us younger ones when she was around that same age!

The scariest part (besides the fact that I myself was still a child), was that the woman who hired me was a complete stranger. I literally went door to door schlepping for jobs. At one home I rang the doorbell and asked the woman who answered if she needed a sitter. She said yes and hired me on the spot (for a whopping 10 cents an hour—a fortune at the time) to watch her baby that afternoon while she ran to the store. I could have been a pint-sized psychopath for all she knew! Fortunately for all involved, I was not, in fact, a prepubescent serial killer and the baby survived my well-intentioned, if haphazard, care.

---

38 CPR = Cardio-Pulmonary Resuscitation. CPR is now an essential component of the Girl Scout babysitting course, btw.

While few people today would hire a complete stranger who showed up on their doorstep to watch their kids, many barely know the people they do end up hiring, having gotten their name from a friend, neighbor, or coworker. And most never ask for references or actually check the ones they're given if offered.

We spend waaay more time researching the latest smartphone than we do the people who are solely responsible for our children's very lives for hours or days at a time. I admit that I myself was guilty of this when I was a young mother who didn't know any better.

On my website[39] I posted a comprehensive guide to vetting caregivers that you absolutely MUST read if you plan to leave your child in someone else's care. Check it out; just not right now, while you're reading this super awesome book.

Who Should You Trust?

You're the parent of a youngster under the age of, say, 13 and you need a caregiver so you can work and bring home the bacon. Your child's school has been shut down for the foreseeable future "out of an abundance of caution" during the Coronavirus pandemic.

Your parents have shuttered themselves in their home to keep from getting the virus themselves and your regular date night sitter, a bubble gum-popping, Tik-Toking teenager, isn't qualified or available to watch a child all day, every day for weeks on end. Plus, her folks don't want her around other people during the outbreak.

You have a few choices: there's the mom who lives next door, there's an older woman who offers sitting services whose name you got from a coworker, and there's your cousin Tito who just got out of the service and is living with his folks until he lands a job.

Who do you choose? For most people, the decision would depend solely on who's available and who answers their call first, even if that means calling Cousin Tito.[40]

Stop. Right. There. Now imagine the sound that irritating buzzer makes on any game show. (I don't know how to write that sound, but you get my drift.)

---

39 www.cjscarlet.com/freebies

40 No offense to Cousin Tito who is, I'm sure, a perfectly nice person, but research shows that the VAST majority of child sex abusers are men. I'm not saying not to hire a man if he meets all the criteria AND passes the background search, but do check in with your gut and be aware that men pose a greater risk to children in general.

Heroic Parenting

The CORRECT answer is the person:

- Who makes your gut (your intuitive sense) do a happy dance.
- Whose references are both favorable and reassuring.
- Who possesses the necessary skills to do the job.
- Who your child actually likes.

Let's address each of these one by one.

Making Your Gut Happy[41]

Your gut is quite literally a second brain in your body. (Actually, it was there first. Before the human brain fully developed, your gut was already on the job, sensing and reacting to danger.) Your gut produces specific hormones (like cortisol, norepinephrine, and adrenaline) when it senses danger that notify the brain to take action and prepare your body to protect and defend itself.

To assess whether someone "feels" okay or makes your tummy twinge you have to actually meet them. Yes, in person and, yes, *before* you need them to sit for you. You can't wait until you have an emergency and are desperate for someone to watch your kid to make a decision. Ideally, you meet with and vet several potential sitters and have them waiting in the wings for when you need them. (If you already have a caregiver you use, you can still put them through the vetting process described below to either validate your choice or weed them out.)

In the event you have an actual emergency and don't have a cadre of trusted sitters waiting to be called upon, you basically have two choices: take your child with you or simply don't go out. Notice that "frantically calling your new next-door neighbor and begging her for help" is not one of those options (unless she's already on the trusted sitters list).

"Meeting" the sitter is self-explanatory. If you can, meet them in person (at least one day before the sitting gig so you can check their references). If you just talk on the phone or do a Skype call, you won't be able to get their vibe, meaning you won't be able to get the opinion of your gut. Remember, your gut is your primary and most essential tool for determining whether someone is to be trusted with the life and wellbeing of your child.

---

[41] Everything in this section on how to trust your gut applies to every person you and your child interact with, not just caregivers.

Checking in with your gut is a very visceral,[42] physical act; it's about how you *feel*. "Vetting" someone is more cerebral;[43] it's about what you *think* of them based on hard data, such as:

- HOW you know them.

- WHO they are (and whether that jives with how they represent themselves on paper or online).

- WHAT their caregiving experience is.

- WHERE else (and for whom) they've worked in the past.

- Only after you've satisfied yourself that they're qualified does the WHEN become important (i.e., are they available when you need them?).

Again, if you're in the market for a caregiver, please download my special guide to vetting caregivers, in which I provide a list of questions you should ask the candidates during their interviews, information on how to check their references, and guidance on how to conduct background checks.[44]

Reassuring & Favorable References

After you interview a potential sitter, *DO NOT hire them on the spot*, no matter how much you like them! Give yourself the benefit of time and distance to think about their responses to your questions and check those references. While you may feel good during the interview, you may experience niggling doubts afterward about their responses to some questions that triggered your gut and made you think twice. *Pay attention to those feelings and trust them.*

The Necessary Skills to Do the Job

People's babysitting knowledge, skills, and abilities differ greatly. One may know child CPR, but not how to save a choking child. Another might not know either of these, but she's willing to play "princess" with your daughter for hours on end and your child adores her.[45]

It can help to make a wish list of the skills and abilities you'd like to have in an ideal sitter and rank those from "essential to have" to "nice to have." Don't compromise on the items you

---

42 Visceral = Based in the body or gut.
43 Cerebral = Based in the mind.
44 Go to www.cjscarlet.com/freebies.
45 She can—and should—learn CPR.

list as essential; the sitter either does or doesn't have those skills and you shouldn't overlook their absence just because you "have a really good feeling" about someone.

Factor in Your Child's Intuition

Children have a great intuitive sense of who feels safe and who doesn't. Always introduce your child to a prospective sitter when they come to your home for the interview and carefully watch how they interact. You're looking for the sitter to engage with your child by being friendly and asking her questions that are appropriate for your child's age and maturity level. On the flip side, you're watching to see how your child reacts to the sitter's attempts to engage with her. If she reacts negatively, that's a clue they might not be a good fit for each other.

Monitoring the Caregiver

So, you've carefully followed the advice in my online Guide to Choosing & Vetting Child Caregivers[46] and you've chosen people you feel 100 percent comfortable with. You rock! You can feel great knowing you're leaving your child in the care of sitters who'll take care of him as if he were their own.

Now you need to follow through to ensure your choice was on the mark. One way to do this is to install video surveillance devices in your home to monitor the sitter when your child is in her care.

"Nanny cams" are small devices that record video and can be used to monitor any activity within the range of the camera lens. They've become quite popular and can be hidden so they look like innocuous items, such as USB ports, teddy bears, picture frames, and so on.

The question is, do you *want* to have a nanny cam (or multiple cameras in different rooms—not the bathroom, please; we're civilized human beings here) and, if so, do you tell the sitter it's there or not?

If I still had young children and were leaving them in someone else's care, I'd choose to use nanny cams and I would absolutely tell the sitter that I had them. This gives her fair warning that she's being monitored "for security and training purposes" as they say, although I guarantee she'll totally forget that in no time and will revert to her usual, hopefully good, behavior.

Many a bad act has been captured by nanny cams that helped convict child abusers. With that being said, if you decide to get a nanny cam because you fear or suspect the sitter is abusing your

---

46 www.cjscarlet.com/freebies

child in some way—back away, slap the silliness out of yourself, and listen up! If your intuition is telling you something's off and you're STILL using that person to watch your child, then your biggest problem isn't the sitter, it's *YOU*.

Kill—and I mean smother with a pillow till it stops moving—that need to make nice and give sketchy people the benefit of the doubt. Act like the parent your child deserves!

Stop using that caregiver at once. No need to explain why or tell her you're not going to call her anymore; just don't call her ever again. She may wonder why you dropped off the radar, but I promise she's not going to bang on your door demanding to know why. Stop worrying about what she thinks and start trusting your gut. You don't even have to know what your gut is reacting to; the mere fact that you feel uneasy is enough reason to stop using someone to care for your child.

Got it? Good. Thus endeth the lesson.

Daycare and After-School Caregivers[47]

With few exceptions, everything I wrote earlier in this chapter applies to vetting daycare and after-school programs as well. Remember that just because the workers were hired by an agency or facility doesn't mean they get an automatic pass. When hiring, the employers are looking for how candidates meet their requirements. You are also looking for how they *don't* meet your requirements.

When checking out a daycare or after-school program, ask to see their license and actually check it out with the licensing authority. *Please do this.* It'll only take you, like, two minutes. Check also to see if there have been any complaints against them or their facility.[48]

Once you're sure you're dealing with a legitimate, licensed center or program, you'll want to find out how they screen and evaluate their workers. Make them show you an actual written process for this. Be sure every employee has had a formal background check done and that their references were actually checked before they were hired.

Make them show you that every employee has been checked against the National Sex Offender Registry. Get the names of every person at the facility who'll have access to your child and when you get home, run your own check of the registry.[49] It's quick, it's free, it's a no-brainer.

---

[47] This section is largely based on the great information I found in Gavin de Becker's *Protecting the Gift*. This and his other outstanding book, *The Gift of Fear*, are essential reading for every parent.
[48] Cheerios offers a cool service for parents called Child Care Aware that will provide the phone number of an agency that can explain licensing in your area. The number is 800-424-2246.
[49] www.nsopw.gov

Heroic Parenting

Ask for a copy of the facility's policies and procedures. Look for clear rules on conduct and the consequences for bad behavior (on the part of the staff). Ask if they inform all parents when an employee is suspected of abusing a child in their care and let them know you want to be notified in all cases.

In *Protecting the Gift*, Gavin de Becker makes even more recommendations that will help you ensure your child is in safe hands. I've never met anyone who's actually gone through all the trouble to vet their child's daycare or after-school care program the way de Becker suggests, but you can bet I'll be advising my son and daughter-in-law do this before they enroll my grandbabies in a new school.

When Your Child Is Home Alone

More than 15 million kids—1 in 25 of whom are between *kindergarten* and 5th grade—take care of themselves after school until their parents get home.[xxxviii]

Before you get all judgy, consider that many parents, especially single parents, don't have access to affordable childcare. Some don't have extra money for anything beyond the rent and food. And because of government cuts, there are fewer after-school programs. *(Jerk move, legislators.)* Some parents just don't have a choice.

Personally, I squirm when I think of little kids sitting in a state of high anxiety while they wait for something terrible to happen in their parents' absence. My oldest son has never forgiven me for leaving him home alone for an hour-and-a-half while I took a college final exam when he was young. He brings it up all the time. I mean like, *all the time*. It was a terrible, risky move on my part, but in my defense, I was an idiot.[50]

Please don't leave your young child home alone. Do everything in your power to find and afford childcare for her so you both can rest easy. Generally, children older than 13 can handle being alone for short periods. For kids between 10 and 12, it depends on their level of maturity and responsibility. For example, is your child comfortable being alone or is she terrified? Does she know what to do and who to call for help if something does happen? Can she handle an emergency situation if, for example, she cut herself while preparing a snack?

Here are some suggestions to keep your child safe when she's home alone and some scenarios you need to train her to deal with. Ask her how she would handle each situation and tweak her answers, as needed:

---

50 Sorry, Sean!

- Buy a cool lanyard or key chain and put the (unlabeled) house keys on it for your child to have handy when she gets home so she can get in the house quickly.

- Even better, get one of those smart locks and security cameras from a good home security company so you can use your phone to watch her safely arrive and see if she goes out.

- Teach her not to enter the house if something doesn't look or feel right (e.g., the door is ajar, there's a broken window, etc.).[51]

- Ensure she has a backup plan, such as going to a trusted neighbor's house and calling the police, if something does look or feel wonky.

- Tell her to call you the minute she gets home so you'll know she's safe.

- If someone calls on the phone, teach your child to tell them something like, "My mom's in the bathroom/busy in the kitchen/on the treadmill. Can I take a message?" If the person starts asking questions, tell your daughter to just hang up. Or, you could tell her to not answer the phone at all unless she recognizes from the number that you're the one calling.

- Teach your child to never, never, never EVER let someone in the house, even if they claim you sent them to pick her up (unless they know the code word you and your child agreed upon ahead of time, which I'll describe in a later chapter). Even if they ask to use the phone because there's been an accident (or other potentially bogus claim), she shouldn't let them in, but can offer to call the police instead.

- Before you ever leave your child home alone, make sure she knows basic first aid, fire safety, and how to call 911 in the event of an emergency.

---

[51] Side story about the power of intuition: One time when my sons were 5 and 8, we came home from a T-ball game in broad daylight and started to enter the front door. Something didn't feel right so I put out my arms and told the boys to back away. I heard noises inside the house, like the scurry of panicked buffalo, so we ran to a neighbor's house to call 911. When the police went inside, they found that we'd been burglarized. (They also found the floor covered with SpaghettiOs and a week's worth of clothes and toys, which I bald-facedly blamed on the burglars. The policeman looked at me like, "Yeah, lady. Whatever you say," and added vandalism to the list of crimes that had occurred.) Missing were my kid's video game console, my jewelry *and my .357 Magnum*. The perps had entered through my sons' bedroom window (that was nightmare material, let me assure you) and left through the sliding glass door in my bedroom. We couldn't find someone to fix the broken window and door until the next day, so the three of us huddled all night, terrified and sleepless, on the floor of my bedroom closet—me with a large kitchen knife clenched in my fist. All I could think of was what might have happened if I had let my sons run into the house with those clowns who had my gun in their shaky hands.

Heroic Parenting

- Write down your home address and landline number; your cell phone number; your company's name, address, and number; and the contact information for emergency contacts if you can't be reached. Post this information on the fridge where she can find it easily.[52]

Your child is basically serving as her own babysitter, so make sure she knows everything you would expect a regular sitter to know. Write down the rules she's expected to follow, such as not having anyone over, how much screen time she can have, whether she has to do her homework before you get home, whether she's allowed to use the stove, what snacks are allowed, etc. Post these on the fridge too.

Badass Grandma's Two Cents

The time you spend ensuring your caregivers are safe for your kids will give you peace of mind and help you sleep better at night, knowing you've done everything in your power to protect your child. I'm mean, who wants to admit they've done a poor job of protecting their kid? Parent up!

---

[52] Use the same Babysitter Checklist I have available for you on my website at www.cjscarlet.com/freebies.

CHAPTER 6
Other Adults & Authority Figures

It Takes a Village Idiot

As parents, we rely on other adults to help us raise our kids and mold them into responsible people. Every day we hand our children off to teachers, coaches, scout masters, doctors, and religious figures. Nearly all these people will be safe, but some of them won't be and we need to be on the lookout for threats.

Human beings tend to get full of themselves when they're put in positions of power. To paraphrase Sir John Dalberg-Acton, "Power corrupts; absolute power corrupts absolutely." Most of the time that manifests as irritating ineptitude, but sometimes it leads people to believe they can use and abuse others, including innocent kids.

Whenever there's an imbalance of power, as there is between your child and any older youth or adult leader of a class, group, team, or religious institution, those in charge may feel powerful and entitled—a bad combination that may lead them to abuse their charges without compunction.[53]

Teach your child that just because he respects or even reveres someone doesn't mean he has to let his guard or his boundaries down. Occasionally ask your child, "What does your gut say about so and so?" This will cause him to start paying attention and teach him to automatically check in with his intuition, especially when interacting with new people.

Check to see if the school or organization conducts background checks on their employees and volunteers. If not, do your own background check on anyone who will regularly interact with your child. It's only around $20 to $30 a month for unlimited searches, depending on the service you choose.

---

53 Compunction = Acting without a second thought for what's right.

Note: Know that you may need the person's permission first before you can do a background search on them. If they refuse to offer their permission, that's a good clue they're not to be trusted. Don't let them anywhere near your child.

Not the Kind of Schooling You Want for Your Kid

An estimated *4.5 million* K-12 students have experienced inappropriate behavior by a teacher or other school official, including lewd comments, exposure to pornography, peeping, and grabbing. And 3 million students have experienced sexual touching or full-out assault.[xxxix]

Here's a breakdown of school employees who have assaulted students:[xl]

- 31 percent were teachers or subs.
- 15 percent were coaches.
- 12 percent were bus drivers.
- 11 percent were teacher's aides.
- 10 percent were security guards.
- 6 percent were principals.
- 5 percent were counselors. (*Seriously?*)
- The remaining 10 percent were other school employees.

These incidents have very serious implications, not only for the sexual, emotional, and mental health of the victims, but for their academic success as well. Another survey reported that students who experienced some form of abuse by teachers and other school employees reported they:[54]

- Felt embarrassed (51 percent), self-conscious (39 percent), and less confident (37 percent).
- Felt afraid (36 percent).
- Felt confused about their sexual identity (29 percent).
- Doubted whether they could have a happy romantic relationship (29 percent).
- Tried to avoid the abuser (43 percent).

---

54 By the Afterschool Alliance and JC Penney Afterschool entitled *"America After 3PM."*

- Didn't want to go to school (36 percent).
- Didn't talk much in class (34 percent).
- Had difficulty paying attention (31 percent).
- Stayed home from school or cut class (29 percent).
- Found it hard to study (29 percent).
- Experienced health effects, including trouble sleeping and loss of appetite (28 percent).
- Experienced academic or disciplinary repercussions (about 25 percent).
- Scored a lower grade on a test or assignment (25 percent).
- Felt less likely to get a good grade (23 percent).
- Changed schools (19 percent).

Despite these troubling results, *94 percent* of students who experienced sexual abuse by a teacher or other school employee never reported it to school officials. When allegations WERE made, only a few ever reported the incidents to law enforcement.[xli]

Scout Masters & Other Group Leaders & Volunteers

Here's a seriously disturbing fact: nearly 90 percent of youth organizations don't conduct any type of criminal records check on volunteers and almost half don't even check their references! At the same time, some organizations want to ban gay people from being volunteers because they (falsely) believe they're more likely to abuse children.[55]

As for the victims of group leader and volunteer abuse, it's impossible to reliably estimate how many there are out there. Very few cases are ever reported and in only a fraction of those is action taken to prosecute the abuser. Instead, rather than firing the abusers, organizations (I'm looking at you Boy Scouts and churches!) often choose to move the alleged perps to other troops or parishes where they're free to molest even more kids. It's shocking and shameful and it needs to stop.

---

55 Research shows that kids are far more likely to be sexually molested or assaulted by so-called "straight" people. In fact, gay individuals are responsible for less than 1 percent of child sexual molestations and assaults.

Abuse in Religious Settings

Speaking of churches, NO religion or place of worship is free from child sexual abuse. If you believe it isn't happening somewhere in your church or synagogue or mosque or temple (whether by the clergy or congregants), you are sadly mistaken. Media stories about abusive priests make it appear the problem lies solely within the Catholic Church (which has documented more than 100,000 victims in the US alone!). But child abuse can flourish in any type of religious organization.

It's such an unfair fight. Religious leaders are held in such high esteem and hold positions of power over their flocks, which look up to them for moral guidance and salvation. Religious organizations offer the perfect storm of conditions that nurture abusive leaders, who:

- Operate with little oversight, and those organizations that *do* provide oversight are often willing to overlook immoral behavior.

- Have free access to emotionally vulnerable populations of children.

- Have the trust of parents—who may not believe their children's allegations.

- Often know their congregation members' deepest secrets, which they can use to manipulate or threaten victims.

- Are often viewed as God's intermediaries, giving them ultimate power over their victims.

No wonder survivors of abuse by religious figures are less likely to report it (nearly 70 percent never tell) than victims of abuse by people in other types of organizations (54 percent of whom don't tell).[xlii]

Medical Professionals

Larry Nassar, the now infamous doctor for the USA Gymnastics national team, sexually molested and assaulted more than 250 young athletes over a 25-year period, despite numerous reports that were ignored by Olympic and Michigan State University officials. Another case involved Dr. Earl Bradley, a pediatrician, who drugged and assaulted over 1,000 tiny tots—and videotaped his crimes!

Doctors, nurses, dentists, hygienists, physical therapists, and mental health professionals are people we turn to when we're most vulnerable because we're usually in physical or emotional pain. We *need* them and we trust them with our wellbeing.

It's so easy even for us, as adults, to be too intimidated to say anything if these people step over the line. We tell ourselves that we must have misinterpreted what happened or that it's no big deal that our gynecologist touched us inappropriately "down there." Heck, most women aren't even honest with their stylist when she messes up, so how do we expect to be able to speak up to a medical professional who's in an even greater position of power and trust?

Again, very few adults and even fewer children tell anyone when something inappropriate occurs. It doesn't help that when allegations are made, the perps are rarely held to account and the number who actually lose their license to practice is pitifully small.

At least with doctors, dentists, and mental health providers you can usually find online reviews that will help you learn more about any complaints that have been made against them. There are several sites you can check out:

- Federation of State Medical Boards offers a search function at www.DocInfo.org that shows actions taken against a specific physician.
- Then there's the Bad Doctor Database at https://baddoctordatabase.tumblr.com.
- You can also conduct an online search on Google for other types of medical professionals by typing in the search box: [his/her name] + complaints + [your state].

Please, please, please never leave your child alone with a medical professional during an exam unless she's old enough to want you out of the room, and even then, always ensure there's a nurse present.

Ways to Thwart Abuse by Authority Figures

Below are some ways to keep your child safe from predatory authority figures:

- Educate your child about what constitutes inappropriate behavior and teach her that it's okay to say "no" to adults, even doctors and religious leaders. (I'll cover this in Part III.)
- Teach your child about the importance of telling you if she's asked to keep "not-so-good secrets" (also covered in Part III).
- Get involved. The more present you are in your child's activities, the less access a perp will have to her and the less likely it is something will happen.
- Closely watch the leader's interactions with her young charges. Watch for grooming behaviors like those I described in Chapter 1 and call them out when you see them. Let

the leader know you're paying attention. Strong parental oversight is a HUGE predator repellant!

- Make sure coaches and troop leaders are adhering to the "Rule of 2," which states that there should always be at least two adults present at all times when working with a lone child.

- Never allow coaches or other group leaders or volunteers to be alone with your child on an overnight trip, such as an athletic competition or band trip, for example.

- Regularly check in with your child and ask what was good and bad about practice. On occasion, ask if anyone makes her feel uncomfortable.

- Be alert to changes in your child's personality or behavior, such as suddenly wanting to drop a club or sport she was enthusiastic about before.

It's so very important to teach your child that it's okay to say "no" to authority figures if they're making her feel uncomfortable or unsafe. Again, I'll tell you how to do that in Part III.

PART II

Where Danger Lurks

In this section, I go into detail about specific dangers you might worry your little one will encounter. This is pretty deep stuff, but it's important that you become educated about these types of threats so you know how to protect your child against them.

Later in the book, I refer often to the chapters in this part, so please be sure to read it all. Hang in there! We're working our way to the solutions.

CHAPTER 7

Bullying

Imagine if every morning as you got ready for work, you knew you were going to be bullied by your boss. Every night you'd worry about what was in store for you the next day and every morning you'd positively dread going to work. You'd feel fearful and anxious; you might even throw up.

Now, what if no one believed you or if other people who witnessed your humiliation did absolutely nothing to defend you? What if they told you to respond to your boss in kind, which YOU know would only make things worse? What if some of those people, secretly relieved that the boss' attention wasn't on them, started treating you badly too? You'd feel isolated and helpless. And as the abuse relentlessly continued, you'd become depressed, hopeless, and maybe even suicidal.

What would you do? Well, as an adult you have several options:

- Report the abuse to HR.[56]
- Quit and find a new job.
- File criminal charges if the abuse turns physical or sexual.

Now imagine you're 5 or 7 or 9 and you're dealing with this kind of nightmare every day. As a kid, your options are far more limited. You can't always count on the school to put a stop to it and you may get a less-than-helpful response from your parents who may tell you to stand up for yourself or work it out on your own.

This is the reality for millions of kids every day in the US.

---

56 HR = Human Resources.

We're Gonna Need a Bigger Boat

While researching bullying, there was SO much information that it was agonizing work trying to capture all the pertinent details and fit it all into one chapter. I read dozens of books and studies on the topic and found them to be all over the board with their advice.

I'm going to cover as much information here as I can so you'll have an overview of what bullying looks like, who the offenders and victims are, how to help your child deal with bullies, and the short and long-term consequences of bullying.[57]

There are thousands of excellent books on this subject you can choose to read, some of which I reference in this chapter and on my website. I provide great basic information, but if your child is being bullied, I urge you to read other books devoted to that topic to help guide you.

A Very Wrong Rite of Passage

I'm guessing that as long as there have been humans on the planet there have been bullies. In my Disco Queen heyday in the late 70s,[58] the worst we had to worry about was being challenged to a fist fight behind the school gym. Although every young man had a shotgun on a rack in the back window of his pickup truck (this was Arkansas, mind you), no one ever brought a gun into the school. I never even heard of a knife being used.

Bullying is most simply defined as aggressive behavior that can be verbal or non-verbal, physical, or relational (I'll explain that term in a sec) that targets victims, often based on their perceived weakness, appearance, race, religion, gender, sexuality, or disability. In some cases, there's no apparent reason someone is chosen as a victim.

For too long, bullying has been perceived as a rite of passage that kids have to deal with as a normal part of growing up. But when it involves threats of harm or actual physical assault, bullying is a form of criminal behavior and should be treated as such.

Many people believe bullies are social outsiders who secretly suffer from low self-esteem, anger issues, and poor self-control. Certainly, some bullies are like that, but others are popular and confident; if anything, they suffer from an overabundance of self-esteem and an inflated sense of entitlement.

---

57 I'll address cyberbullying in my soon-to-be-published book for parents of kids 10 to 18.
58 Man, did I ROCK those Danskins!

Heroic Parenting

Yes, I Actually Said That Out Loud

I'm gonna take a hit for this, but I'm going to say it anyway because it's true: kids can be total jerks sometimes—to their parents, to their siblings, and most of all to each other. Of course, not all kids are schmucks, but almost every child goes through phases (think the "terrible two's," puberty, or any time you try to get them to put down their electronic devices). They're just... so... grrrr... that you want to pinch their little heads off. You wonder what happened to your sweet, affectionate child.

Wake up, momma! Move on, dad! Those golden days are over. Until they grow a fully formed frontal lobe and get a clue, most adolescents have to be survived, much like an 18-year-long bout of COVID-19.[59]

Surviving the Grade School Gauntlet

- Fact: *Millions* of kids are bullied each school year.

- Fact: 85 percent of the time, no one—not friends, other children, teachers, or other adults—tries to intervene to stop the bullying.[xliii]

- Fact: 60 percent of elementary and secondary school students rate bullying as a major problem affecting their lives.[xliv]

- Fact: Most 5th through 12th graders are more concerned about emotional maltreatment and social cruelty from peers than anything else, including academic achievement.[xlv]

I think it's safe to say that we've got a serious problem on our hands.

What Bullying Looks Like

It's shocking to me that when an adult physically assaults someone it's a crime, but when kids do it to other kids, it's called "roughhousing."

This is true even at school, and yet schools aren't that great at keeping tabs on what's happening in their halls. In North Carolina where I live, for example, 72 percent of the state's K-12 schools reported ZERO bullying incidents to the federal government in the 2015-2016 school

---

[59] I KNOW you know what COVID-19 is (also called Coronavirus). I'm in the throes of social isolation as I edit this chapter and am about ready to chew through a chain link fence, I've got cabin fever so bad. Even my dogs can't stand me at this point.

year![60] Compare this with the 19 percent of NC students who say they were bullied. This isn't just ludicrous; it's putting our kids at risk.

According to experts Deborah Carpenter and Christopher J. Ferguson,[61][xlvi] bullying behavior shouldn't be confused with horseplay, good-natured teasing, or brief clashes between kids on the playground. "Friendship troubles, squabbles between classmates, and the all-in-good-fun wrestling match that gets a little out of hand are normal; sticking a foot out to intentionally trip (and possibly hurt and humiliate) a younger child is not."

Bullies are inventive and bullying comes in so many creative forms, from "direct" bullying (involving face-to-face interactions) to "indirect" bullying (involving emotional, verbal, or social mistreatment that turn victims into social outcasts).

Boys and girls exert social control differently, which means they bully differently. Girls generally use relational aggression, while boys are more often physically aggressive. Girls also tend to control or dominate by social exclusion—withdrawing friendships, not inviting others to birthday parties, or giving the silent treatment. Boys tend to be more direct in expressing anger. They can be verbally aggressive, using names like "stupid" or "idiot." Boys tend to get over it more quickly, while girls tend to carry resentment longer.

Let's cover these in greater depth.

Direct or Physical Bullying

Physical aggression tends to get the most attention from schools, parents, and the media. It includes physical acts or "in-your-face" threats of harm between an aggressor and victim.

Deborah Carpenter describes it this way:

"Typically, the behavior is action oriented, involving such behaviors as hair pulling, pinching, pushing, shoving, slapping, kicking, tripping, poking, stabbing, spitting, hitting, punching, head butting, choking, imitating wrestling holds, throwing an object at someone, pushing books out of one's hands, and hiding or destroying of property. Girls

---

60 Apparently, school officials don't want to besmirch their perfect "zero tolerance" records, but I'll bet they'd cry like babies if they were ever bullied themselves!
61 According to Deborah Carpenter and Christopher J. Ferguson, PhD, in their very informative book *The Everything Parent's Guide to Dealing with Bullies: From playground teasing to cyberbullying, all you need to ensure your child's safety and happiness.*

are more apt to use mild physical aggression such as pulling hair, slapping, and scratching; boys are more likely to punch, shove, and throw objects.

"Physical bullying can occur even when there is no actual physical contact. The bully can shake his fist in your face, slam a book down on your desk, or invade your personal space. This is referred to as posturing. Posturing is a common scare tactic bullies use to intimidate and frighten their victims. Once a bully gets a reputation for being violent and cruel, a simple threatening move like a fisted hand or a mock air punch can strike fear into a bullied child's heart. The threat of physical violence is sometimes just as effective as actual physical violence.

"Another form of physical bullying involves actions that are meant to sexually intimidate or harass. A sexual bully might lift up a girl's skirt, 'pants' a boy, push the bodies of two kids together, pinch someone's bottom, grab a girl's breasts or snap her bra, make unwanted sexual advances, or pressure someone into unwanted sexual activity.

"One of the biggest problems with the continuation of physical bullying is the potential progression and escalation of violence. If the bully trips or shoves you today, what will he do to top it tomorrow? The danger for ever-increasing levels of violence exists."[xlvii]

Although bullying can happen anywhere, it occurs mainly where there's little or no adult supervision, such as at the bus stop or on the bus, and at school in the hallways, bathrooms, or on the playground. It also happens wherever groups of kids play unsupervised.

Relational Bullying

This type of bullying is more insidious and can be even more damaging to a child's self-esteem than emotional or physical aggression. "Mean" girls, especially, love to use this method to terrorize and demoralize their chosen victims.

In her Popsugar.com article,[62] Sara Ahmed[xlviii] says that relational bullying focuses on the victim's discomfort and humiliation for the entertainment of the group. This can be excluding the victim from conversations or activities, gossiping about her, highlighting her supposed faults, or flat-out spreading false rumors about her that cause her social harm.

The hurt is often compounded by the fact that the victim's "friends" will often join in with the bully's tactics in order to fit in and deflect negative attention from themselves.

---

[62] From *Why Aren't We Talking About This Dangerous Type of Bullying?*

Ahmed offers a list of examples of relational bullying that make me wince just reading them:

- Excluding a member from their own social group: "The rest of us didn't ask you to go camping because we thought you wouldn't be interested."

- Making friendship conditional: "You can sit with us if you promise not to laugh like a donkey."

- Using negative body language around the victim: Constant eye-rolling or smirking among each other when that child is talking.

- Making fun of the victim's appearance: "You're so ugly… just kidding."

- Discouraging others from being sympathetic to the victim: "Are you in love with him or something? We're just playing around."

- Not allowing the victim to make any type of mistake: "Did you see how she tripped on her own shoelaces? This girl is the shoelace tripper. Remember the time you tripped over your shoelaces?"[xlix]

Most kids are desperate to fit in and be considered popular. What's so awful about relational bullying is that it can destroy the victim's reputation and social standing for days, weeks, or even years.

Who the Bullies Are

Bullies Who Suffer from Shame

Children who believe they're unlovable, incompetent, or somehow inadequate often suffer from low self-esteem and even shame. To explain shame, compare it with guilt—guilt is "I did something wrong," whereas shame is "there's something wrong with *me*." Big difference. The latter points to feelings of inadequacy so deep that they make the person feel inherently flawed and loathe themselves.

To compensate, children who live with shame may bully others in an attempt to cover their own sensitive feelings or divert attention from their perceived shortcomings.

Bullies Who've Witnessed or Are Victims of Violence at Home

Kids who witness or are victims of domestic violence at home often embrace the victim mentality or bully persona themselves. Seeing a parental figure yell at, threaten, or hit others in the family teaches children that this is how people treat each other.

Heroic Parenting

Some may carry that behavior to school and bully their peers because they don't know any other way to relate to them. Others may become bully-victims (described below) who are done with being the victim and morph into bullies to gain a sense of control and power in their very disempowered lives. And some may bully their peers because they'd rather be like the more "powerful" abusers in their lives than the "weaker" victims, having seen the price the victims pay.

Bully-Victims

Bully-victims are children who have themselves been bullied by peers, siblings, or parents. They're tired of being the one without power, so they flip from being the victim to being the aggressor, targeting the most vulnerable kids in order to gain a sense of power and control. Their aggressive behavior keeps them at the bottom of the social ladder, which feeds their anger and sense of powerlessness. This is called the bully-victim cycle because it feeds on itself.

Bullies Who Are "Good" Kids

This type of bully is confident and believes he's superior to his peers. He may be a star athlete or on the Student Council and feels entitled to lord it over other students. He loves to show off his superiority and power by bullying kids he considers weak. He has plenty of friends who encourage his aggression, either because they're bullies too, or because they fear becoming his next target if they don't go along with his antics.

Bullies Who Have Learning or Behavior Disorders

Kids who live with attention deficit/hyperactivity disorders or some type of learning or developmental disability that makes it hard to control their emotions and impulses often have few friends and feel lonely and frustrated by their poor social skills. When stressed, some may go into a rage and act out by harming or threatening to harm other kids. Their excess energy, poor impulse control, and frustration and embarrassment over their learning difficulties just exacerbate their volatile nature.

Bullies Who Are Sociopaths or Psychopaths

Few people understand the difference between sociopaths and psychopaths. Both suffer from deep psychological issues that cause them to lack empathy for others or feel little to no guilt for their bad actions. Both may superficially appear charming and glib, while on the inside they care only about getting their own needs met, up to and including the desire to intentionally hurt others.

While sociopaths may be able to form deep bonds with those they care about and their antisocial behavior may lessen over time, psychopaths, on the other hand, feel no remorse for their crimes and care about no one. These people don't bully out of retaliation, to preserve their social standing, or to gain the respect of their peers. They bully "simply because they can," Carpenter writes.[1]

Group Bullies & Toadies

Unlike other types of bullies who act alone, bullies in the "good kids" and "bully-victim" categories may bully as a group, egging each other on as they pick on their victims. Being part of a crowd, led by an alpha male or female, encourages the group members to do and say things they likely wouldn't do on their own. The relative anonymity of the group has a disinhibiting effect, which can lead to truly heinous behavior (think gang rapes or group fights targeting a single victim).

Many bullies have "toadies" or other kids who follow them around and tacitly or overtly encourage their attacks on other kids. Often, these groupies side with the bully to avoid becoming his victim.

Girl Bullies

If I asked you to envision the typical school bully, chances are high you'd picture a boy. But girls are just as likely to be bullies, especially when it comes to dishing out emotional, verbal, and relational punishment. "Sticks and stones may break my bones" is bunk. Everyone knows physical wounds can heal, but emotional scars can leave a lasting impact on victims. And girls can be positively *vicious* when it comes to dealing out indirect abuse.

Once they get into middle school, girls begin to rate themselves and each other by who's in their inner circle and how many friends they have, how pretty and cool they are, and how popular they are. It's an *all-out war* and the prize is popularity and loyalty. To ensure she wins, a girl bully will choose who the losers are and then mercilessly exclude them. Her friends back up her bullying behavior because they don't want her critical eye to fall on them.

Who the Victims Are

There are two main types of bullying victims—children who are passive and those who are considered "provocative."

According to Carpenter, passive victims tend to be anxious, non-aggressive, and physically weaker than their peers, with few or no friends to turn to for protection or support. They may suffer from low self-esteem and are unlikely to try to defend themselves.

Provocative victims are both anxious and aggressive, with poor impulse control or social skills, and a tendency to irritate and alienate others. These victims may have a developmental disability like attention deficit/hyperactivity disorder or autism that makes them prone to react angrily, and sometimes violently, if they're taunted.

Bullies love to provoke these kids and then sit back and watch them spin out of control. And because the victims may already have a bad reputation for acting out, teachers are often quick to blame and punish *them*, rather than the offenders, sometimes even when they witnessed the bullying that led to the outburst.

Special Classes of Victims

LGBTQA+[63]

The spectrum of gender and sexuality is amazingly diverse. Sadly, out of ignorance or fear (usually both), some people choose to target and victimize LGBTQA⁺ individuals. People who identify as lesbian, gay, bisexual, transgender, queer/questioning, asexual, or other gender/sexuality identity (about 5 percent of the US population) are at tremendous risk of being bullied and/or assaulted.[li]

Here are some stats to consider:[64]

- 74 percent of LGBTQA⁺ students were verbally bullied (e.g., called names or threatened) in the past year because of their sexual orientation and 55 percent because of their gender expression.

- 36 percent of LGBTQA⁺ students were physically bullied (e.g., pushed, shoved) in the past year because of their sexual orientation and 23 percent because of their gender expression.

- 49 percent were cyberbullied in the past year.

- 30 percent of LGBTQA⁺ students missed at least one entire day at school in the past month because they felt unsafe or uncomfortable, and 11 percent missed four or more days in the past month.

Sexual identity is one of the most central aspects of a person's personality and it can be devastating and even traumatic to have one's gender identity or sexual preference mocked and punished

---

63 LGBTQA+ = Lesbian, gay, bisexual, transgender, queer/questioning, asexual, plus anything else that doesn't fit within those or the "straight" categories.
64 From the 2013 National School Climate Survey.

by others. It's tragic but not surprising that the suicide rate for LGBTQA+ youth is four times higher than for heterosexual youth.[lii]

Children with Physical, Learning, and Developmental Disabilities

Children with disabilities are at a greatly increased risk of being bullied due to their physical vulnerabilities and compromised social skills. In extreme cases, for example those involving bullies who expose children with allergies to the items they're allergic to, it could even result in the victim's death.

Some children, due to the type of disability they have, are considered "provocative," meaning their poor social skills and low impulse control tend to alienate their peers. It can also bring out the worst in bullies, who get a kick out of harassing these kids until they lose it. The teacher then punishes the victim, having not witnessed the bullying behavior that prompted the outburst.

If your child has a disability or special health issue, you'll want to ensure his Individualized Education Plan (IEP) includes a solid plan to protect him from being bullied. If bullying does occur, it may be considered "disability harassment" which is prohibited by the Americans with Disabilities Act.

In Chapter 14, I'll talk in detail about how to empower and protect kids with disabilities.

Clues That Your Child Is Being Bullied

On an average day, kids can be moody, surly, and uncommunicative. So how do you differentiate between "normal" anti-social behavior and symptoms that your child is being bullied in some way?

You know your child better than anyone. Look for behavior that's different or inconsistent with her usual personality and ask questions to determine whether it's a temporary phase or something more serious that needs your attention or intervention. Deborah Carpenter details a number of symptoms to watch out for, which are listed below. (Seriously, read Carpenter's book; it's one of the best ones I found on bullying and cyberbullying.)[liii]

When kids are victimized in any way, they tend to blame themselves and internalize their feelings. Bullying is incredibly stressful. When your child's body is under stress, it produces too much of the "fight-or-flight" hormones (adrenaline, norepinephrine, and cortisol), keeping her in an aroused state of hypervigilance that leads to a host of physical and psychological symptoms, including:

Physical Symptoms

- Anxiety and nervousness.
- Sleep disturbances, such as insomnia or night terrors.
- Digestive issues, including constipation or diarrhea.
- Fear of using the bathroom at school, causing her to run home to use the toilet.
- Eating disorders, such as anorexia, bulimia, or binging (with or without purging[65]).
- Nervous tics or habits, such as sudden nail biting or stuttering.
- Changes in body posture or body language.
- Torn or soiled clothing (indicators of physical bullying).
- Scratches, bruises, or other injuries.
- Frequent stomachaches or headaches.
- Refusing to go to school or to ride the bus.
- Trying to bring a weapon to school to protect herself.
- Faking illness to get out of going to school.
- Cutting or hurting herself.

Emotional Symptoms

- Isolating herself.
- Clinging or reverting behavior, such as bedwetting.
- Dissociation (being mentally "checked out").
- Unexplained emotional outbursts.
- Depression, sadness, lack of interest in activities or hobbies she used to enjoy.
- Behaving out of character.

---

65 Purging = Intentionally making one's self vomit after eating.

- Secretive behavior.
- Trouble establishing and maintaining healthy relationships.
- Loss of confidence and self-esteem.
- Sudden or chronically bad grades.
- Skipping or dropping out of school.
- Expressions of helplessness and hopelessness.
- Negative self-talk.
- Seeming happy on the weekends but anxious on Sunday nights or at the end of a holiday when she has to return to school.
- Sudden interest in personal safety.
- Talking about or attempting suicide.

Consequences of Bullying

Bullying hurts everyone involved; it even hurts our society by making the world more dangerous and threatening.

Effects on the Victim

For the victims of bullying, most physical wounds will fade over time, but the emotional wounds can last a lifetime. Even short periods of emotional or relational abuse can cause a child to harshly blame himself and decide he really *is* a loser. This loss of self-worth and self-esteem can impair your child's ability to be successful in school and, later, in his career and relationships.

Children who internalize their abuser's voice in their head may engage in self-sabotage and develop learned helplessness, in which they no longer try to make things better because they believe their efforts are futile.

There's a true story about elephants that illustrates this: In the olden days, when a baby elephant was sold to a circus, the owner tied a rope around one foot and the other end around a tree. The baby would try over and over to wander but was always thwarted by the rope. Over the years, the elephant learned the limits of the rope until, eventually the owner would untie the rope from the tree. The elephant could go as far as he liked now but wouldn't wander beyond the length of the original rope because he'd become so used to it.

That is learned helplessness and it can affect your child in much the same way. He can essentially give up hope that things will change or get better. He accepts his fate as a victim and enters into a vicious cycle in which he's likely to be further victimized. It can also lead to severe depression and even suicide.

On the other hand, your child might become hypervigilant, making elaborate plans to avoid the bully to the point that it occupies all his attention. As a result, his school and other relationships begin to suffer. He may become so obsessed with his safety that suicide or revenge seem like the only escape from the torment. Many school shooters were bullied and chose to act out vengefully to stop it. Hundreds of kids have died as a result.

Bullycide

When a child is bullied relentlessly and no one intervenes to protect him, he may not see a way out of the torment and might attempt or actually commit suicide. This has become common enough that there's a term for it: "bullycide." Kids who are bullied are more than twice as likely to attempt suicide as kids who aren't being victimized.[liv] (Boys are 7 *times* more likely to successfully kill themselves.)[lv]

One suicide can create a domino effect, with other kids who are also living in despair following suit. Kids who've lost a classmate to suicide are five times more likely to attempt suicide, even when they didn't have a personal relationship with them. It's like the first suicide gave them *permission* to end their own suffering. Sadly, 12- to 13-year-old kids are at the highest risk.[lvi]

If someone at your child's school has committed suicide and your child has talked about suicide or you fear he'll attempt it, I urge you to find a local therapist who can work with you both to find a way to stop the abuse and heal from it.

Why Kids Don't Tell

Sixty-four percent of kids who are bullied don't report it to their parents or authorities.[lvii] While you want your child to tell you if she's being bullied, in her mind she may have good reasons for not telling:

- Embarrassment over being a victim.
- She doesn't want to worry you.
- She may assume you'll tell her to work it out with the bully, ignore him, or tell her to "toughen up" and move on.

- Fear that you or others won't believe her or, conversely, that you'll overreact and stop her from communicating with her friends. (This would be a common, if knee-jerk reaction that could keep her silent the next time something happens. Better to reward her for showing good judgment and being mature enough to recognize when she's in danger and asking for help.)
- Fear that you'll try to confront the bully or his parents.
- Fear of getting the school authorities or police involved.
- Fear of being seen as a narc[66] or tattletale.
- Fear of retaliation or becoming even more vulnerable to the bully and others if she tells.
- Fear of being blamed, especially if she did or said something to instigate the bullying (by making a mean comment herself, for example).
- And, most disturbing of all, the belief that she deserves it.

Why Parents Don't Take Action

Parents also don't always react appropriately when they learn their child's been bullied. They may:

- Feel helpless to do anything themselves and tell their child to ignore it or handle it on his own.
- They may not know how to react appropriately and so do nothing.
- They may think bullying is a rite of passage that their child has to learn to deal with on his own.
- They may lack sympathy, as in, "I was bullied and I survived. So can you."
- They may fear making things worse for their child if they intervene (although it usually gets worse if they don't).

If your child confided in you that he was being bullied and you reacted badly, you can repair the damage by talking to him and apologizing. Assure him that you'll protect him from now on. Ask for his opinion about how he thinks the two of you should handle the situation. Just

---

66 Narc = A person who turns people in (to the authorities or their parents) for something they did wrong.

remember that YOU are the parent and that you'll most likely need to report the incident(s) to his school and possibly the police.

How to Bully-Proof Your Child

Kids see and understand so much more than what we give them credit for. They know what's up and unless they're just starting school, they've likely already seen bullies at work. Studies have found that bullying and teasing are among kids' top worries (along with school shootings). Teaching your child how to deal with bullies will empower her to quickly nip it in the bud.

Talk Early & Often

The best time to talk to your child about bullying is *now*, whether she's being bullied or not. The sooner you start the conversation, the better prepared your child will be to deal with bullying if she encounters it.

Asking your child what she's witnessed or experienced opens the door for her to come to you if something happens. Talking through scenarios and roleplaying her responses will teach her how to react in the moment if something happens. If she does get bullied, you can read age-appropriate books together on the subject and talk about what you've read.

It's important to define for your child what bullying is and what it's not. Teaching her the difference between occasional teasing (done in good fun), rudeness (done out of thoughtlessness), meanness (done with the intent to wound, but not rising to the level of threatening behavior), and actual bullying can help her put other kids' behavior into perspective.

The first thing to teach your child is that no one deserves to be bullied and that there's nothing she does that causes her to deserve being targeted. *It's not actually about her.* Tell her that bullies act out because they want to appear cool and powerful, because they're insecure and choose to hurt others to make themselves feel better, or because they're afraid if they don't join in the bullying they'll be targeted themselves. It could even be a combination of these.

Bullies want to inflict damage on their victims' confidence and self-esteem and say things that usually aren't true to get a reaction. Most books about bullying advise kids not to take it personally. Heck, even adults take things like that personally, so how can we expect a child to be more mature than we are?

That's why it's good to talk about this before something happens, so you and your child can discuss it when things are calm and she's not in crisis mode.

If your child has been or is actively being bullied, assure her that it gets better and show her how to defend herself verbally and physically (if necessary),[67] which I'll talk about shortly.

Encourage Your Child to Remain True to Himself

The most important thing you can teach your child is to be true to himself, no matter what's happening around him or to him. Here in the US (unlike in some other countries), individuality and uniqueness are valued and celebrated.

This is a difficult concept for school-age kids to grasp because many of them so desperately want to fit in. They fear that if there's something about them that makes them stand out, they'll be shunned and even punished by their peers. Wearing glasses, dressing out of fashion, being shy or dorky, being a nerd, having a different sexual orientation, or having some type of disability—anything that makes them appear different—can make them a target.

What makes me saddest about this is that the very things that can make a child a target for bullies are often the very things that make them special and most lovable. Having their peers use those traits against a child can destroy his sense of worthiness and self-esteem in ways that can take years to repair.

If your child is obviously different from his peers in some way (e.g., super shy, socially awkward, or physically different), you'll need to work extra hard to bolster his confidence and help him appreciate his special contribution to the world.[68]

Because the consequences are so great, most kids try to fit in, even if that means contorting themselves into pretzel shapes to do so. But to do this, they have to hide their true selves, and that leads them to become inauthentic. And people, especially kids, can easily spot inauthenticity and it can bring the hammer down on the victims even harder.

What's ironic[69] about this is that nearly all kids feel like dorks and are faking it just as hard as everyone else. Even the bullies are afraid of not fitting in, which is why they act like such toads in the first place. By making their victims the focus of everyone's attention, they're hoping to distract other kids from their own perceived shortcomings.

---

[67] In Chapter 17, I'll show you how to teach your child to physically defend herself using my signature "Taz" moves that don't require any formal martial arts or self-defense mastery.
[68] I share ways to increase your child's confidence and self-esteem in Chapter 15.
[69] If I'm using the word "ironic" incorrectly here, it's fine to GENTLY correct me. Just don't be a jerk about it or I might not-so-gently advise you to re-read this entire chapter and write a 500-word essay on the value of kindness.

Heroic Parenting

Fact is, other kids aren't thinking about your child much, if at all. They're thinking and worrying about themselves. So tell your snookums to stop obsessing over what other people think! Encourage him to wear his dorkiness like a badge of honor. Teach him that in the real world, outside of grade school, kindness and generosity are what help people get ahead and find happiness and success.[70]

Remind your child how adorable puppies with crooked smiles are and how much we treasure rocks and animals and trees that are different from all the others. Bolster his confidence by telling him that when he's true to himself and acts with authenticity, he'll feel and appear cool to others because confidence is as cool as it gets.

The way to be cool is to glory in not fitting in.

Point out how his idols (e.g., musicians, movie stars, even superheroes) all have flaws and are dorks too; that it's okay, and even better than okay, to be different. Remind him that these people wouldn't be famous if not for their unique qualities. Remind him that not everyone can be popular and of the high cost of popularity (again, inauthenticity). Does he *really* want to be like that?[71]

Jennifer Hancock says:

"The great thing about embracing your inner dork is that it takes all the stress off of you. Once you stop trying to fit in, you can relax and be yourself. So what if someone calls you a dork. You are – 'nuff said. Teasing simply doesn't work on someone who has embraced the fact they are a dork and they are different. It also frees you up to really enjoy the things you like. Even if what you really enjoy is classical music and you dream of being an opera singer someday, you don't need to hide that from your friends. Not everyone has those talents or dreams and it is pretty darned cool if you do. So embrace that about yourself and pursue the things that truly interest you. The point is, when you accept and embrace whatever it is that makes you different, you inoculate yourself against the bullies because they can't make you feel ashamed of something you aren't ashamed of."[72]

I love that. But what if your child has a physical or developmental disability or other attributes (e.g., being smaller, bigger, being poor, etc.), which make him more likely to be targeted by

---

[70] Yes, yes. Power and money can sometimes do that too, but do they bring *genuine* happiness? Okay, so they might do that as well, but do they create peace? Checkmate.
[71] Be prepared for him to say "yes" to this question. If so, impress upon him that there's always a high cost to fame that few are really ready to pay.
[72] Jennifer Hancock, *The Bully Vaccine: How to Inoculate Yourself Against Bullies and Other Petty People.*

bullies? The same rules apply. There are kids out there with these types of challenges who refuse to apologize for who and how they are, and they're more respected as a result.

Of course, being confident and authentic doesn't guarantee your child won't be bullied, but it will help him not to take it so personally. Combine that with the proactive and defensive tactics I teach next and he'll be better able to respond to bullies in ways that are more likely to quickly put an end to the taunting.

Talk to Your Child about How to Respond to Bullying

The bullying cycle usually begins with verbal harassment before escalating to more serious behavior. Your daughter's reaction to the bully's very first attempt may determine whether she goes from a one-time target to a long-term victim.

The most common advice bullied kids receive from well-meaning parents is to just "ignore it and they'll go away." That's helpful if the bullying is limited to simple name-calling or teasing, but when it involves physical harm or threats of harm, all bets are off.

Just ignoring the bully usually doesn't work. After all, if your child is constantly exposed to this person at school or on the bus, the threat of harm is ever-present. Better to tell your child not to positively reinforce the bully's behavior, which is very different from simply ignoring it.

Positive reinforcement means reacting in any way that's satisfying to the bully—whether that's crying, cowering, acquiescing, or getting angry. Your child's best course of action is to deny bullies what they're looking for by not giving them the satisfaction they're hoping to get. When your child reacts like a victim, the bully gains power and may continue to pick on her because he's "rewarded" when he does.

When your child denies the bully that satisfaction, she becomes less interesting as a victim. By denying the bully his emotional reward, your child will make it less worthwhile for the bully to pick on her. She's basically "retraining" the bully to leave her alone.

Teach your child specific things to do and say in response to bullying behavior that will deny the bully his satisfaction, such as:

- **Embracing being the butt of the joke.** When your daughter makes jokes about herself based on what the bully says it puts her in control of the situation and denies the bully the upset reaction he was looking for. For example, when I was 5, a friend called me

"Cinderella," riffing on the real name I went by at that time of Cindy. It hurt my feelings because it wasn't meant as a compliment but was being used to tease me, so I began to cry. This led the other kids to tease me too. If I had joined in the teasing, saying something like, "Yes! I'm Cinderella! Now fetch my glass slipper!" we all would have had a good laugh and it would have ended with me feeling empowered and not like a victim.

- **Responding with as little emotion as possible.** Advise your lamb to wear a poker face and not give the bully the satisfaction of an emotional reaction.

- **Responding with good humor or positive emotions.** Teach your child to act like she's thrilled that the bully noticed her, agree with the bully, thank the bully for his interesting perspective, act with boredom or disinterest, or respond with the same phrase every time (for example, "Thanks for sharing."). This will suck the oxygen out of the bully's fire and cause him to give up on his quest to get a reaction from your child.

- **Teaching your child to be fearless**, to accept that she's being targeted and to not care so much. Help her realize that since it isn't about her or what she does or doesn't do, the bully has some measure of power over her. However, she has the power to choose how to react. Tell her to use that power to free herself from worry and fear.

There are a number of other ways your child could respond to a bully, including:

- Avoiding the bully whenever possible. If she must, she can ask for a different locker to avoid bumping into him in the halls.

- Buddying up with a friend to keep from being alone around him.

- Agreeing with the bully ("You're right, I am a klutz.") and walking away.

- Rolling with the taunts ("You're right, my last name *does* rhyme with 'butt.'") and walking away.

- Making a self-deprecating joke ("You're right, I suck at math!") and walking away.

- Owning her personality ("You're totally right, I'm a dork and proud of it!") and walking away.

- Ignoring him and walking away.

- Telling the bully to stop in a clear, firm voice AND WALKING AWAY.

You may have noticed the repetition in the examples above. Prefacing her responses to the bully with "You're right" shows confidence and takes the wind out of his sails. And walking away after responding puts distance between her and the bully.

Practice these responses at home using roleplay where you and your child take turns acting like the bully and the victim until she feels comfortable saying them in a strong, firm voice. Even have her practice walking away while you try (pretending to be the bully) to get her to react.[73]

If she can't walk away from the bully because she's cornered, she can continue using the verbal responses above until (a) the bully gets tired of the game he's clearly not winning, or (b) the bullying escalates into an attack, in which case she has a decision to make about whether to fight back or not. Let her know that fighting back if she must, to keep from being assaulted, is the last resort. But, if she feels it's necessary to protect herself, she can choose to do so. Assure her that the consequences from the school are less important than her safety.

Know that when your brave child uses these tactics, the offender might not give up right away and may even escalate his attempts to bully her. Teach her to expect this and tough it out until he gives up. The bully may frantically attempt to reassert control, but if your child continues to deny him a reaction, he'll eventually give up and leave her alone. *But she has to be consistent and not give in!* Giving him what he's looking for will only make the situation worse.

Be sure your child doesn't post the anti-bullying tactics she's employing on social media or share them with other kids so they don't come to the attention of the bully and lead him to increase the abuse.

Jennifer Hancock[74] warns that, "Once you stop responding to bullies the way they want, their obnoxious behavior spikes and becomes more frequent and more severe as they try to get you to respond. This is known as a blowout. If the blowout fails to get the desired response, their attempts will fall off quite rapidly. Eventually they stop trying altogether. The good news is that the blowout means you are close to extinguishing the behavior. The bad news is that because we are all humans with real human emotions, not broken vending machines, most people give in at this point and respond to the bullying."

---

[73] Please don't take your mock bullying too far so you don't end up seriously hurting your child's feelings.
[74] Jennifer Hancock, *The Bully Vaccine: How to Inoculate Yourself Against Bullies and Other Petty People.*

If, on the other hand, the bully acts in a way that's positive, by being nice for example, advise your child to reinforce his behavior by being nice in return. Bullies seek attention, and giving him positive attention when he behaves is a great way to retrain him to behave appropriately.

It's just like with an animal you're trying to train—you give negative reinforcement when they disobey and yummy treats when they do something right. If the bully goes through a period of being good, encourage your child to keep reinforcing it. If he reverts to his old bullying tactics, she should go back to reacting with humor, boredom, or disinterest.

"The beauty of doing this," Hancock writes, "is that it puts you in control. Yes, they are still being mean, but you are the one in control of the situation, not them. In short, you are training your bullies to not be such jerks. That's pretty darned cool when you think about it. The bonus is that you get to be the cool, calm, collected individual who was able to find compassion for the rudest jerks in the school. And that's something to be proud of."[lviii]

It can take days to months of doing this before the bully stops, depending on how persistent or insecure he is. This is why it's so important to nip bullying in the bud the moment it starts.

When Self-Defense Is Necessary

When bullying turns physical, your child may need to defend himself to prevent further harm. Two things are important here:

1. Your child needs to know that if he's in imminent danger of being physically (or sexually) assaulted and needs to defend himself against an attacker, he should do what he must to protect himself and worry about the consequences later. His immediate safety is paramount!

2. Your child also needs to know *how* to defend himself properly, so his actions are effective yet don't go to the extreme.

Enroll your child in self-defense or martial arts classes, which will give him not only skills, but confidence. It's important that he take these classes long enough to become proficient. Taking just a class or two won't help him. He needs to continue to practice these new skills for the lessons to become ingrained in his memory and accessible in a moment of crisis.

For those who can't or don't want to take formal lessons, teach them to use my signature "Tasmanian Devil" self-defense moves, which I describe in Chapter 17. Unleashing his "inner Taz" is as simple as using his own bodily "weapons" to repel bullies and other predators. The tactics I recommend are easy to remember and use, and they're quite effective. Any child (or adult!) can quickly learn and apply them.

What to Do When Your Child Is Being Bullied

If you learn your child is being bullied, the first thing to do is tell her how sorry you are this happened to her and promise you'll work to protect her moving forward. Don't get overly emotional or angry, which could make her regret telling you.

Calmly draw her out to get the whole story and decide together whether she can handle the situation on her own or if you should report it to the school. Your child may beg you not to get involved or report the bullying. If the bullying is mild and your child isn't overly upset by it, you can teach her ways to handle it on her own, such as those I just suggested. Letting her deal with a minor bullying situation can increase her confidence in her ability to take care of herself.

Be sure to keep the lines of communication open and encourage her to tell you if the bullying doesn't stop or things get worse. Watch for signs that things are escalating and be prepared to intervene at any point you feel your child is endangered.

However, if your child has been injured or has been threatened with injury, or if the bully is mentally unstable, has a weapon, or has threatened to use a weapon, it's imperative that you immediately report it to the school (and even the police, which I'll talk about below).

With your daughter's help, document everything leading up to the incident(s) and exactly what happened during and afterward. Include attempts your child made to protect and defend herself. Stick to the facts and try not to get emotional or take an accusatory tone in your document or any interactions with school officials. This can come off as overly hysterical and put the authorities on the defensive instead of in your corner.

Keep a running log of all phone, electronic, and in-person interactions with school authorities and the police, including who was involved in the conversations, when and where they occurred, and what was discussed and promised. You'll need this record when you meet with school authorities or the police.[75]

Clueless kids, especially bullies, often document their bad acts to show off to their friends and get social media likes. This is to your advantage because their videos, texts, emails, or social media posts provide great evidence you can use to bolster your child's claims.

---

[75] I've created a Word document you can use to record information about the incident(s) and all interactions with the authorities that you can find on my website at www.cjscarlet.com/freebies.

Heroic Parenting

Also document any injuries to your child, including taking photos of her injuries over time until they completely heal. Consider recording a video of your child telling what happened and showing her injuries.

Recognize that your precious angel may not be totally innocent in the matter. While she doesn't deserve to be unduly harassed or abused, she may have contributed to the situation through her own mean or inappropriate comments or posts. Own up to those while emphasizing the need to stop the situation from escalating.

Don't try to talk to the bully's parents unless you know them well. It probably won't go the way you expect it to, meaning the parents are likely to defend their child rather than apologize and make them stop. Better to let the school handle it.

Reporting to the School

When dealing with school officials, you may get a tepid response at first. Ask for a meeting with the principal, your child's teachers, and the guidance counselor to talk through what happened and come up with a solution.

Bring an ally with you—an advocate or close friend who can support you. That will lead the school authorities to behave more respectfully and make them more likely to take action. Just having another person there will make them sit up straighter and treat you with greater respect. Plus, if you meet with them alone, it's their more-authoritative word against yours if there's a disagreement over what is said or promised in those meetings.

If school officials still try to sweep the situation under the rug, maintain your cool and get the school board or police involved. If the school isn't able or willing to protect your child from the bully, you may need to consider changing your child's school or homeschooling her.

Your job is to do whatever it takes to keep your child from being harmed. If that means getting a bad rep[76] as "that parent," so be it.

A Word on Zero Tolerance Policies

When I got the call from the middle school saying my oldest son, then 12, had been in a fight, I couldn't believe it. *Sean? My Sean? He wouldn't harm a soul!* I rushed to my son's side and found him holding a bloody cloth to his mouth where his broken tooth had been shoved through his gums.

---

76 Rep = Reputation.

According to both Sean and the principal, he was walking to class when another boy pushed him from behind to the concrete and he landed on his face, hence the injury. The attack was totally unprovoked and nothing else happened, but both boys were given a week of in-school suspension.

I. Was. *Furious!* My son was the victim of an assault and he was going to be punished? The principal explained that it was the school's "zero tolerance" policy to punish both children involved in a fight, regardless of who started or finished it. Despite my pleas and threats to take it to the school board, the principal wouldn't budge. In the end, he gave Sean three days of in-school suspension and the bully was suspended (out of school) for two weeks.

If that happened today, knowing what I know now, I would have pressed criminal charges and fought harder to keep my son from being punished at all. He was the victim of a crime and should never have been treated like a criminal himself.

In an effort to curb bullying and other bad behavior, many schools have adopted similar "zero tolerance" policies, which deal out severe punishments for rule violations regardless of the circumstances. When bullying is a "he said, she said" matter because there are no witnesses (or witnesses refuse to talk), innocent victims may be punished too, as my son was.

As impressive as it sounds for schools to employ zero tolerance, it's not fair to victims and may discourage them from trying to defend themselves for fear of being suspended or expelled. And it may discourage school officials from reporting incidents because they want to appear to be on top of problems in their schools.

Another tack schools take is to require both the bully and victim to go through mediation or conflict resolution. First of all, it's *not* a "conflict," which implies both parties are responsible for the problem. It's a victimization, and the victim needs to be protected from the bully and not forced to sit across from her and be responsible for stopping her behavior. The number one priority should be stopping the violence and keeping the victim safe. Your child's school may need you to remind them of that.

Actions that are more effective include graduated sanctions, which provide more appropriate consequences for the bully, as well as counseling and peer mentoring that can modify her behavior.

If your child has been bullied or tells you it's a problem at her school, talk to the principal about how the school addresses the problem and encourage him to implement bullying prevention training and strategies, which are known to reduce bullying by as much as 50 percent.[lix]

When to Take It to the Next Level

If your child has been physically assaulted or received dire threats of harm, you can always take legal action, ranging from obtaining a restraining order to filing a police report to suing the bully's family in civil court.

Deciding whether to report bullying incidents to the police can be a tough call—except when your child has suffered physical harm or threats of harm. In those cases, you *must* get authorities involved before a tragedy occurs.

In any event, if your child's school isn't being responsive and doesn't effectively protect your child, you can file a formal complaint with the US Department of Education's Office for Civil Rights. Your child is protected by Title IX, which is a federal civil rights law that prohibits sex discrimination in any K-12 school, online school, college, or university that receives federal funding. Title IX provides protections and remedies for victims of gender-based harassment,[77] bullying, sexual harassment, dating abuse or intimate partner violence, and stalking.

When your child is granted protection under Title IX, she may be eligible to receive accommodations, such as having the bully moved to a different classroom. (I go into detail about Title IX in my handout on Legal Remedies, which can be found on my website's Freebies page.)

If Your Child Is the Bully

If you find out your little angel is more of a little monster, don't panic. Check out the free handout about What to Do If Your Child Is the Bully on my website at www.cjscarlet.com/freebies.

---

[77] "Gender-based" harassment or bullying occurs when a student doesn't conform to gender stereotypes (e.g., targeting a person because of their gender or sexual identity, or because they don't act the way a boy or girl "should").

CHAPTER 8

Digital Dangers

The dark world of online child sexual exploitation is not a pretty topic, but it's an essential one to cover given the fact that your child is a digital native who will spend an increasing amount of time online as he grows older.

The Internet is arguably the greatest invention of all time. It's brought the global community together in amazing ways, but it's also made us—and especially our children—more vulnerable to bad people who want to take advantage of us.

While most other types of crime are decreasing, online sexual exploitation of children is one area where the statistics are going up in a seriously bad way. For example, the number of documented complaints of online enticement of children has gone up by almost 250 percent since 2004![lx]

This is definitely when teaching your child to be wary of *all* strangers is a good thing. I'll talk more about this below, but first, let's ensure we're all on the same page.

- There are close to a *million* registered sex offenders in the US (and those are just the ones who've been caught and convicted!).[78]

- The FBI estimates that there are close to a million predators (registered and unregistered) online every day looking for people to victimize.[lxi] And the younger the victim, the more severe the abuse.[lxii]

- Nearly 90 percent of all sexual advances toward children take place in Internet chat rooms and through instant messaging.[lxiii]

---

78 According to the FBI, around 100,000 sexual predators have not registered in their communities as required and law enforcement has no idea where they live.

- Young children are becoming addicted to online pornography, with their first exposure occurring as young as 8 years old.[lxiv]

A Few Definitions

Some of the definitions below look obvious, but many older caregivers will also read this book and may benefit from a better understanding of what these terms mean. (And watch it with the "Okay, Boomer" snark. We're older, but to paraphrase Kathy Bates' character in the 1991 classic movie *Fried Green Tomatoes*, we're wiser and can kick your butt at Trivial Pursuit! Towanda!)[79]

Internet

The global network that connects computers to storehouses of electronic information and enables people all over the world to communicate and share information.

Internet Service Provider

Companies (like AT&T and Spectrum) or governmental, educational, or non-profit organizations that offer full access to the Internet, usually for a fee.

Internet Browser

A browser is a gateway to the Internet. Services like Google Chrome, Internet Explorer, and Firefox provide software programs you use to view web pages on your computer.

Search Engine

A search engine is a website that allows users to look up information on the World Wide Web (Internet). The top three search engines are Google, YouTube, and Amazon.com.

Online child sexual exploitation includes:

- The production, possession, downloading, and distribution of child sexual abuse and exploitation materials online.
- Grooming children for sexual purposes.
- Streaming of live online child sexual abuse.
- Sexting (texting sexual content and conversations).

---

79 Only those who have seen the movie will know what "Towanda" means. It's one of the many perks of being a member of the Boomer generation.

- Sextortion (extortion using sexual images of the victim for leverage).
- Online child sexual abuse and exploitation in real-time.

Social Media

Websites and apps[80] that enable users to create and share content or to participate in social networking.

Chat Rooms

Chat rooms are online spaces where users communicate with one another through text-based messages. It's like a virtual party where strangers congregate to talk about shared interests, discuss hot topics, flirt, ask for and offer advice, or just hang out.

Cybersex

Engaging in online sex-oriented conversations and materials.

Trolling

Antagonizing others online by deliberately posting inflammatory, disruptive, or offensive comments or content.

Cyberstalking

Using electronic communication to harass or threaten someone with physical harm.

The World Wide Web Is the Wild, Wild West

When your child goes online—through her computer, laptop, tablet, e-reader, smartphone, Apple iTouch, or gaming console—she instantly has access to every piece of information that can be found on the world wide web (unless you've smartly put filtering software on those devices).[81] This is great if she's looking to research the natural habitat of bonobo chimpanzees for a school project, but not so great if she sneaks in a search for videos of their mating habits (which are seriously impressive, btw).

---

80 Apps = Applications.

81 I simply don't have room in this book to go into great detail about the pros and cons of the various electronic devices or the types of vulnerabilities these create, so I highly recommend you read *The Boogeyman Exists; And He's in Your Child's Back Pocket: Internet Safety Tips for Keeping Your Children Safe Online, Smartphone Safety, Social Media Safety, and Gaming Safety* by Jesse Weinberger. It's a super informative and highly entertaining read.

And it's free, free, FREE! Or at least it doesn't cost *money*. Never forget that if you're not paying for a product, you *ARE* the product!

Are *YOU* Ready for Your Child to Be Online?

Before you ever let your child touch any electronic device that connects to the Internet, you need to be sure that YOU'RE ready. What do I mean by that? I mean that you must accept your solemn responsibility as a parent to teach your kid what's okay and what's not okay online, and you must be willing to set meaningful boundaries that are backed up by real consequences. You need to supervise his online activities and regularly monitor his conversations and provide corrective advice to keep him within bounds.

If he goes beyond those boundaries and breaks the rules you set, you must then be willing to be the bad cop and dish out appropriate punishment and consequences, up to and including smashing his phone or computer. Yes, I said *smash* and I meant it. I'll talk more about when this is warranted in a bit.

The big question is *when*. When is your child ready to have access to the Internet through a computer, tablet, smartphone, or gaming console? Well, that depends on several factors, including:

- Your personal beliefs about when kids should be allowed to have access to online content.
- Your willingness to set and enforce strong rules around that access.
- Your confidence that your child can be trusted to follow your rules.
- Your willingness to talk candidly with your child about digital dangers *before* he ever lays a finger on a keyboard and to spend time with him to create safe profiles (which I'll cover below).
- Your willingness to police your child's online activity and to bring the hammer down when he breaks the rules.
- Your child's maturity level.

Only one of these depends on your child; the rest are all on you, mom and dad. No doubt you noticed that I used the word "willingness" three times in this list. Willingness implies choice, and it comes down to just that—you get to choose whether to set your child up for safety by putting in a bit of time and effort to ensure he has a positive online experience. Or, you can choose to set him up for failure and potential victimization by allowing him to freely surf the web with no supervision. (And not choosing is also a choice you make, BTW.)

Seriously, you'd be amazed how many parents either don't care or don't have a clue what their kids are doing online. But clearly, you're not one of those parents or you wouldn't be reading this book, am I right? Don't worry, I make it easier for you by providing you with a list of rules to get you started.

So, I ask again: Are YOU ready to be the adult in the room and provide your child with the guidance and appropriate consequences he needs to stay out of trouble or, worse, harm?

I hope you said yes, because if you said "no" or waffled because you'd rather be your child's BFF than his parent, then you're putting him at serious risk of being damaged—emotionally, physically, sexually, and/or legally. If you just "can't" have the digital dangers conversation with him, then don't let him have any devices that can access online content or conversations. Otherwise you're being willfully obtuse.[82]

Jesse Weinberger[83] says it perfectly:

"Your goal as a parent is to educate your child as to the risks of having a particular device. You should also encourage input from your child as to how they intend to use the device, how they feel about specific risks, and what their real-world digital experience has been thus far. Leave the lines of communication with your children open so that they always feel comfortable in being honest with you. However, do not confuse this conversation with a 'negotiation' of digital terms with your child. Make it clear to your children that part of your job as a parent is to keep them safe and to ensure that they are interacting with the world in a way that you find appropriate according to your own family's values. These safeguards are every bit as important to their healthy development as eating vegetables and getting enough sleep."

PLEASE step up here. Reading *Heroic Parenting* (and the other books I reference in this chapter) is a great way to don the mantle of authority and do right by your child.

Is Your Child Ready?

Have you ever compared today's movies—with their action scenes transitioning so quickly—to those made in the 70s? Or watched your kid text? His little thumbs fly so fast your eyes can barely detect it![84]

---

82 Obtuse = Intentionally stupid. I also like the way Urban Dictionary defines it as "the state of being simultaneously high and in a reclined position." HAHAHA!
83 Jesse Weinberger, *The Boogeyman Exists; And He's in Your Child's Back Pocket.*
84 In the meantime, I'm fumbling in slowmo because, unlike your digital native of a child, I—a digital immigrant—wasn't born with a cell phone in my hand. I didn't even own one until I was in my late 30s! Cut me some slack; I'm a grandma.

Heroic Parenting

Your son's growing brain has developed to ingest large amounts of data in a short span of time. It's a quantum leap from the way things were 25 years ago when you were young, but it's your child's reality and it's all he's ever known or can even imagine. Just as fish don't realize they're surrounded by water because they're so immersed in it, your child can't see the difference between the real world and the digital world.[lxv]

Your son's job is to be a kid, which means testing boundaries, making mistakes, and figuring out who he is. Your job as a parent is to help him do all these things. That means setting firm boundaries that allow him to make and learn from his mistakes and encourage him to form his unique identity. Believe it or not, kids actually crave fair and consistent boundaries because it gives them a framework to work within and, yes, something to push against.

You crave them too. It's helpful, is it not, when your boss gives you parameters to work within when you're working on a new project, as well as regular feedback to let you know you're on the right track? It's also helpful to get kind, constructive feedback when you're off base. It works the same way for kids. They want and need your guidance, and even your punishments, to help them learn how to navigate the world they live in.

Giving your child unfettered access to the digital world without educating him about its dangers or how to safely navigate that world is like giving him a loaded gun and not teaching him how to use it properly. That last sentence may seem hyperbolic[85] but it's not—kids are literally killing themselves because of online threats and harassment. This is super serious stuff.

If you position online access as a privilege and rite of passage your child can earn by demonstrating maturity and responsibility, he'll be more likely to take that responsibility seriously. Telling him, for example, that once he turns 7 AND has shown you he can follow other household rules he can create an online profile on GeckoLife will give him something to work toward. Nothing motivates a child to do chores and homework like the promise of screen time!

I want to make sure you hear me on this. Nothing, and I mean NO THING will motivate your child to follow the rules, do chores, and complete his homework like the promise of screen time. Smart parents use this fact to their advantage. On my website, I provide a chore list you can use that rewards your child with screen time for checking off the boxes.

---

85 Hyperbolic = Over the top.

Jeepers Creepers How the Lingo Has Changed!

Every generation of kids has their own lingo they use to sound cool and trendy. Nowadays, when something is awesome, it's "sick," and if you say, "it's da bomb," you're clearly out of touch.[86]

Our clever kids have devised a whole new lexicon[87] using acronyms to communicate online and on their cell phones. The ostensible reason is that SMS[88] only allows a certain number of characters in messages, so people have to keep their messages super short; think Twitter with its former limit of 140 characters.

The more likely reason, however, is that these acronyms act as a secret code kids use to communicate with each other in a language parents don't understand. For example, did you know that "9" stands for "parent watching?" If your child writes "9" in a message while you're peeking at her online activity, she's telling the person on the other end to keep it clean and appropriate until you're no longer looking, at which point she'll type "99" (for parent gone).[89]

How Predators Decide Who to Exploit

Just like IRL,[90] online predators carefully choose their victims with intention, based on signs they're looking for, such as a child's obvious lack of self-esteem or confidence, susceptibility to flattery, and statements she makes that indicate she's lonely and desperate for attention and affection.

Perps also get additional info online by paying attention to sexy profile names, images, and posts that are provocative and send the message that a child is open (knowingly or unknowingly) to engage in sexually explicit conversations or in-person meetings. And just as your child can lie on her profile and claim to be older, most online perps will lie to appear and even sound (sometimes using voice changing technology) closer to the victim's age, so that cute 16-year-old boy could actually be a repulsive 50-year-old man sitting in his skivvies and shoveling Cheetos into his gaping maw.[91]

---

86 I still say it. Sue me.
87 Lexicon = Vocabulary.
88 SMS = Short Messaging Service.
89 To learn what these acronyms stand for, go to www.netlingo.com for a comprehensive, up-to-date list. As with the Urban Dictionary, be prepared to either laugh your head off (if you have a good sense of humor) or for your eyes to bug out (in which case you might want to have a trash can nearby to throw up in).
90 IRL = In Real Life.
91 Maw = Mouth.

How Perps Get Access to Your Child

Usually, to gain access to chat rooms and instant messaging platforms, your child has to fill out a profile where he might unknowingly give out personal information that can entice predators. Below are the most common ways predators use technology to connect with children:[92]

- **Chat Rooms**: The most popular chat rooms for both children and pedophiles are game rooms, child-oriented sites, and teen sites.

- **Instant Messaging (IM):** IM sites are similar to chat rooms, but the communication is more private and one-on-one. It's also live, so the conversation can quickly escalate into inappropriate comments, suggestions, and requests.

- **Email:** If your child gives out his email address to someone he doesn't know, their communications become private and he can hide their conversations from you simply by saving them in a hidden folder and then deleting them from his email inbox, so if you look just in his inbox or sent folders, you won't find anything suspicious.

- **Websites:** While websites aren't used for direct communication, your child can run across content that promotes hatred, violence, sexual images, or pornography. Many websites ask for personal information that naïve children often provide, and they usually leave cookies[93] on your computer so they can track your activity.

- **Blogs:** Blogs encourage readers to offer their opinions, communicate with others, and even post photos which, again, can entice predators and enable them to develop a relationship with your child.

- **Mobile Phones:** A whopping 95 percent of teens have access to a smartphone and 45 percent are online "constantly."[lxvi] Smartphones are kids' favorite way to access all the above because they can do so anywhere, anytime, and out of sight of their parents.

Chat Rooms Are the Devil!

Remember that 90 percent of sexual advances toward children are made through chat rooms and Instant Messaging. Chat rooms are so appealing to predators because the conversation can

---

92 From *Child Safety & Protection: Child Security for Parents & Children* by Brian Cox and Rob Knight.
93 Internet "cookies" (not to be confused with their distant buy yummy baked cousins) are messages that web servers pass to your web browser when you visit Internet sites that may contain information about your visit to the web page, as well as any information you've volunteered, such as your name and interests.

take place in real-time, one-on-one, or with multiple people. It's fun, it's fast, it's engaging. No wonder kids love it.

Your child can also hide behind her profile, so there's a level of anonymity, which tends to have a disinhibiting effect that encourages people to be more outgoing, candid, vicious, and sexual. This anonymity gives your child a false sense of security that could lead to real trouble.

That PlayStation Isn't Just a Game

Video gaming systems have changed significantly from the time I bought my sons their first Nintendo in the early 90s.[94] Now they can stream movies and shows and enable players to compete and talk trash with other players across the planet. Fun? Yes! Potentially dangerous? Most certainly.

Online predators use that chat feature to meet and groom unsuspecting kids. There's even a video chat feature that provides visual access to your child, so the perp can see him. (The video chat feature has the added benefit, for the creepers, of ensuring they're talking to real kids and not undercover cops posing as children in order to catch predators.)

You need to protect your child when they're gaming just as you would when they're on their computer or smartphone. Through the gaming console settings, you can enable parental controls and disable Internet access and video streaming features. You can also install other parental control software to ensure your child is fully protected while gaming. Apps like Bark[95] will notify you if harmful or inappropriate content is detected.

An interesting and essential exercise would be to play along with your child or watch him play. Ask him to show you how he uses the chat and video features to communicate with other players. Of course, it's totally up to you whether you allow him to use those features, but know that thar be dragons and use those parental controls!

And for the love of Mike, *please* don't let your child play games that aren't rated for his age! I know of parents who cave in and let their young kids play mature-rated games like Grand Theft Auto where they can kill cops and prostitutes and commit other mind-numbing mayhem. Your kid may throw a screaming tantrum when you try to limit his gaming options, but let that heroic parent flag fly! It's better to have an angry kid than a damaged one.[96]

---

94 Great. Now I can't get the theme music from Mario Brothers out of my head!
95 www.Bark.us
96 Ooh! Great Tweet material!

Special Lures Predators Use Online

Criminals can be so crafty and sexual predators are the most creative of all. They've always been adept at grooming children in all the ways I've covered to this point, but the online world offers entirely new methods to lure kids into giving them what they want.

For example, in one famous case involving an international child pornography ring that was ultimately busted, the ring members used three creative techniques to encourage their victims to provide sexual content:

- **Dares**—Ever play Truth or Dare? Well, this is a bit like that, involving ring members daring the children they were talking to online to do small things, like taking off articles of clothing and then graduating to bigger dares, like engaging in actual sex acts which, of course, were being recorded and shared among group members.

- **Polls**—Ring members created "fun" polls to engage the children, asking them to vote on the attractiveness of a particular child. These polls would then get more sinister, asking the children to vote on what the person should do next (for example, remove clothing, masturbate, or engage in sex acts).

- **Competitions**—Ring members would pit one child against another and give points to them for doing "daring" things, such as taking off their clothes, showing their private parts, or performing specific sex acts—all on camera, of course. The kids were encouraged to win as many points as they could in order to get to the next "level."

These types of lures are so insidious and so effective because kids enjoy games, they love to win, and they're eager to please others. It must have been like shooting fish in a barrel.

Pornography

In the Stone Age, a kid's first exposure to porn most likely occurred when he stumbled on his dad's or older brother's stash of dirty magazines. The photos could certainly be shocking to an innocent child seeing a fully nude woman for the first time, but the magazines usually didn't show full-on sex acts (except for the really raunchy ones).

Fast forward to the Internet Age and we have a totally different game on our hands. Online pornography leaves *nothing* to the imagination and a shocking amount of it features illegal images of children being sexually abused and tortured.

The average age when a child is first exposed to porn (by accidentally stumbling upon it online, through friends, or by seeking it out) is around 11, but some kids as young as 8 are "regularly consuming pornography online."[97]

Kids under 10 account for 22 percent of porn consumption, according to one study.[98] The study also found that while 97 percent of parents used parental control software to block access to adult websites, 12 percent of their teenagers succeeded in uninstalling or unlocking this software.[lxvii]

It's not a question of *if* your child will be exposed to porn, it's a matter of *when*. Roleplay with you child what she should do and say if someone tries to show her pornography (in a magazine or online). For example, she could say, "I don't want to see that. It's gross," or "I'm not looking at that. My Mom/Dad would kill me," and then walk away.

Child pornography—now called Child Sexual Abuse Imagery (CSAI) to better reflect what it really is—is any depiction of a minor or an individual who appears to be a minor engaged in sexual or sexually-related conduct. This includes pictures, videos, and computer-generated content. Even altering an image or video so that it *appears* to be a minor can be considered child pornography.[lxviii]

The FBI's Child Victim Identification Program has received nearly 300 *million* videos and images of child sexual abuse acts since it launched in 2002. And these images get around through any of the untold numbers of child porn forums and networks or via live streaming, which show the abuse of children *as it's happening* to an eager paying audience. Because it's streamed in real-time, it's even more difficult for authorities to detect and stop it.

Porn has always been popular with a certain crowd, but the advent of the Internet has made pornography instantaneously accessible and even free. It's also made more people perceive viewing porn as a socially acceptable activity.

Why Porn Is a Big Deal You Should Care About

There are two types of pornography that should concern you as a parent: (1) pornography your child can readily view in magazines or online through his phone, tablet, computer, or gaming console; and (2) pornographic images (photos and videos) of your child that he himself or someone else takes of him.

---

97 According to Jesse Weinberger in *The Boogeyman Exists; And He's in Your Child's Back Pocket*.
98 According to a study commissioned by BitDefender®, an Internet security solutions provider.

Heroic Parenting

Porn Your Child May View

Chances are really high that your child over 7 has seen pornographic material. According to GuardChild.com, *90 percent* of kids 8 to 16 have seen online pornography. Most accidently ran across it while entering innocent search terms on the Internet and got the surprise of their life. And since 20 percent of all online porn involves sexual images of children, there's also a good chance your child may have seen another child being abused.[lxix]

Here's the kicker—you can't blame your child's dodgy friends for exposing him to porn because 79 percent of the time that exposure *occurs at home*. Yes, YOUR home.[lxx] Makes you want to run out and buy some parental control software, doesn't it? Good! I'll talk about how to do that later.

Your child could also be shown porn by a predator who's attempting to groom him. Pedophiles like to view porn and online sex acts with their victims to normalize that behavior and try to sexually arouse them. Research shows that those who view child sex acts may be more likely to act out what they see.

Pornographic Images of Your Child

Seeing pornographic images at a tender age is bad enough, but what predators are really interested in is obtaining sexual images of your child that they can keep for personal use or share with or sell to others.

Many of the online sites dedicated to so-called "kiddie porn" encourage or require members to upload their own images of children being sexually exploited. Sickeningly, they trade images like kids used to trade Pokémon cards.

Sexting

You're putting your head in the sand if you think your child's too young to learn about sexting. Kids as young as 11 are doing it and you want to nip this alarming little practice in the bud.

Get this: 15 percent of teenagers have sent or posted nude or semi-nude images of themselves to someone *they **only** know online!* What most adults would consider a stupid move is considered by many kids to be a great idea. (Actually, many adults do this too! Way to be great role models, guys.)

Your child probably carries the means of her own destruction with her 24/7. It's her smartphone, and with it she can sext with others and send and receive explicit photos and videos all day and all night long. One Texas study warns that, "Sexting is the new first base."[lxxi]

Aaaand this is how sextortion begins.

Sextortion

Here's the general pattern: a predator poses as a younger kid or trusted older mentor and grooms a child for as long as it takes to gain her trust. Next, he tests the waters by throwing out a few sexual jokes or comments to see how the child reacts. If she reacts negatively by setting a boundary and telling the offender to stop, he'll likely move on. If she reacts positively or even neutrally, the perp will press on, eventually asking her to send one sexy photo "just for fun."

Once he gets the nude or semi-nude photo, the predator threatens to reveal the photo on social media and/or tell the girl's parents. The child naturally freaks out because she doesn't want to get in trouble and lose her online privileges for life, and she certainly doesn't want to experience the embarrassment and harassment that would surely follow the photo's release, so she does whatever the creep asks, sending more—and more explicit—photos and videos (which can include the victim performing sex acts and could number in the hundreds or thousands!) or agreeing to meet him in person.

The more images she sends, the more the predator asks for, until the child is in so deep and feels so hopeless about finding a way out, that she may even consider suicide to stop the harassment, constant anxiety, and fear. In the meantime, the predator is using the photos and videos for his own enjoyment, while almost certainly passing them on or selling them to other predators.

And then there's good old revenge porn. This occurs when two people break up and one (or both!) of the former partners posts sexual images or videos of the other without their consent to enact revenge by embarrassing them, causing them distress, threatening them, or even blackmailing them.

Over half of older child victims know their offenders in person, often as a romantic partner. About a third of them are threatened with physical harm and tormented for more than six months. Half didn't disclose the incidents, and few reported them to the police.[lxxii]

Don't forget that when your child sends sexual images to anyone, including intimate partners, she runs the risk that her former object of adoration will share those images with his friends (as 38 percent do). And it can get much worse if she ends up being charged with a federal child pornography crime because she sent a naked selfie! (I'll talk more about this below.)

As a result of sextortion, child victims commonly experience a range of negative outcomes, including hopelessness, fear, anxiety, and depression. The CyberTipline reports that about 1 in 3 child sextortion targets engaged in self-harm, threatened suicide, or attempted suicide as a result of their victimization.[99]

Bully Heaven

Your child could become the victim of bullies or cyberbullies if they get their hands on revealing or embarrassing photos or videos of him and shares them with others. These humiliating images can range from photos taken of a victim being bullied (imagine him being stuffed into a locker or being pummeled in front of a cheering crowd) or of the victim in a compromising position (like being naked in the locker room).

When the child realizes these images are out there for all the world (and most importantly to him, his peers) to see, the humiliation is compounded exponentially. A really creative bully can even alter an innocent photo to make it appear that the victim is doing something immoral or illegal.

That "Innocent" Sexy Photo Could Land Your Angel in the Big House[100]

Did you know that in most states, if your child is under 18 and sends a sexually explicit photo of himself to his girlfriend, he could be charged with a felony under current child pornography laws? And be sentenced to actual prison? AND be listed as a registered sex offender for the rest of his life?

Heck, if your child just reposts or forwards even a "sexually suggestive" photo or video that someone sent him, he could also be charged with felony possession and trafficking of child pornography. This is *serious* stuff, people.

---

99 If your child received sexually explicit images over the Internet or has been sexually solicited by someone who knows your child is under 18, immediately contact your local or state law enforcement agency, the FBI (www.fbi.gov/resources/parents/resources-for-parents), and the National Center for Missing & Exploited Children (www.missingkids.org/gethelpnow/cybertipline).
100 The Big House = Jail or prison.

This information really shocks and scares me because it could happen to any child, even those with the most vigilant parents. And if you consider that 20 percent of kids admit to having sent genital pics to other people,[lxxiii] we could fill our prisons with child "offenders."

I totally get why the laws are so tough; it's imperative that the government do something to try to curb the sexual exploitation of minors and there are plenty of victims among that 20 percent, but not ALL of them are perpetrators. They're just kids being stupid kids. But no matter how much the parties involved protest that they were willing participants, your child could still be charged with the creation and trafficking of child pornography.

And it gets worse. Kids who are found guilty of violating child pornography laws can blow their chances of being accepted into a decent college, lose their scholarships, or lose their jobs or internships—just for sending a revealing photo of themselves.

The worst news is, once those photos or videos are "out there" in cyberspace, there's no getting them back. They're online forever.[101] Any potential college admissions agent or employer could (and probably will) look over your child's social media profiles and see shots of her partying like it's 1999 or posing for a nude selfie. And potential employers will very likely do a criminal background check, and you certainly don't want them to find a conviction on your child's record or see that she's on the sex offender registry.

Did I scare the pants off you? Good. You MUST teach your little darling to not post or send sexual images to anyone. Ever. Seriously, let's talk about how to keep your child out of trouble online.

Laying Down the Law

Great! You've decided to parent up and you're ready to have a candid conversation with your child about digital do's and don'ts. If he's already happily surfing in cyberspace, start having that conversation at once to ensure he knows what the new rules are (or reinforce the existing rules—that's a gold star for you!).

Below I share with you some of the most important rules you should enforce to keep your child safe. Know, however, that your little imp may look you dead in the eye and lie his butt off when you ask him the questions I suggest here. For every social media account and log-in detail he shares, he's likely hiding two more he knows you wouldn't approve of. Just know that going in.

---

101 I thank God every single day that we didn't have Snapchat or Girls Gone Wild when I was a teenager or my boobs would be all over the Internet! Don't gag; they were awesome back then, thank you very much!

Heroic Parenting

If You Have a Hard Time Saying "No" to Your Child

If you're worried about saying "no" to your child—because you don't know how to set consistent boundaries, because you were terrorized as a child or grew up with no rules at all, or because you're afraid that if you bring the hammer down your kid won't like or love you anymore, this section is for you.

Over the course of his lifetime, your child will be told "no" thousands of times—by you, by teachers, by bosses, by friends, and by romantic partners... you get my drift. The sooner he learns to deal with the "no's" in his life, the better off your son will be. And the bonus is, if you start teaching him when he's young, he'll have your guidance and love to cushion the blows and setbacks along the way. Children who aren't told "no" don't develop strong coping skills and have a cosmic head slap in store for them when they enter the real world.

When a child gets his way all the time, the "yeses" become meaningless and lose their value. It's a bit like having candy with every meal. The pleasure begins to wear off after a while and the sugar high loses its appeal. Although he'll almost certainly protest when you say no, he won't stop loving you and he'll get over it faster than you think.

Kids are so resilient and adaptive. When you put up a boundary in one direction, they'll usually find a more creative, more constructive way to have fun than the one you denied them. Trust that your budding entrepreneur will find a way to act within the boundaries you set and have fun in the process.

With great power comes great responsibility. This is true in all areas of life, and the word "responsibility" needs to be ever-present in your child's mind. Trust me on this, you can't know everything he does online.[102] Your best bet to keep him safe is by ensuring he knows the truth about what goes on online and how to navigate that busy jungle filled with determined predators.

One of the best ways to keep him in line is to allow him to access his (or the family's) computer or laptop *only* in the living room or den, or wherever your family hangs out the most. Your presence and the constant traffic will serve as a deterrent. It'll drive him crazy, but he'll get over it. Also require that he also ask permission first to use the computer.[103]

---

102 If you think you can, you're wrong.
103 And if you're *really* smart, and I know you are, you'll make him earn his screen time by doing chores and/or homework first.

What to Teach Your Child about Digital Dangers

- Don't trust anyone—and I mean N-E-1 with his username and password, not even his best friends or siblings. The only person he can share his passwords with is you, the parent (of course your partner as well, if you have one). This must be mandatory. Tell him that his best friend today could be his worst enemy tomorrow, and that so-called friend could access his social accounts and wreak havoc.

- Ask him what he thinks "sexy" means. Talk about what kinds of photos and videos are considered inappropriate.

- Make sure your son knows the legal consequences of sexting, which I spelled out above—even when the photo isn't nude (remember, it just has to be *suggestive*) and even if he didn't take the photo himself. Be brutally honest with him about the fact that he can be arrested, charged, convicted, and imprisoned for a federal felony if he sends so much as one genital pic to his girlfriend. (I'm being a bit dramatic here, but the feds have successfully prosecuted kids as young as 10! They're not messing around and neither should your child.)

- Be absolutely 100 percent clear that sending a sexy photo to someone online could end up all over the web on his friends' social media and make him vulnerable to sextortion.

- Tell him that sexting will be interpreted by predators to mean he's willing to have sex with an adult.

- Talk about how predators lie in their profiles and communications and talk about what grooming behavior looks like. Warn him that perps may try to manipulate him by giving him compliments and gifts—a well-known and effective tactic to get your child to feel like he should give the predator something he wants in return.

- Teach your child to trust his intuition; if something doesn't feel right, it's not, and he needs to stop all communications with that person.[104]

- Your child must always notify you immediately if a stranger wants to meet him.

- Warn him to neverneverNEVER meet with anyone he meets online without you, the parent, being present. This is SO important!

---

[104] I'll tell you how to teach your child to trust his intuition, set and maintain strong boundaries, and act to protect those boundaries in Chapter 16.

Heroic Parenting

- Don't "friend" anyone online who he doesn't know in real life.

- Help him select an appropriate profile photo and write a good profile that isn't provocative to predators.

- Teach him how to choose strong passwords. You can create acronyms that have special meaning to him, like the names of his favorite movies or songs.

- Together, choose the social sites he'll join. Lookup (together) on Google the pros and cons of each site you consider and select the ones you both agree on. Remember, you're the parent here and you have the final word!

- Cover or turn off his webcam when he's not using it. People can hack into the webcam and watch your child get undressed, pop his pimples, sleep, etc.

- Set limits on what your child is allowed to do online, what sites he can visit, what kind of content he can post, who he can "friend" and chat with, and what chat rooms he can go to.

- Install parental monitoring software and tell your child it's there to put him on notice that his online activity is being monitored.[105]

- Learn which apps and social sites are bad news by visiting www.FamilyEducation.com.

- Talk about how sexting can lead to sextortion.

- Remind your child that the photos he posts have location information embedded in the files. This can lead perps to other info that can identify where the child goes to school, who his friends are, etc.

- Teach your child to check in with the "internal cop" in his head before disobeying one of your rules, accessing a chat room or site that you wouldn't approve of, or entering into or continuing a conversation that involves sexual content. Advise him to ask himself: "Will my parents or grandparents be upset or disappointed if I do this?"

- Make it crystal clear why he should never meet someone in person he only knows online if you're not also present. In addition to thinking they know everything under the sun, kids

---

[105] I HIGHLY recommend the Bark app (www.bark.us), which flags you when anything inappropriate pops up on your child's profiles without you having to monitor every post and social interaction.

tend to think they're invulnerable and don't believe they could ever be duped or abducted into a sex trafficking ring, for example.

- Encourage your child to tell you if another kid is being sexually exploited or bullied online so you can let that child's parents know. Explain that seeing and not reporting these crimes makes him guilty of wrongdoing and may make him legally liable, depending on the nature of the exploitation. Let him know you want him to be part of the solution, not the problem.

- As he grows, talk to your child to help him understand that his online reputation is one of his most important assets, one that needs to be closely guarded. Photos of him partying or that contain sexual content will live on the web forever and could ruin his future prospects.

- Tell him not to retaliate if he's provoked by someone online or he may also be guilty of criminal behavior himself.

- Show him how to block, flag, and report abusive content. This is the most effective way to stop bullying behavior. If you don't know how to do these things, Google the answer and teach your child what to do so he can handle bullying incidents quickly and neatly.

- Reinforce how much you respect him and how much he should respect himself. Teach him that how he behaves online is a reflection of how he expects to be treated by others.

Your child's computer, tablet, and phone time should be limited to a set amount per day, at your discretion, and be *completely* off-limits overnight. At bedtime, make him turn them over to you to keep in your room every single night.[106] Yes, he'll whine and complain, he might even cry and pitch a fit, but stick to your guns, mom and dad! Whether he believes it or not, you're doing him a favor. The earlier you implement this rule, the quicker he'll get used to the idea as just a fact of life.

Questions You Need to Ask Your Child Who's Already Online

- What social media accounts does she have, including her passwords?
- What are her profile handles for each account?

---

[106] My friend once confiscated her 15-year-old stepdaughter's phone and it pinged at 1:30 in the morning with sexts from her boyfriend, shattering her parents' naïve image of her as a totally innocent angel, which led to a necessary conversation that should have been had much sooner.

- Which photos is she using for her profile avatar?
- Has she ever posted something and then immediately or later regretted it? What did she do about it? What would she do differently now that she knows better?

Should You (Gasp!) Spy on Your Child?

My short answer to this question is *Heck yes!* Your precious gosling isn't as innocent as you might like to think. Yes, most kids are genuinely great human beings, but they're still kids and kids across the board do stupid stuff. It's part of their learning experience. Remember, good judgment comes from experience and experience comes from *bad judgment*. It's their job to experiment and make mistakes.

So, don't be afraid to spy on, ahem, *monitor* your child's online activity, if only to save herself from herself. And let your daughter *know* she's being watched; it'll keep her on her toes. Be aware that she'll very likely try to create profiles you don't know about, which is why monitoring software is a must-have. She won't like it one bit, but stand firm!

I have another bonus handout for you on my website that lists the highest-rated monitoring and protection software. You can find it at www.cjscarlet.com/freebies.

This Isn't a "Turn the Other Cheek" Moment, It's an "Eye for an Eye" Moment

Rather than simply punishing your child when he breaks an unspoken rule, which will feel grossly unfair to him and likely spark a rebellion, it's far better to lay out clear rules and the consequences for breaking them in advance and then stick to them.

Of course, you can't foresee every scenario and you'll have to wing it sometimes, but you can predict a lot of what might happen (because you read this book!). Remember that if you install monitoring apps or software, you'll be able to detect when he's gone off the reservation and you'll have time to come up with an appropriate punishment.

If your kid breaks a rule you hadn't anticipated, take the time you need to figure out a reasonable punishment and then hand down your verdict. Stick to your guns when you deliver the news. Your child will squeal like a wounded piglet when you tell him you're taking his phone. He'll beg and plead and promise it will never happen again. He'll yell that you didn't have a rule in place and that it's not fair that he's being punished for something he didn't know was against the rules. He may even threaten to harm himself or run away if you impose your punishment.

I urge you, dear parent, to *stand your ground*. He'll eventually get tired and head upstairs or get hungry and come downstairs. Either way, the onslaught will end… for now. After that, he may not speak to you for a while and his glares may jab a knife in your heart, but you have GOT to stick with your ruling. Otherwise, you're teaching him that the cost of doing what he wants is to make you suffer. You're the only loser in that scenario.

Ensuring the Punishment Fits the Crime

But the punishment has to fit the crime; you don't want to smash his phone because he went to a forbidden website. In that case, you might instead calmly reinforce the rule and then suspend his online privileges for a week or two, depending on the type of site he went to. Save the big guns for when he deviates from the plan in a big way that exposes him or has already exposed him to real danger.

Here are some examples of punishments, just to give you an idea of what's possible. Of course, you alone can decide what constitutes an appropriate punishment for your child, just please make sure you've told your kid what these consequences will be *in advance*, if possible.

- For posting private info, like his real name, address, or phone number, make him close down the respective accounts. Watch him actually do this and don't let him open new accounts for at least a month. If he does it again, ditch the smartphone and get him a flip phone.

- If he shares his password with anyone other than you and your partner, make him close the respective accounts and don't let him create a new profile on that site for at least a month.

- If he cyberbullies or encourages the cyberbullying of another, take all his digital devices away (that includes his phone, tablet, computer, laptop, and gaming system) for at least a month. Make him apologize, in person if possible, and make amends to the victim. Make him read one of the bullying books you'll find on the Resources tab of my website (that's appropriate for his age and developmental level) AND write a short report on what he learned (to prove he actually read and absorbed it).[107]

---

[107] Wow. I *like* this idea of having kids do research to learn why their actions were dangerous and to have to write a report to prove they understood what they learned. It's both informative and suitably painful. You can use this with kids as young as 8.

- If he includes sexual images or content in his profile name, handle, or avatar, have him close down the respective accounts and don't let him open new accounts for at least a month or more and only with you standing over his shoulder as he chooses new ones. Also confiscate all his digital devices for a couple of weeks. Then, talk with him about the relevant dangers I cover in this chapter and write a report on what he learned.

- If you learn your child sent sexual content of any kind (including sexting or sexual harassment, or sexual images or videos) to another person, take away all his devices for at least a month and his smartphone FOR.EVER! After your electronics boycott has ended, buy him a flip phone that can't access the Internet. Yes, you can smash his smartphone if you like, just to bring the point home.[108] Again, talk with him about the relevant dangers I cover in this chapter and write a report on what he learned.

- If he receives sexual content (communications or images/videos), take a screenshot, document the communications that led up to that moment, and call law enforcement. Put a two-week embargo on all electronic devices to put some time and space between your child and the lure of cyberspace.

- If he plans to or actually meets someone he only knows online, you're on Defcon 5.[109] In this case, he loses all breathing[110] and electronic device privileges for at LEAST a month and his smartphone forever. Be sure to put monitoring software on all his electronic devices so you can be sure he's not communicating with that other person. Ban him from tagging photos on social media sites or sharing his GPS location (which tell perps where he is). Make him write that report (seriously, do it!) so he knows what kind of trouble this could lead to.

What to Do if Your Child Is Being Exploited Online

Be on the lookout for signs your child is being exploited online (e.g., engaging in inappropriate conversations, sexting, being sextorted, etc.). For example, you daughter may suddenly avoid

---

108 Better yet, sell the smartphone and keep the cash or donate it to a women's shelter (which will give it to a domestic violence victim so she can call for help if she's in danger). Be sure to wipe all the data off the phone first and remove any memory chips.

109 Defcon 5 = The most serious state of affairs.

110 Okay, so maybe don't take away his breathing privileges, but hit him where it hurts (not literally, of course. No corporal punishment, please!). By removing access to his favorite things or activities, even if that means he can't go to the prom or play in the big game, you'll leave a lasting impression that will discourage him from doing that sort of thing again.

going online or answering her phone, become secretive and try to hide her online activity by changing what's on the screen when you enter her room, or quickly delete messages when you walk by. She may also try to erase her screen history or other files.

As with any of the dangers I talk about in this book, whether your child comes to you or you learn another way that she's being exploited online, you have to work to appear calm, even if you're totally freaking on the inside. Do NOT overreact by screaming, sobbing, blaming or shaming your child, or by threatening to do severe bodily harm to the offender. This will only make your child feel awful and possibly keep her from being completely honest with you about all that happened for fear of making you even more upset.

Her biggest fear is that you'll take away her phone or computer privileges—a real possibility—but refrain from immediately taking her devices away or smashing them until you get to the bottom of the story. Remember, if she came to you for help, you need to take into consideration that (a) it took a lot of courage for her to do so, and (b) she's showing a large measure of responsibility and good judgment by telling you at all. Oh, and (c) she's *talking to you*, which beats the alternative (her silence or a suicide attempt) by a long shot.

Document What Happened

As I wrote in the last chapter on bullying, it's important to keep a log of every interaction your child has had with an offender, as well as all interactions with school or law enforcement officials, so you'll have something concrete to show if you decide to press charges.[111]

Here are other things you can do:

- Tell your child to ignore but not delete hurtful comments (so you can maintain a record in the event the harassment escalates).

- Save and print out copies of all online communications to provide a record for schools, police, lawsuits, etc.

- Try to ID the offender. If a crime has been committed and you know who's responsible, that information will jumpstart any law enforcement investigation. If you don't know who that person is, leave it to the police to investigate; don't play private eye and possibly escalate things or compromise the investigation.

---

111 There's a sample log you can find on my website under the "Freebies" tab.

- Clearly and firmly send a message to the online offender to cease and desist his harassment, sextortion, or sexually inappropriate behavior. Tell him you've reported him to the police and that they're investigating the incident(s). Immediately change your child's email and other profiles and block the bully. Ban your child from visiting sites where the offenses occurred.

- Report the offender to the phone company, Internet service provider, and owner of the website in question. The sexual exploitation of people of any age is against most digital companies' policies and can be prosecuted.

- If the offenses are being committed by another student, report them to the offender's school. Additionally, if the behavior is severe or threatening, report it to the police right away.

If your child has been the victim of sexual exploitation, in addition to reporting it to the police you can file a report online to the National Center for Missing & Exploited Children's CyberTipline at www.cybertipline.com.

Badass Grandma's Two Cents

I just can't stress enough that if you're concerned about digital dangers, you need to read Jesse Weinberger's book, *The Boogeyman Exists; And He's In Your Child's Back Pocket: Internet Safety Tips For Keeping Your Children Safe Online, Smartphone Safety, Social Media Safety, and Gaming Safety*. Jesse's book is the most informative and interesting of the books I've read on online safety. It's also real and realistic, and a fast read. It definitely gets the Badass Grandma's Seal of Approval!

CHAPTER 9

Sexual Molestation and Assault

I saw the horrified look on my 13-year-old son's face from all the way across the Olympic-sized pool and knew something was very wrong. As I made a furious beeline around the perimeter of the pool, the middle-aged man who was swimming next to him scrambled out of the water and sprinted off in the opposite direction.

For a second, I was torn—do I chase down the man and tackle him without knowing what had happened, or do I rush to my son to ensure he was okay? I chose to go to my son, pointing madly and screaming all the way, "Stop that man!" As I reached my son's side, I looked up and saw the man run out of the front door and disappear. *Darn it!* My son was shaken, but okay. The scumbag had sidled up next to him in the pool and tried to fondle him beneath the water.

I wanted to weep with frustration and sorrow; I had tried so hard to break the cycle of abuse I'd experienced, but I still couldn't keep my son safe, even when he was just a pool's-width away from me.

Yes, I had worked hard on *me*, but I had neglected to teach my children how to protect themselves when I couldn't. My son didn't know how to react when the man approached him, and he didn't know he could say "NO!" to an adult. I felt like a total failure as a parent.

Kids Are Super-Resilient

Back in the mid-1990s I ran a child advocacy center for abused children. It was some of the most rewarding work I've ever done, but also the most difficult. My agency welcomed children of all ages who'd been neglected, beaten, molested, and sexually assaulted, most often by family members. While my clinical staff provided counseling for them, I worked with other social services and criminal justice agencies to ensure each child was protected and that the offenders were prosecuted.

Heroic Parenting

I was a single mom then, raising two young boys while at the same time dealing with my own history of childhood molestations and sexual assault. My emotions were roller-coaster crazy as I alternately wept for our clients and myself and celebrated as they and I navigated the healing process. It amazed me how quickly these kids bounced back when they were believed, told the abuse wasn't their fault, and then were given the counseling and protection they needed. And while I struggled for years to work through my own trauma, over and over again I saw these incredibly resilient kids leave our agency mere months later largely healed from their emotional wounds.

I share this with you to emphasize how important it is to prevent your child from being molested or assaulted by arming her with the information I teach in this book and, if abuse does or has occurred, how important it is to believe and support her and seek professional help right away.

This story also reinforces that for every evil predator on the planet, there are hundreds of good-hearted people on the right side of the law working to make the world safer for your child. Like Mr. Roger's mother taught him when he was a child, "Look for the helpers. You will always find people who are helping."

Definitions

Child Sexual Abuse

According to StopItNow.org, child sexual abuse includes "all sexual touching between an adult and a child, and sexual touching between children when there's a significant age difference (usually 3 or more years) between them, or if the children are very different developmentally or size-wise.

"Sexual abuse doesn't necessarily involve penetration, force, pain, or even touching. If an adult engages in any sexual behavior (looking, showing, or touching) with a child to meet the offender's interest or sexual needs, it's considered sexual abuse. This includes the manufacture, distribution, and viewing of child pornography (now called child sexual abuse material)."[lxxiv]

Sexual abuse also includes, among other things, having a child pose, undress, or perform in a sexual manner; spying on a child in her bedroom or bathroom; having a child look at or watch sexual acts in person, in movies, or in magazines; and having non-educational, sexually-explicit conversations with a child.

Abusive Non-Touching Acts

Abusive "non-touching" acts include: showing sexually suggestive images or porn to a child; talking to her in sexually explicit or suggestive ways via phone, Internet, text, or in person; taking sexually explicit or provocative photos or videos of a child; viewing or violating private behaviors such as bathing or dressing; or exposing oneself to a child in a lewd way.

Sexual Assault/Rape

Sexual assault, a nicer term for "rape," is defined by Merriam-Webster as illegal sexual contact that usually (but not always) involves force upon a person without their consent, or is inflicted upon a person who's incapable of giving consent (because of age, or physical or mental incapacity or impairment) or who places the assailant (such as a doctor or priest) in a position of trust or authority.

Sodomy

The term "sodomy" refers to oral and anal sex acts of any kind.

Incest

Child sexual abuse is considered "incest" when the perpetrator is a biologically or non-biologically related person who's functioning in the role of a family member.

Online-Mediated Sex Crimes

Sex crimes against children that are facilitated through online means include the possession, distribution, or production of child pornography; sexual solicitations (online interactions with minors for sexual purposes, including plans to meet offline); and conspiracy crimes such as collaborating with others to distribute or produce child pornography, or sexually solicit or traffic minors.[lxxv]

When It Really Counts, Everyone's Counting Differently

Estimates of the number of children who are victims of child sexual abuse are impossible to pin down because so many kids never tell an adult they've been victimized. They may have been threatened by the perp or they may be so filled with shame that they fear being blamed for the incidents.

When I researched the statistics on this, they were all over the place. Every time I looked at government agency or non-profit advocacy sites, the stats were so different it was confusing and frustrating. Some of them even contradicted their own statistics in the same document!

What I *can* tell you from my professional experience in the criminal justice field is that the number of child sexual victims is appallingly high. In my 30 years working with survivors, virtually *every single woman* and a surprisingly high number of men I have spoken to about this subject have shared that they were either molested or raped, most as children or young adults. Of these, only a handful ever reported the crimes. And of the ones who say they did report it, I can remember only *two* that ended up with the offenders being arrested, tried, and convicted.

I will share a bit of good news: the number of child sexual abuse cases, like other violent crimes, has been declining—by 65 percent between 1992 and 2016.[lxxvi]

Who the Perps Are

If you read Chapter 1 about predators, you already know that perpetrators can be found in every shape, size, color, gender, age, socioeconomic level, religion, educational background, group, club, sports program, school, college and university, and church. They can be family members, friends, neighbors, teachers, coaches, religious leaders, or (less likely) strangers.

Here's what we know about the perpetrators:

- About a third of child sexual abuse victims are abused by family members.
- Knock that up to 50 percent when the children are under 6.[lxxvii]
- The younger the victim, the more likely it is that the offender is another child, (40 percent of child sexual abuse cases)[lxxviii] who may be older or bigger, making it a criminal offense.
- Boys make up 93 percent of juvenile offenders; girls make up 7 percent.[lxxix]
- An incredible *70 percent* of child sex offenders have between 1 and 9 victims, while 20 percent have 10 to 40 victims.[lxxx]

Who the Victims Are

No child is immune from the possibility of child sexual abuse. I don't care how nice his neighborhood is or how much money his parents make. I don't even care how hypervigilant his Tiger Mom is; every child is at risk. That's the bad news.

The good news is, because you're reading this book, you're learning how to protect your child *and* empowering him to protect himself to the best of his ability when you're not around. By educating him about the dangers the world presents and teaching him how to thwart predators, you're doing the very best you can possibly do for him.

Risk Factors

One thing researchers and agencies *do* agree on is the risk factors that make children vulnerable to sexual abuse. Please remember that just because a child has some or even all of these risk factors doesn't make it his fault if he's sexually abused. It's *always* the perpetrator's fault for choosing to commit the crime. It also doesn't mean your child *will* be abused; it just means he's more vulnerable to predators because of these factors.

Here we go:

- Family structure is the biggest factor in a child's risk of sexual abuse. Kids who live with both parents are at the lowest risk of abuse, but that risk goes up by 20 times or more when there's a stepparent in the picture.[lxxxi]

- Children living in foster care are 10 times more likely to be sexually abused than children who live with their birth parents.[lxxxii]

- Girls are five times more likely to be sexually abused than boys.[lxxxiii]

- Boys younger than 12 are three times more likely to be abused than older boys.[lxxxiv]

- Both genders are the most vulnerable between the ages of 7 and 13.[lxxxv]

- African American children are nearly twice as likely to be abused as white children.[lxxxvi]

- Children in low-income households are three times more likely to be sexually abused, and those in rural areas are twice as likely to be abused as those who live elsewhere.[lxxxvii]

- Children who've witnessed or have been the victim of other crimes are significantly more likely to be sexually abused.[lxxxviii]

These are just the factors that have been measured. There are more risk factors I want to list here. Your child is at greater risk of abuse if she:

- Has low self-esteem and lacks confidence in herself.

- Is lonely and craves attention and affection.

- Has been physically or sexually abused before.[lxxxix]

- Is also the victim of physical or emotional abuse.

- Has special needs, such as a physical or intellectual disability, chronic illness, or mental health issues.[xc]

- Hasn't been taught the basics of human sexuality, so she doesn't know what constitutes healthy and unhealthy touching and behavior.

- Spends unsupervised time with others, at or away from home.

- Is exposed to or has easy access to X-rated material or pornography.

- Has siblings or parents who've been sexually abused in the past, *whether or not it was ever talked about.*[112]

- Has parents or siblings with drug, alcohol, or mental health issues.[xci]

Please pay attention to these. If your child has any of the risk factors above, I urge you to read Chapters 15, 16, and 17 to learn how to teach your child to develop a stronger sense of confidence and self-esteem, set and maintain solid boundaries, develop and use her intuition, and protect and defend herself so she doesn't become one of the statistics.

Signs & Symptoms of Abuse

Kids can be tricky to read; some are open books and express every emotion they feel, while others are more reserved by nature. When a child's been sexually abused, the experience is often very traumatic and he may even dissociate and become numb, showing no emotion at all.

Still, there are some signs you should watch for that *may* indicate your child has or is being sexually abused. You'll note that these symptoms are almost exactly the same as those for bullying and other types of abuse. Trauma is trauma and it leaves clues.

Again, just because your child displays some or even many of these symptoms doesn't necessarily mean he's been sexually abused; it may just be normal kid behavior as he transitions from adolescence to puberty. Regardless, if your child is displaying any of the symptoms above, it *does* mean you need to get to the bottom of whatever's causing his distress. Even if your child stubbornly refuses to share with you, I promise you—and I know this from personal experience—he's hoping you'll find out and stop the abuse.

---

[112] Kids are so intuitive and can pick up on the most subtle cues, so even if they haven't been explicitly told that a parent or sibling was abused, it's like they can be "contaminated" by that energy and it makes them more likely to be abused too.

By being observant and keeping the lines of communication open with your child, you increase the likelihood that any incidents will be identified quickly. Better yet, keep reading and I'll show you how to teach your child to set and maintain such strong boundaries that he can stop predators in their tracks *before* anything bad happens.

Back to the signs and symptoms of abuse. I'll jump right in with the big ones:

- Pregnancy.
- Being diagnosed with a sexually transmitted disease or infection (like herpes, syphilis, gonorrhea, vaginal infection, etc.).
- Genital or rectal pain or bleeding.
- Underwear or sheets are stained with blood or other discharge.
- Urinary tract infections, or abnormal vaginal or penile discharge.
- Pain while urinating or with bowel movements.
- Obvious difficulty walking or sitting.
- Fearful behavior, such as nightmares or new fears of certain people, places, or things.
- Depression or social withdrawal.
- Extreme increase or decrease in appetite, or the development of an eating disorder.
- Sudden lack of self-esteem or confidence.
- Frequent stomachaches or headaches with no medical cause.
- Bedwetting (if they're already toilet trained).
- Sudden personality changes (e.g., a normally outgoing child stops speaking, a well-behaved child develops discipline problems).
- Bullying others or being bullied.
- Extremely aggressive or passive behavior.
- Overly affectionate or clingy behavior.
- Regressive behavior (e.g., thumb sucking, bedwetting, etc.).

- Sudden interest in sex or sexualized behavior that seems inappropriate for his age, including excessive touching of his own private body parts, persistent sex play with friends, toys, or pets; drawings with sexual content; or asking age-inappropriate sexual questions. (See Chapters 12 and 13 to learn about what kind of sexual behavior is appropriate for your child's age.)
- Sexual promiscuity.
- Drop in school performance.
- Seems to be hiding something.
- Attempts to run away or skip school.
- Self-harm of any kind (e.g., cutting, burning, or otherwise injuring one's self, or careless behaviors resulting in self-harm).

The Consequences

Below are some of the short- and long-term consequences your child may experience if she's been or is being sexually abused. Keep in mind that not all survivors are traumatized or negatively affected by the incident(s); it depends on the length and severity of the abuse and the child's ability to cope and adapt. Also know that many of the problems may not manifest until your child is older. It's not uncommon for puberty to be a trigger.

Compared to her peers, when a person has a history of childhood sexual abuse, she's:

- Far more likely to develop post-traumatic stress, which can lead to abnormal development, dysfunction, and distress well into adulthood.[xcii]
- More likely to engage in high-risk behaviors, such as engaging in risky sex or drinking and using drugs. Her likelihood of abusing drugs or alcohol is three to four times higher than for people who were never abused.[xciii]
- More likely to get pregnant as a teenager. In fact, two-thirds of pregnant teens have a history of sexual abuse, and boys who've been sexually abused are more likely to get a teen girl pregnant.[xciv]
- Nearly 25 percent more likely to drop out of school.[xcv]
- Twice as likely to be arrested for a violent crime.[xcvi]

- Twice as likely to attempt suicide and three times as likely to develop a psychiatric disorder.[xcvii]

- At greater risk of developing serious health conditions, such as diabetes, cancer, stroke, and heart problems.[xcviii]

Badass Grandma's Two Cents

It's important that you know that being victimized doesn't mean your child is doomed to a terrible life. Many, if not most, survivors—even those who struggle for some time through the healing process—go on to be successful and happy. Because I didn't seek help for my post-traumatic stress until I was in my 30s, it took years of therapy to work through the trauma. But once I did, I was on fire and I never looked back! My life today is so sweet and peaceful and filled with joy and gratitude that I can hardly believe it myself. There is a light at the end of the trauma tunnel!

CHAPTER 10
Child Abductions

Sleepless Nights and Random Coconuts

As a grandparent, my greatest fear and the one that used to keep me worrying late into the night was the thought of my grandchildren being kidnapped by a nameless, faceless stranger who would hurt and sexually abuse them or sell them into a child sex trafficking ring. The thought that I might never see them again or know what ultimately happened to them was my second worst nightmare; the first was that my precious grandchildren would wait endlessly for a rescue that would never come. The image of them crying out my name and waiting for me to come get them rips my heart into jagged little pieces.

I literally want to curl into a fetal position and whimper just thinking about it. It truly is my worst nightmare. When my grandtwins were born, I spent many nights trying in vain to will those terrible thoughts away. What finally stopped them were two things: (1) I realized that worrying was what I did when life got too good. When I felt too happy I would begin to wonder when the other shoe would drop and things would get chaotic again. Worrying was my way of "putting myself back in my place." And (2) I researched the actual statistics on child abductions and learned that fewer than 100 children are taken each year in stereotypical stranger kidnappings.

Please know I'm not trying to minimize the impact of this; even one child abduction is one too many. But I falsely believed that the annual total of missing and exploited children, over 400,000 each year, were all stranger kidnappings, which they are *not*.

Definitions

Abduction (aka Kidnapping)

The term "abduction" refers to any act in which a child is wrongfully removed, retained, detained, or concealed through methods including persuasion, fraud, or open force or violence.[xcix]

This generally includes incidents in which a child is abducted and held for a period of time while the family and police frantically look for her, as well as situations in which a child is kidnapped by a perpetrator on the way home from school, taken to a remote area, sexually assaulted, and released without being "missed" by a caregiver or having the incident reported to police.

In cases involving family member abductions—most often by non-custodial parents—the situation is considered an abduction when the offending person fails to return the child to the custodial parent in violation of a custody order, conceals the child, transports the child out of state with the intent to prevent contact, or threatens or intends to deprive the custodial caretaker's right permanently or indefinitely.[c]

Stereotypical Kidnapping

A "stereotypical kidnapping" involves the abduction of a child by a stranger or slight acquaintance in which the perp detains the child overnight, transports the child at least 50 miles, demands ransom, expresses the intent to permanently keep the child, or murders the child victim.[113]

Runaway & Throwaway Children

A runaway is a child who leaves home without permission and stays away at least overnight, or who is away with permission but chooses not to come home and stays away for at least one night (for children under 15 or those who are considered "mentally incompetent").[ci]

A "throwaway" is a child who is thrown out of their own home and the caretaker hasn't arranged for adequate alternative care, and the child is prevented from returning to the home for at least one night.[cii]

Missing Involuntarily, Lost, Stranded, or Injured Children

This includes children whose whereabouts are unknown to their caretakers, causing the caretakers to spend at least one hour trying to locate them, and who contacted the police or a missing children's agency to locate the missing children. Meanwhile, the children were trying to get home or make contact but were unable to do so because they were lost, stranded, or injured, or were too young to know how to return home or contact the caretakers.[ciii]

---

113 FYI, someone of "slight acquaintance" includes a non-family perpetrator whom the child or family doesn't know well enough to speak to, or a recent acquaintance whom they've known for less than six months, or whom they've known for more than six months but seen less than once a month.

The Stats

As I explained in the Introduction to this book, of the 424,066 children reported missing or exploited in 2018:

- 94 percent simply misunderstood directions or miscommunicated their plans, were lost, or ran away.[civ]

- About 4 percent were kidnapped by family members in custody disputes.[cv]

- Non-family members abducted 1 percent of the missing children, and the kidnapper was someone the child knew.[cvi]

- Just 105 children (.00007 percent of all missing children) were kidnapped in the kind of stranger abductions that are sensationalized on the evening news.[cvii] And of that number, *only 65 percent were complete strangers to the victims.*[cviii]

- 99.8 percent of the children who go missing (whether abducted by someone known to them, abducted by strangers, or who are runaways) make it home.[cix]

Once I grasped that my grandchildren were more likely to die by being hit on the head by a random coconut than to be abducted by a stranger, I stopped worrying myself to a frazzle and got a full night's sleep for once.

Hopefully, now that you've read these stats, you'll be able to sleep better too. But this chapter is about the reality of child abductions, so let's talk about it.

Who the Perps Are

Kidnappers come in all shapes and sizes, with varying motives for their crimes. Here's a list of their characteristics:

Strangers

- 95 percent of abductors are men, most of whom are unmarried.[cx]

- 42 percent are between 19 and 29 years of age.[cxi]

- Most perpetrators of stereotypical stranger kidnappings are male between 18 and 35 years of age and are white or black in equal proportions. About 70 percent are unemployed, and roughly half have problems with drugs or alcohol.[cxii]

- Women abducted 10 babies in 2018 to raise the child as their own, sometimes to preserve a relationship with a man by claiming the baby was his.[cxiii]

- About a third of stranger kidnappings are carried out for ransom, while others are unintended, such as a child being caught in the backseat of a carjacking.[cxiv]

- Most kidnappers aren't pedophiles, meaning they don't "love" and crave sexual contact with children. They usually don't care if they cause harm to their victims, unlike pedophiles who choose to sexually engage with children because there's a strong attraction. Strangers resort to kidnapping children because they often lack the social skills to develop adult intimate relationships.[cxv] Most kidnappers have difficulty winning over adult women because they're socially awkward. They may not have the social skills to attract and befriend women and have very few friends. Abductors go after children because they're easier to lure and usually can't defend themselves.[cxvi]

- Upwards of 70 percent of strangers who kidnap children for sexual purposes were sexually abused themselves at some point.[cxvii]

- For incidents in which a suspect was identified or arrested, 13 percent were registered sex offenders at the time of the incident.[cxviii]

Non-Custodial Parents

As I mentioned above, about 4 percent of missing and exploited children are abducted by family members who break custody agreements, keeping children from their legal guardians.

In a small percentage of these cases, the abductor may believe the child needs protection from the person who has legal custody, but most cases involve acts of revenge against the legal guardians, and the abductors have no consideration for the children's welfare or happiness.

Here are some characteristics of non-custodial parents who commit abductions and some warning signs that they may be capable of kidnapping their own child:

- Fathers (53 percent)[cxix]
- Mothers (25 percent)[cxx]
- Grandparents (14 percent)[cxxi]
- Other relatives (8 percent)[cxxii]

- Children are usually abducted from their own home or yard, or the yard of a friend.[cxxiii]

- Only 7 percent of children are abducted from school or daycare.[cxxiv]

- The non-custodial parent may have legal rights to unsupervised visitation or joint custody of the child and may take her out of the state or country while having a legal right to be with her. In 63 percent of cases, the non-custodial parent took the child during an approved visit.[cxxv]

- The offending parent may have threatened to abduct or had previously abducted the child.

- The non-custodial parent may have no strong ties to the child's home state but does have ties to friends and family living in another state or country.

- They appear to be planning something (e.g., selling a home, securing the child's school or medical records, etc.), or researching the laws in other states or countries.

- There's a history of contentious marital issues.

- They consider themselves the victim in the separation or divorce and feel justified in taking the child.

- They have a history of committing domestic violence or child abuse.

- They're prone to outbursts of anger, their behavior is irrational and unstable, and revenge is a priority in their lives.

- They change jobs or homes without letting the custodial parent know.

- They begin to pay attention and display affection toward their child when they haven't done so in the past.

Non-Family Members Whom the Child Knows

This category includes anyone the child knows who isn't a family member, which accounts for just 1 percent of kidnapping cases. The list includes neighbors, authority figures, delivery drivers, bus drivers, babysitters, friends, and acquaintances, among others.

Who the Victims Are

According to the US Department of Justice's 2011 National Incidence Studies of Missing, Abducted, Runaway, and Thrownaway Children (NISMART) study:[cxxvi]

- About 81 percent of the victims of stranger child abduction were girls.

- Half of all stranger abduction victims were girls between 12 and 17. Girls 11 and younger accounted for 30 percent of victims.

- Around 12 percent of victims were boys under 12.

- Over 60 percent of victims were white, 31 percent were black, and about 24 percent were Hispanic.[114]

- Children who've been abducted were more likely to be from low-income households and have separated, estranged, or divorced parents. In two-parent families, less than 1 percent of children were abducted compared to 8 percent from single-parent households.[cxxvii]

- In non-custodial parent abductions, younger children (under 6) were especially vulnerable, making up over 44 percent of abductions.[cxxviii]

Where & How Incidents Occur

According to the National Center for Missing & Exploited Children's website, here is where and how child kidnappings occur:[cxxix]

- In 68 percent of attempted child abductions, the perpetrators were driving a vehicle to transport the child victims.

- 31 percent of attempts were made when the children were going to and from school or school-related activities.

- 34 percent of attempts were made between 2 and 7 pm, when children were out of school and were likely unsupervised.

- In an overwhelming 80 percent of stranger abductions, the first contact between the abductors and child victims occurred within a quarter mile of the victims' homes.[cxxx]

- The street near the children's houses is where 62 percent of abduction attempts took place, regardless of the victim's age.

- At the time of abduction, the youngest victims (under age 5) were more likely to be walking with or being carried by a parent or other adult. School-aged children were more likely

---

[114] I know, that adds up to way more than 100 percent. Good on you for paying attention! I guess the researchers counted biracial and multiracial children in multiple categories. I honestly don't know.

to be walking alone or with peers heading to or from school, the bus stop, or their homes on school days, or to the home of a friend, activity, or simply walking on non-school days.

- 7 percent of incidents occurred outside, away from the child's home, while they were playing, hanging out with friends, or doing chores.

- 5 percent occurred at school bus stops, and another 5 percent at parks and playgrounds.

- 4 percent occurred at or near the child's school while they were playing or waiting for a ride or the bus.

- 3 percent of victims were taken from inside their homes.

- 2 percent were taken from parking lots and garages.

- 2 percent were abducted in stores.

- A small number were taken from daycare facilities, campgrounds, public pools, libraries, grocery stores, fairs and festivals, parades, bathrooms and changing rooms, medical centers, and hotels/motels.

- Infants and toddlers under 2 were the most likely to be taken from homes and medical centers. The younger the child, the more likely he was to be taken from inside his own home.

- When the child victim was taken to a secondary location, it was most often a secluded area, such as behind buildings or in alleys, cemeteries, parking lots/garages, woods/bushes, parks or playgrounds, and indoor locations such as vacant buildings, bathrooms or changing rooms, in the offender's vehicle, house, place of business, or hotel/motel rooms.

Online-Mediated Abductions

Surprisingly, online-mediated abductions (where the victims meet the offenders online) account for just 9 percent of child abductions.[cxxxi] I thought that number would be a lot higher, but youth homicides and abductions committed by strangers that the victims met online can be counted on one hand.[115] The vast majority of abductions are perpetrated by people the children know in real life—family members, neighbors, romantic partners, and rivals.

---

115 According to the Crimes Against Children Research Center's study.

According to Andrea Sedlak et al, "The Internet may even be part of the reason for the decline. Before the prevalence of messaging apps, unwanted sexual solicitations online decreased from 19 percent in 2000 to 9 percent in 2010. The Internet has allowed law enforcement to conduct stings and catch offenders before they can physically reach kids. It may keep kids closer to home than they would have been in an era when their search for diversion meant being out in the world. The tracks criminals leave online can also be used as evidence for later prosecution. We shouldn't assume the online environment presents greater risks than other spheres our young people inhabit."[cxxxii]

Nice to have some reassuring news!

Ploys Predators Use to Lure Children

Predators can be majorly slick characters, although many of those who commit crimes of opportunity (meaning they jump at the chance to kidnap a child because the opportunity presents itself) are just fumbling along.

- In 34 percent of abduction attempts, the offenders used force to kidnap their victims, including physical force, or used a weapon of some kind to threaten them into compliance.

- Force was used 57 percent of the time against kids under 5 (who were often near their parents!) and in half of the cases against kids in high school.

- Children between 5 and 14 were mainly manipulated or coerced through verbal lures,[cxxxiii] which I describe below.

Whereas the predators your child knows are likely to groom her through more subtle techniques (see How Predators Groom Their Victims in Chapter 1), a stranger is more likely to use alluring promises to convince your child to go with him. He wants her to go with him voluntarily, rather than kicking and screaming which draws attention to him. And it's *so* easy to convince an innocent, vulnerable child to comply with their requests.

Here are the most common verbal lures predators use to coerce children, according to a variety of resources I found on the Internet, including KidGuard.com:[cxxxiv]

The Gift Ploy

Hey, kid. Would you like some candy?

Few children can resist the lure of free treats, money, or toys, and virtually all of them will take a stranger up on his offer, *even when they've repeatedly been warned by their parents not to.*

Heroic Parenting

Children need to be aware, no matter what their age, that accepting gifts from others without your permission is unacceptable and that most "harmless" people wouldn't offer these things without talking to you first.

Teach your child to bust this ploy by telling the person "NO!" loudly and then running to tell you.

The Cute Animal Ploy

Would you like to see my new puppy?

It's hard to resist this appealing trick. Even adults go up to strangers and ask if they can pet their animals. It's so easy for a kidnapper to gain a child's attention and trust just by approaching her while carrying an animal. They'll often tell the child the animal's name and ask her if she wants to pet it. Of course she does! Then, once the child comes close, it's easy to snatch her and run.

Teach her to bust this ploy by coming directly to you to ask permission before going toward anyone she doesn't know well. This will enable you to check out that "opportunity." If it was a ploy, the predator will be long gone before you go outside.

The Emergency Ploy

I need you to come with me right away! Your mom's hurt and she sent me to pick you up.

Any child would fall for this lure.[116] Without giving it a second's thought, she'll go with a kidnapper who pretends there's been an emergency involving her parent. Caught up in worry and fear, it's easy for a child to forget the rules she's been taught about not going anywhere with others without your permission.

Tell your child to bust this ploy by refusing to go with that person until he or she says the correct code word that you taught her in advance. (I talk more about this in Chapter 13.)

The Assistance Ploy

I lost my puppy. Can you come help me find him? I'll give you a reward!

Children are compassionate by nature and will usually jump at the chance to help someone in need. Crafty kidnappers play on that desire by pretending to be injured or needing help finding something. Teach your child that adults don't ask children to help them; they ask other adults.

---

[116] Heck, *I* would fall for this lure if someone told me one of my grandchildren had been hurt! Okay, maybe not to the point that I'd blindly get in their car and go with them without hesitation, but you get my point.

Don't be afraid that you're teaching your child not to be helpful and compassionate. Rather, help her bust this ploy by teaching her that the best way she can help is to find a trusted adult to assist someone in need.

The Name Ploy

Hi, Jessica! It's great to see you!

Bedazzling your child's name on her backpack or lunchbox is cute, but it could give predators a way to approach your child by saying her name as if the perp knows her. If you want to label your child's belongings should they get lost, put the labels somewhere where they can't be seen from the outside and bust that ploy!

The Friend Ploy

I'm a friend of your dad's and he asked me to pick you up from school today.

This is a tough one to resist for kids who are afraid to say no to adults. Help your child bust this ploy by asking the person to say the secret code word you taught her in advance. (I'll teach you about code words in Part III.)

The Bad Child Ploy

I'm a police officer. You're in big trouble. Come with me!

How scary is this ploy? And what child wouldn't fearfully follow the instructions of an officious-sounding adult who told her to come with him "or else?" Help your child bust this ploy by insisting she go to you (or other trusted adult) immediately if anyone, even someone claiming to be a police officer, tries to take her away.

The "Open the Door" Ploy

Hello? I just had a car accident and I need to call for help. Can I come in and use your phone?

This lure is similar to the assistance and emergency lures and is used to appeal to your child's desire to help someone in trouble. Your child can bust this ploy by *always* refusing to let anyone in the house, no matter how much they beg and plead. Instead, tell her to call 911 immediately and then to call you.

How to Protect Your Child from Abduction Attempts

The most effective way to protect your child from being abducted is to teach him to recognize the above ploys. Of course, how you talk to him depends on his age and maturity level. In

Part III, I break it down for you by your child's age group so you'll know what to say and how to say it.

In Chapter 2, I talked about how important it is to teach children how to safely interact with people they don't know and how to trust their own gut when deciding whether strangers are "safe." Your child will encounter new people throughout his childhood, so simply telling him not to talk to strangers is impractical and unwarranted.

That being said, it's critically important that you also teach your child that even when he thinks someone feels safe and seems nice, he is NEVER to go with them ANYWHERE for ANY REASON. That means your angel can nevereverever:

- Accept any gifts without your permission, no matter how appealing.
- Try to help an adult they don't know well, even if they appear injured and are begging for help. Your child's response should always be to summon an adult to help that person.
- Keep a bad secret, even if the person threatened them or made them promise not to tell.
- Go with someone who asks them to come with him, unless they know the secret code word.
- Give in to any threats someone makes—even if they have a weapon (which predators will almost never actually use). If the predator tries to use physical force or threatens to harm your child, your would-be Power Ranger absolutely must yell and fight as if his life depends on it—because it just might.[117]

If any of the above happen to your child, teach him to yell and run, and to come tell you or another trusted adult right away.

Practical Tips to Thwart Abduction Attempts

There's a LOT you can do to keep your child safe from kidnappers. Here are some practical things you can teach him to lessen the chance that he'll be approached by a potential kidnapper:

- Be clear with your child's school or daycare that no one is allowed to pick him up without your permission. Provide them with a list of people who *are* allowed to pick him up.

---

[117] In Chapter 17, I help you teach your child how to unleash his inner "Taz" to increase his chances of getting away from the kidnapper. I promise to make it into a fun hands-on game that you'll both enjoy practicing.

- If your child walks to school, walk the route with him to identify landmarks and safe places—such as stores or the houses of neighbors you both know—where he should go if he's being followed or needs help. Practice walking the route with him so you can point out places he should also avoid and where he can go for help.

- Have him buddy up with other kids when walking to and from the bus stop, school, or around the neighborhood.

- Encourage your child not to hesitate to ask for help when he senses that someone or something doesn't feel right.

- Teach your child how to call 911 on a cell phone AND a landline phone and tell him what to say if he has to make that call. Ensure he knows his and your full name and address.

- Create an ID kit with your child's fingerprints, physical description, and recent photo. Many local police stations offer child ID kits, or you can make one yourself.[118]

- Get a personal safety device or app for your child.

- Roleplay scenarios with your child from the ploys I shared. (In Part III of this book I'll talk more about using roleplay to teach your child to recognize and respond to tricky situations.)

How Kids Have Escaped Abductions

I've already said it twice before, but it bears repeating: 99.8 percent of the children who are reported as missing, for any reason, make it safely home[cxxxv], whether by thwarting[119] the kidnapping attempt, escaping from the kidnapper's control, being rescued, or returning home on their own (as in the case of runaways).

Many attempted abductions were thwarted by the children themselves, who did something proactive to stop the predators. For example, according to NCMEC, kids used the following actions, which helped them get away 83 percent of the time:[cxxxvi]

- Ignoring or refusing the predator's demands.

- Screaming or yelling to get attention (which is the most effective means for getting adults to intervene and most often leads to the arrest of the offender).

---

118 Learn how by visiting www.klaaskids.org/safety/idkit/.
119 Thwarting = Stopping it from happening.

- Physically pulling away from the predator.
- Using their cell phones to threaten intervention.
- Fighting, which worked in 29 percent of the escapes.
- Walking or running away, which occurred in over half of the escapes.
- Being rescued by a parent, other adult, or other child, which happened in 20 percent of the cases.

It's imperative that you talk to your child about how to react if someone attempts to lure or forcibly abduct them. Politeness and passivity virtually guarantee your child will be taken if he's approached by a would-be kidnapper. You want to train your kid to be a mini hero who knows how to avoid and deal with dangerous characters!

If Your Child Goes Missing

If your child goes missing, call the police at once! Despite what you've heard, *there's no waiting period in cases involving missing children,* so don't hesitate for a second if you fear your child has been abducted. Here's what to do:[120]

- If you have a visitation order in place and the other parent hasn't returned the child as ordered, send a certified letter with delivery confirmation to the court stating that visitation is being revoked because your child wasn't returned to your custody. This helps parents, especially when they're telling the truth and not intentionally making false claims.

- If you lose your child in a store, know that many chain stores will issue a "Code Adam" which alerts all employees to guard all exits until your child is found and/or police arrive.

- If you have reason to be certain your child has disappeared and isn't happily playing at a friend's house, don't waste precious time searching for him yourself. Call the police first and then conduct your search along with whatever friends or volunteers you can muster.

- If the police prefer to organize the search and bring in tracking or air-scent dogs, let them do so. An unsupervised and unorganized search party might trample valuable evidence and clues.

---

[120] Again, I rely on experts Brian Cox and Rob Knight to lay out what to do in this situation.

- Trust the police to do their job. It's okay to monitor their progress and ask for updates, but try not to harass them or interfere with their investigation.

- If you feel they're not doing a thorough enough job, don't be afraid to go up the chain of command to their boss. Your child's life might be at stake and you should expect to be taken seriously.

- Contact Child Find of America and any other agencies you can identify that are dedicated to locating children.

Badass Grandma's Two Cents

I loaded you down with a lot of really scary statistics and information in this chapter, but there's no way to sugarcoat the facts. Sorry 'bout that. It's about to get a lot more fun because we're now moving into Part III of this book, which is all about how to empower your child. Thanks for hanging in there!

PART III

How to Talk to Kids at Their Level

A Note about This Section

We want our kids to be safe, so we teach them to wear their helmets when they get on their bikes and to look both ways before crossing the street. But very few parents teach their children about body safety, or they wait until they think their kids are "old enough," when it may be too late. In my case, my parents NEVER talked to me about body safety or sex, even after I became pregnant at 15.[121]

I'll put myself on the spot and admit, with tremendous regret, that although I had a VERY thorough sex talk with my boys[122] and bought them condoms when they started dating, I didn't teach them a single thing about how to protect themselves from predators because I didn't know how to do it for myself at that point.

If you haven't been talking to your child about body safety—because you didn't know how or what to say, or you were too embarrassed, or you were afraid of frightening your child—don't feel badly; you can correct that right now.

---

121 What the heck, Mom?
122 Separately, of course, while they sat on my bed with a pillowcase over their heads to hide their embarrassment. I'm not joking.

In this section, I break down the most important things to teach your child according to her age and maturity level, and I promise you it's not as hard or embarrassing as you think. I'll talk about how kids in each group process information, the greatest threats they face at each age, how and what to teach them, and examples of what your conversations might look like.

I hope you choose to read every chapter, but I encourage you to at least read the chapters that come before and after the one in your child's age group. Each chapter is different and may contain information that applies to your child, who may be at the younger or older range of her particular age group.[123]

I've included an entire chapter just for parents of children with disabilities. If you're the rockstar parent of a child with a disability, please read that chapter AND those that apply most closely to her age group and maturity level.

When I talk about the threats to your child (e.g., babysitters, digital dangers, and so on), you should refer back to those chapters in Parts I and II for detailed information about each threat.

Obviously, I couldn't cover every single scenario in this section. To learn more about any given topic, I encourage you to refer to the resources I offer on my website.[124]

Your Child's Brain Isn't Fully Cooked Yet

If you ever took Psych 101, you've heard of Maslow's hierarchy of needs. For those who haven't, psychologist Abraham Maslow developed this theory to illustrate the five levels of human needs that must be met for a person to thrive.[cxxxvii] Needs lower down on the hierarchy must be satisfied before you can attend to needs higher up.

At the base of the five-tiered pyramid are physiological needs—food, water, warmth, and rest. Next are security and safety needs, followed by belongingness and love needs (intimate relationships and friends), and esteem needs (feelings of esteem and accomplishment), with self-actualization (achieving one's full potential) being at the top of the pyramid.

As you can see, security and safety needs are second only to the most basic survival functions. Obviously, you can't be concerned about personal security (e.g., running away or fighting off a predator) if your body can't physically function, just as you can't bother with creating relationships (level 3) if you're under immediate threat of harm.

---

[123] I will soon publish a second *Heroic Parenting* book about empowering kids from 10 to 18 that you'll want to read after you finish this book.

[124] www.cjscarlet.com/resources

Heroic Parenting

Since your child's brain won't be done cooking (developing a fully functioning prefrontal cortex) until they're in their mid-20s, it's up to you, the parent, to help him fulfill those security and safety needs by teaching him what he needs to know to stay safe.

Kids learn in diverse ways: 20 to 30 percent are auditory learners who respond to verbal information, 40 percent are visual leaners who like to read or see information, while the remainder are kinesthetic, meaning they learn by doing. I'll tell you how to use a mix of these methods to teach your child to protect and defend himself.

But know this: kids learn most from watching your example, so be sure you're walking your talk! When I wrote my last book, *The Badass Girl's Guide: Uncommon Strategies to Outwit Predators*, I realized I wasn't practicing everything I was teaching my readers about personal boundaries and had to step up my own game!

Remember that teaching your child about danger and how to thrive safely in the world is a process; you'll need to have ongoing conversations over the years. You only retain about 25 percent of what you read, so please consider this book to be your parenting bible—read it through to the end and refer to it often to ensure you absorb and can teach the information it contains.

CHAPTER 11

Infants up to 24 Months

This is going to be a shorter chapter than the two that follow, simply because much of what I suggest you teach your child needs to wait until she's verbal and can understand what you're saying. Still, you're constantly interacting with your infant and she's learning about language and safe touch from you, and she'll pick up a lot during these pre-verbal months.

How This Age Group Learns & Processes Information

Infants up to 24 months learn by *doing*. Every moment they're awake they're hearing, looking, sucking, grasping, and touching. As they do these things, they're learning the concept of cause and effect—*if I do this, that happens*.

Initially, everything infants up to 4 months do is largely reflexive and accidental, but that doesn't mean they aren't paying attention. As they learn that those initial smiles[125] make mommy and daddy coo happily and smile back, babies begin to intentionally repeat those actions. This is the genesis of your child's ability to differentiate "good" behavior from "bad." Through trial and error, she learns what pleases you and what elicits disapproving frowns.

Beginning between 12 and 18 months of age, babies intentionally manipulate the things and people around them to get their needs and desires met. They also begin using simple words and become very demanding. Watching my grandchildren when they were this age, I could see the wheels turning in their little noggins and their frustration as they tried to communicate their very big thoughts with their very limited language skills. No wonder babies throw tantrums!

Infants and toddlers understand language before they can speak it. Their baby babble isn't just adorable, meaningless chatter; it's their first attempt to verbalize their thoughts. *Your* words, the

---

125 Debbie Downers claim those early smiles are due to gas bubbles, but that's just because they don't like babies. I'm kidding. Or am I? Hmmm?

things you say to your child, lay the foundation for everything that follows. Positive, encouraging words make your child feel happy and loved, whereas harsh, negative talk teaches her the world is a scary, unsafe place.

Choose your words wisely because your little one will parrot them back to you sooner than you think! (Ask any parent who's ever uttered swear words around their child thinking she's too young to understand. They know well the sting of hearing their lil' chipmunk drop the f-bomb around the in-laws!)

My point is, it's never too early to start talking about body safety with your infant. No, she won't understand what you're talking about… at first. But if you start with the basics when she's tiny, by using proper body terms when you bathe her, for example, she'll grow up knowing what's what and she'll be much safer as a result.

Sex & Sexual Development

You might think that sexual development in babies is a non-issue. They are, after all, totally innocent and unaware of their sexuality. Or are they? Babies actually begin exhibiting sexual behavior and showing interest in their bodies while they're still infants. They explore their world mainly through touch, and the more nurturing that touch is the more he'll view human bodies, his in particular, in a positive light.

Don't be alarmed or embarrassed if your baby touches himself when he's in the bath or being changed (or toddling around naked, as babies are wont to do); he's just trying to understand how his body feels and functions. Don't scold him or tell him he's being "bad" for doing what comes naturally.

If you're uncomfortable seeing your little one touch himself, you can always say, "Your private parts are just for you and you should only touch them when you're not around other people. Let's get you dressed now." Then redirect him with a new activity or toy. Of course, he won't understand what "private" means until he's a bit older, but you're training him early on to set healthy boundaries around his body.

Greatest Threats to Your Child at This Age

Molestation & Sexual Assault

(Refer to Chapter 9)

Child Abductions

(Refer to Chapter 10)

Pornography

(Refer to Chapter 8 on Digital Dangers)

There's a sick subculture of pedophiles lurking on the deep dark web who love to take sexually explicit photos of children and trade them back and forth. The younger the victims (infants and toddlers), the more violent the acts depicted tend to be. Be mindful of whom you leave your child alone with!

Strangers

(Refer to Chapter 2)

Older Children

(Refer to Chapter 3)

Partners, Stepparents & Non-Custodial Parents

(Refer to Chapter 4)

Relatives

(Refer to Chapter 4)

Babysitters & Other Caregivers

(Refer to Chapter 5)

Discussing Body Safety

There's no such thing as starting too young when it comes to teaching your child about body safety. Yes, she's preverbal, but she's learning at the speed of light and may begin to understand what you're saying before you're even aware that she does.

The body safety discussion isn't a one-time talk; it's a two-way conversation you'll have with her throughout her childhood. (Don't worry; I'll teach you how throughout this and the next few chapters.)

When to Teach Your Child About Body Safety Issues

The best time to talk to your infant about body safety issues is when you have to do something to care for his body, like diapering or bathing him. For example:

- When changing diapers. When you're changing his diaper, you can make it a habit to (occasionally) say something like, "Time to cover up! Your private parts are just for you, right? Remember, no one else should look at or touch your privates except [mommy/daddy/grandma, etc.], when you need to get clean, or the doctor when you need help to stay healthy."
- During bath time. This is a great time to talk to your child about his body parts, using the correct terminology that I'll cover below in the section on Body Words.

What to Teach Your Child

Below you'll find information on the broad categories that cover what you'll want to teach your infant as he grows from baby to toddler.

Boundaries

Physical and emotional boundaries are meant to protect your child and keep him safe from infringement by others. I'll talk more about this in the section on Body Autonomy below.

Emotions & Feelings[126]

Babies are ruled by their emotions and they communicate by expressing each and every feeling the moment they become aware of it. The best way to begin teaching your baby about his intuition and emotions is to recognize when he's having strong feelings and validate them.

For example, if your son gets angry because he doesn't want to eat his strained peas (and who would; am I right?), name his emotions for him by saying: "You don't want to eat your peas and you feel angry because I'm trying to make you eat them. Hmm?"[127] Or, if he's playful and giggling, you might say: "You look so happy! Are you happy to play with daddy?"

Toddlers often struggle to name their emotions, which is part of the reason they throw tantrums—it can be really frustrating not being able to communicate what you want in a way adults can understand. Over time, as your child grows older, he'll begin to associate the words for feelings with the feelings themselves.

---

[126] Emotions and feelings are the same thing.
[127] If he truly doesn't want to eat the peas, it's because he thinks they taste terrible or he's full. Don't sweetly validate his feelings and then continue to force him to do something (unessential) that he doesn't want to do. Of course, if it IS essential, like taking a bath or taking medicine, he'll just have to learn the hard lesson that sometimes there's just stuff we have to do whether we like it or not.

Heroic Parenting

Resilience

You can foster your baby's resilience by allowing him to work through challenges on his own without running to rescue him every time. When he falls on his butt and cries while trying to stand up, calmly assure him he's okay and encourage him to try again. The same goes when he experiences a disappointment, say, not getting his way when he tries to stuff his waffle into the DVR. Let him grouse about it for a few seconds and then redirect his attention to something he *is* allowed to do.

I'm not advising you to ignore real injuries here, I'm just saying that rushing in to save him from the slightest fall or disappointment could make him feel anxious and impact his self-confidence, whereas reassuring him that he's just fine teaches him to shake it off and keep on going.

Body Words

For babies under 2, stick to the basics by saying things like: "I'm going to wash your penis/vulva[128]/bottom now to keep it clean."

Body Autonomy

Learning about physical boundaries is one of the very first lessons your baby learns. During his time in the womb, he was "one" with mom, and learning that he's a separate being takes a bit of figuring out. It can be scary to feel that stark sense of individuality, as you can imagine, and it's part of why infants can experience separation anxiety. As your baby begins to differentiate himself from you and others, he'll look to you for reassurance that everything's okay; that he's okay.

You can introduce your son to healthy boundaries, first and foremost, by teaching him that his body is to be respected—by himself, by you, by everyone. When diapering him, for example, talk him through what you're doing before you do it, saying: "Time to clean your private parts! Okay? Here we go!" Tell him everything you're going to do, from removing his diaper, to wiping him, to applying cream, to putting on a fresh diaper. It's not only respectful, it's a great way to talk about body safety while you have his undivided attention.

A word about forced affection: I remember the first time my granddaughter refused to hug me. Granted, I asked her first if she wanted a hug, but when she gave me an emphatic "No!" I was crushed. At the same time, I was quite proud of her for setting a boundary with me. I've started

---

[128] Yes, it's actually the vulva that you clean. I'll explain in the next chapter.

asking my grandkids if they want a hug, a kiss, a fist-bump, or a handshake. They love having a choice and they enjoy mixing it up.

When we force children to be affectionate with others without checking in with them first, we're sending the message that we expect them to prioritize the wants of others over their own feelings and wishes. Don't force it.

If You Have Concerns Your Child Has Been Victimized

A child under 2 simply can't tell you if someone is sexually molesting or assaulting her, at least not in words. Often there are no signs you can point to that clearly show abuse has occurred. Sometimes, though, there are clues your child gives off that may indicate something serious has happened. Here's what to watch for:

- She has redness, bleeding, bruising, or soreness around her genital area.

- She has trouble walking or sitting, potentially due to pain in her genital or anal areas.

- Your child cries inconsolably or throws a fit when it's time to drop her off at daycare or with her sitter, or she appears frightened around her caregivers or other people (don't forget that juveniles are responsible for one-third of child sexual abuse incidents).

- She suddenly becomes super clingy or refuses any affection. It's not uncommon for abused children to exhibit extreme behavior, meaning a normally calm child starts acting aggressively or an outgoing child becomes passive and listless.

- She experiences night terrors or other sleep disturbances.

Some of the above signs may be perfectly normal for your child. For example, my oldest granddaughter has night terrors, just as her mother did when she was a toddler. You know your child better than anyone; trust your gut and if you sense something's wrong, get help to investigate it.

Reporting Sexual Abuse

See the Appendix for information on how to report child sexual abuse. And check out the many resources I list on my website.[129]

---

129 www.cjscarlet.com/resources

CHAPTER 12

Young Children 2 to 5

I'm the mother of two grown sons and have three grandchildren (a 3-year-old and 5-year-old twins, a boy and a girl), whom I see several times a week, so I know well what a fun but chaotic time this is for you as a parent. Your precocious toddler is a mercurial[130] creature—an itty-bitty Dr. Jekyll and Mr. Hyde.[131]

Your child's doing something cute and Facebook-worthy one minute and reprising a scene from the Exorcist the next, pea-green vomit included. Keeping up with him takes all your energy and you spend half your time chasing him down to keep him from stuffing pennies in the light socket and giving the cat a buzzcut.

Because your child is so ambulatory and tricky, it's hard to keep your eye on him every second, no matter how vigilant you try to be. You may not even realize he's not in the room with you until you hear the oh-so-sad sound of your cell phone being flushed down the toilet.

When your little terrorist finally goes to sleep (after five stories and a half dozen songs—for the love of God, go to sleep already!) and makes that magical transformation to a sweet cherub again, you can finally fall into bed. But just as you're drifting into the sleep of the dead yourself, that evil voice in your head starts whispering.

Images of every godawful scenario of harm that could befall your baby boo begin flashing through your mind—that kid who bites him at daycare, the new babysitter who might secretly be a serial killer, dark strangers who could kidnap him and sell him into a life of sexual slavery. The scenes get worse and worse, gathering steam until you're sick to your stomach with anxiety. You

---

130 Mercurial = Like mercury, in that it changes depending on the conditions.
131 *The Strange Case of Dr. Jekyll and Mr. Hyde* was published by Robert Louis Stevenson in 1886. The book and its more than 120 stage and film adaptations explore the good and evil that reside in the hearts of all human beings.

finally fall into an exhausted version of sleep, only to wake up a few hours later in a fog to do it all over again.

Welcome to parenthood in the era of media and social media mass hysteria (Breaking News at 11:00!). So, what's a parent to do with all this potential danger?

Breathe.

Now close your eyes and listen to me very carefully. *(Wait. If you're reading or driving, please don't close your eyes, just pretend they're closed and continue on.)*

Here we go: You, as a parent, have so much more power than you realize to protect your child from dangerous people. And your child, with your help (and the ideas from this book), has all he needs in his own special little body package to protect and defend himself when you're not around.

If you read the Introduction, you know that the world isn't nearly as scary as the media and social media rants would have you think. In fact, the world is *far* safer today than it's ever been.

Let that knowledge seep deep into your bones and allow it to reassure you and release you from your worries and sleepless nights.

Your child, and you, are going to be okay.

Even in the unlikely event that something bad does happen, you'll both find a way to deal with it and move forward. By reading this book and applying what I share, you're giving your child his best chance of thwarting any predator and effectively reacting to stop any threat.

Feel better? I hope so.

How This Age Group Learns & Processes Information

Every single year of a child's life is important, but when it comes to learning and development, the first five years are the most critical. She's a little sponge soaking up information, and what she learns now—or doesn't learn—about appropriate behavior, compassion and empathy, boundaries, and other social skills will remain with her for the rest of her life, for good or ill.

There's a big difference between a 2-year-old's view of the world and a 5-year-old's, so I'll break it down:

Heroic Parenting

Your 2-Year-Old

Toddlers at this age are sweet and affectionate, curious, chatty, and growing more independent by the minute. Still, your child wants you close by and constantly demands your attention. She lives for songs and books and games and she loves to be silly. She's also age-appropriately egocentric and bossy, and her new favorite word is "no." (More like "NO!!!!!" shouted at ear-shattering decibels.)

As much as this tiny tyrant wants to do things her way, she craves routine. She also needs you to be the one in control so she feels secure. I've learned from watching my daughter-in-law that the way to get my 3-year-old granddaughter to do anything isn't to ask what she wants, but to offer her two choices ("Do you want to wear the pink tights or the blue tutu?"). More than two choices are overwhelming and just makes the decision process take longer.

Most of all, your child craves love and affection, although she may be shy of strangers. While you want her to grow comfortable being around others, don't force her to interact when it's clear she doesn't want to. And, most certainly don't make her hug or kiss others unless she agrees to—after being politely asked first.

Your 3-Year-Old

This age can be described as "energetic!" Life is all about play, play, play, because that's how your child learns best. Your 3-year-is exploring the world and soaking up everything he encounters. He's starting to use his imagination and loves to pretend he's a superhero (or princess; don't judge). He's also interacting more socially, playing along *with* his peers rather than merely playing beside them as a 2-year-old does. He's still learning how to share with others. You can reason a little more with him as he begins to understand how to do things for himself and solve problems.

While a 2-year-old learns better from real life experiences over TV or books, by age 3, your son is able to learn from a variety of sources, including (hopefully age-appropriate) TV shows and cartoons, books, and screen media. It's helpful to talk about what he just watched or what you read to him to help him better understand and process the lessons those hold.

You may look forward to this age because you're past the terrible twos, but I've got bad news for you—the switch doesn't flip when your little terrorist turns 3. No, the terrible twos are merely a prelude of what's to come over the next 15 years.[132]

---

[132] Hey, I'm just the messenger; don't hate.

Your 4-Year-Old

Your preschooler is a tornado of activity and chatter. Creative play is more refined and her artwork is more skillful. She loves to test the limits—hers *and* yours—and will test your patience mightily in the process. She may be interested in organized activities, like sports, arts and crafts, or dance. This is when your tedious side gig as a chauffeur begins (it ends only when she leaves home at 18).

This is the age when your child becomes an interrogator with skills worthy of the "Grand Inquisitor."[133] "Why?" and "how?" are her favorite words. She has questions about *everything* she sees and experiences, and she peppers you with so many questions—most of which you don't have a clue how to answer—that it can make your head spin.

Your 4-year-old is likely engaging in fantasy play and can be quite creative with it. My grandson spends much of his time pretending he's the Hulk and he's convinced he can beat up bad guys.

Your 5-Year-Old

By the time your child is 5, his brain has grown to 85 percent of its capacity, size-wise, and it shows. He's curious and rapidly absorbs new ideas and information. He may already be reading or is on the cusp of it and loves to show off what he's learning.

Depending on your child's personality, he looks forward to kindergarten with either excitement or some anxiety, most likely a mix of the two. How well you handle him going off to school will dictate in large part how well *he* handles it. If you position it as a fun and exciting opportunity to learn and make new friends, he'll likely be less nervous than if you bemoan the loss of your "baby boy."

Five-year-olds like to be seen as independent, but still look to their parents for love and assurance. Your child is capable of understanding body safety issues at a deeper level which, as he enters the rough and tumble world of grade school, become even more important.

Sex & Sexuality

Our bodies are monster tactile sensors and it feels good when they're touched in a pleasurable way. This is just as true of new-born infants as it is of horny teenagers.[134] Our society has made

---

133 The person who was in charge of interrogations during the Spanish Inquisition.
134 And even hornier adults!

sexual exploration and masturbation into dirty topics and some of you may be horrified because I'm talking about the "M" word. Deal with it, honeybun; your child is a human being and human beings are sexual and sensual creatures who like to do what feels good.

Very young children and toddlers will often poke, pull, rub, and play with their genitals, right in plain sight of God and everyone, to the great embarrassment of the people around them. It's up to you (because you're the adult now, dang it!) to be your child's guide to what is and isn't okay in public.

Kids 2 to 4 are naturally immodest and will strip off their clothes at the drop of a hat. They're also *very* curious about the human body and bodily functions. They may want to touch mom's breasts or watch while you go to the bathroom.

Most kids engage in innocent sexual behaviors at some point and it's perfectly natural and nothing to lose your mind over (I'll tell you below when it *is* something to freak out about). That being said, no parent is ever really prepared to walk in on their child exploring her body—or someone else's.

If you catch your child under 6 masturbating outside of her room or the bathroom, say something like, "Grown-ups do that in private and you should too." Then redirect her to another, more socially acceptable activity to divert her attention away from her body. For older kids, you can gently remind them that playing with themselves is something they should do in private and leave it at that.

Party of Two (or more)

Now, what about when it turns into a party? So called "child's play" is usually normal too when it's spontaneous; done in fun and out of curiosity; and the children are similar in age, size, and developmental level. But just because it's normal doesn't mean you have to allow or encourage it when you spot it. Use these situations as teachable moments about respecting their own and others' body boundaries and privacy.

Let me give you a few stats to help you get a little perspective and stop thinking your child is a mutant because he's playing doctor with his BFF:

- 50 percent of the adults surveyed admitted they engaged in sexual behavior before they were 13 (and those are just the ones secure enough to admit it).

- 73 percent of the time it was with other children (often of the same gender).

- 34 percent showed their genitals to another child.
- 16 percent remember simulating intercourse with another child.
- 5 percent inserted an object into the vagina or rectum of another child.
- 4 percent recalled oral-genital contact. [cxxxviii]

If you find your child engaging in normal child's play, calmly say something like, "I see you and Jerry[135] are comparing your bodies. Remember that even though it's interesting to see what other people's bodies look like, we keep our clothes on when we're around other people. Now get dressed."

Again, this kind of behavior is almost always normal, innocent child's play. It's only when there are more than three years difference in the ages of those involved, or the behavior becomes intrusive, hurtful, or age-inappropriate that you have a problem.

If you do stumble upon an incident or learn of one, don't shame, blame, yell, scream, cry, or punish your child for doing what most kids do. Tell him that it's not okay to touch anyone else's private parts except his own, in the privacy of his room. This is also a good time to remind him to tell you if anyone ever touches his private parts. Explain that the "private parts" are the body parts covered by his bathing suit.

Even if the behavior is genuinely inappropriate, abnormal, or dangerous, you don't want to react by panicking or punishing him right in the moment. Rather, you need to calmly tell the children to stop the behavior, separate them, and give yourself a few minutes to decide how to respond.

What's "Normal" & What's Not

Below is a list of normal and "concerning" sexual behaviors for children 2 to 5, provided by the American Academy of Pediatrics.

Normal, Common Behaviors
- Asking questions about bodies and bodily functions.
- Thinking "potty words" are hysterically funny (e.g., calling others "poopy heads").

---

[135] I'm serious, Jerry. We listened to each other's heartbeats and yet you haven't called me in 54 years! Have you no heart left?

- Asking questions about gender differences in body parts.
- Trying to touch their mother's breasts.
- Getting an erection (boys only, duh).
- Touching their genitals or masturbating in public or private.
- Showing their genitals to peers.
- Looking at or touching the genitals of peers or siblings.
- Trying to look at peers and adults in the nude.

Concerning Behaviors[136]

- Any sexual behaviors between children who are more than three years apart or very different in size or developmental level.
- Asking peers or adults to engage in specific sexual acts.
- Inserting objects into the genitals.
- Explicitly imitating intercourse.
- Touching animal genitals.
- Displaying a variety of sexual behaviors on a frequent basis.
- Sexual behavior that results in emotional distress or physical pain to others.
- Sexual behavior associated with other physically aggressive behavior.

Answering Your Child's Questions about Sex

Guess what? If you don't talk to your child about human sexuality and the human body, he'll get the 911[137] from his equally clueless friends or from what he watches on TV or online, and then heaven only knows what kind of erroneous[138] garbage he'll learn and carry around in that brain of his.

---

136 If your child exhibits concerning behaviors, you should seek counseling for him right away.
137 In other words, he'll get it off the "street" from his friends or other non-trustworthy, clueless, or malicious sources.
138 Erroneous = False or incorrect.

When you find your curious little squirrel engaged in sexual exploration, that's a good time to see what questions he might have. This way you can share not only the facts, but your values around sex and sexuality as well. This isn't a time to drop a truth bomb on him about the facts of life. Let his questions determine how much you share, knowing that what you tell him could screw him up for life.

Just kidding.

Mostly.

Kids this age aren't looking for the low-down on sex and all that it entails. They generally just want to know the basics (which can range from, for example: "You came from Mommy's tummy" to "Daddy planted a special seed in Mommy's body that grew into a baby and that baby was you!").

Precocious[139] children may ask for more details. I HIGHLY recommend you buy one of the multitude of books for kids on the topic of "where babies come from." I also provide web addresses in the Resources section of my website[140] to several great, short, articles from the Sexuality Resource Center for Parents.

The Digital Natives Are Restless!

Most toddlers today can use a tablet and do basic navigation on a cell phone. My 3-year-old granddaughter can scroll through my phone's photo gallery like it's her job and has even taught this old dog a few new tricks (like using the "pinch" gesture to go to a grid view of my pics. Who knew?). At 3, your child has the manual dexterity to use a mouse or touch screen to speed through websites and pages, so stay alert to what she's looking at. Using parental controls that are password-protected when she's on devices is important to ensure she doesn't accidentally run across inappropriate content.

Before you put any computer, tablet, or phone in your child's hands for the first time, tell her there are rules about using them. Yes, even if she's only 3. No, she won't understand what you mean, but you need to start the conversation now and continue talking about the rules throughout her life at home. By the time she's 4, she'll begin to understand what the concept of "rules" means, and you can begin expanding the conversation to include more of them (e.g., to stay on pre-approved, password-protected, age-appropriate sites). Under no circumstances should your child of that age be on the open Internet or ANY site where she's interacting with others online!

---

139 Precocious = Kids who are especially curious or advanced in their questions.
140 www.cjscarlet.com/resources

Heroic Parenting

Hulk Angry!

Kids this age can be aggressive and are just now learning how to modulate their feelings and tempers. Violent content (and many kids' cartoons contain a shocking amount of violence!) can motivate them to act aggressively. When my grandson's in superhero mode, he runs around pretending to fight and shoot bad guys, scaring the dickens out of his sisters, me, and the dogs.

When your mini Avenger does mimic the violence he sees on TV, use it as a teachable moment to talk about consequences (for the bad guys) and ways to resolve conflict that don't involve fighting.

What Your Child Needs from You

Toddlers still want and need to stay close to you AND they also want to be independent. They love to test your limits, but giving them room to grow doesn't mean letting them get away with everything.

As the parent, you need to set reasonable limits, both for your child's protection and that of others. That means teaching her that there are consequences for bad behavior. Spankings are painful and humiliating and only teach children that violence is the answer. At this age, time-outs of one minute for each year of age (i.e., two minutes for a 2-year-old) are appropriate, although diverting their attention to a more acceptable activity is often more effective and less likely to end in a tantrum.

Your child needs you to be in control. When you lose your cool, she thinks *she's* in charge and that feels scary and dangerous to her, so she acts out even more, hoping you'll step up and take control. Clearly lay out your rules and stand firm, but try to remain calm when she forgets or stubbornly refuses to cooperate.

Greatest Threats to Your Child at This Age

Bullying

I addressed bullying thoroughly in Chapter 7, so I won't repeat myself here. But I do want to take a minute to talk about how to keep your toddler from growing up to be a bully himself. Toddler temper tantrums are perfectly normal and to be expected, but let's be clear, they *could* be a gateway drug to bullying if you don't help your little monster manage his overwhelming emotions.

For every expert who advises parents to either ignore their tantruming child or redirect his attention to a different activity, there's another expert claiming these tactics will create a tyrant.

One thing's for sure, allowing your child to throw fits or use (or threaten to use) violence to get his way will only lead to more tantrums *if you give in to him.*

Giving in to your child's tantrums by letting him have his way is a HUGE mistake! It teaches him that he can use bullying to get what he wants. Your job is to help him learn impulse control and delayed gratification so he can grow up to be a functioning adult.

If you hold out for 10 minutes but then give in to his demands at 10 minutes and 2 seconds because you're exhausted and you can't stand the ear-splitting screams and door-kicking any longer, you've just taught your son that the price of getting what he wants is 10 minutes and 2 seconds of screaming like a rabid Chupacabra.[141] It also teaches him that he and his emotions are more powerful than you are. Bad juju, that.

My daughter-in-law is a master at handling tantrums. When my grandkids were under 3, Bekki would talk them through their fits, sitting next to them on the floor and saying in a soothing voice, "You've got big emotions, huh? It's okay; you're okay," until they calmed down. Now that the twins are 5, she usually gives them a few minutes to pitch their screaming hissy fit, and when she senses they're running out of steam, she redirects their attention to a different toy or activity (other than what they were freaking over). I'm telling you, she's a pro. Don't get me wrong, she still loses her cool on occasion (I mean, she's not *Gandhi* for goodness sake!), but for the most part, she maintains her composure.

Like it or not, your child pays attention to every single thing you do and say and takes you at your (even unspoken) word. So, when you're not in control, which makes her feel insecure and anxious, she thinks it's okay to be out of control too. Also, if you treat others poorly—talking badly about them or throwing your weight around in front of her—you're teaching her to do the same. This is especially true of your negative words directed toward her and your partner.

Never forget, *your criticism of her becomes her inner voice and determines how she sees herself.* (I would underline that twice if my computer would let me, it's THAT important.) And how you treat your partner teaches her what to expect in her own relationships later.

Pornography

(Refer to Chapter 8)

---

[141] The Chupacabra is a legendary creature whose name comes from the animal's reported habit of attacking and drinking the blood of livestock, including goats.

Heroic Parenting

Please teach your child that no one should ever take pictures of their private parts and that they should tell you right away if someone does or tries to.

Molestation & Sexual Assault

(Refer to Chapter 9)

Kidnapping

(Refer to Chapter 10)

Strangers

(Refer to Chapter 2)

Siblings, Peers & Older Kids

(Refer to Chapter 3)

Partners, Stepparents & Non-Custodial Parents

(Refer to Chapter 4)

Relatives

(Refer to Chapter 4)

Babysitters & Other Caregivers

(Refer to Chapter 5)

Daycare & Pre-School

(Refer to Chapter 5)

Other Adults

(Refer to Chapter 6)

Discussing Body Safety

It's perfectly normal to feel nervous or uncomfortable about talking to your child about body safety issues, but it's super important to do so and you and your child will grow more comfortable with it over time.

The point of this book is to teach you how to talk to your child about danger *without scaring her to death*, so don't think you have to give her any scary stats or stories to get her attention. You can keep the conversation friendly and even light. Below I'll share some examples of things you can say to get the point across without making your child afraid to leave your side.

Don't think this is all about having one humongous safety talk with your child where you do a massive data dump on her and walk away thinking you've done your job and now she's safe. No, you'll want to introduce body safety topics in tiny doses over time, throughout your child's life until she (finally!) graduates from high school and leaves home.[142]

Approach the subject of body safety matter-of-factly: "It's time we went over the rules about body safety" or "I want to have a talk about body safety today." If your child doesn't act interested or seems uncomfortable, you can say, "It's awkward for me too, but it's important that we have this talk."[cxxxix]

Don't worry if you don't get it just "right" or get flustered; you're going to make this part of your routine and you'll get better at it over time. In Chapter 18 I'll help you learn how to incorporate safety talks into your daily conversations and the monthly family meetings I recommend. The point is to make it an ongoing conversation that you start early to make it into a habit for both you and your child that will still work even when they're rebellious teenagers.

When to Teach Them About Body Safety Issues

If you want your little duckling to pay attention to you when you talk to him about body safety issues, choose a time when you're both comfortable and relaxed. Trying to talk when either of you is stressed is a bad idea.

Consider using the following times to have body safety conversations with your child:

- **Changing clothes or diapers.** When your child is changing clothes or you're changing his diaper, you can make it a habit to (occasionally) say something like, "Time to cover up! Your private parts are just for you, right? Remember, no one else should look at or touch your privates except [mommy/daddy/grandma, etc.] when you need to get clean, or the doctor when you need help to stay healthy."

---

[142] When I and each of my siblings graduated from high school, my parents gifted us each with a suitcase. "Here's your hat; what's your hurry?" LOL!

- **Bath time.** This is a great time to talk to your child about his body parts, using the correct terminology that I'll cover below in the section on Body Words.

- **Bedtime/storytime.** Tell or read stories to your child and talk about them afterward to highlight the moral lessons and any safety themes (such as the debatable wisdom of Goldilocks going into a strange house). Ask open-ended questions (ones that can't be answered with a simple yes or no) like, "What would you do if that happened to you?" and use your child's answer for further discussion. Keep it light. (I do NOT recommend talking about danger topics just before bed. I don't know about your child, but deep thoughts tend to keep my older granddaughter awake way beyond bedtime.)

- **Over a treat.** Create a fun routine, like having a chat over hot cocoa or milk and cookies when you talk about any questions or concerns he may have around body safety. This could include asking questions like, "How safe do you feel at school?" followed by, "Are there any bullies at your school?" and "Has that kid ever picked on you?"

- **Before any new situation.** Before your child starts a new activity or goes somewhere where he'll be interacting with new people (daycare, soccer, etc.), talk to him about what he might experience and who he might meet. Make it a fun conversation by wondering together what adventures he'll have. Introduce the most important body safety issues, such as remembering to trust his intuition and telling new people "no" to hugs. Encourage him to ask questions.

How to Teach Your Child About Body Safety Issues

Using Stories

Children *love* stories (mostly they love the attention you pay them when you're reading to them). Here's a short list to give you an idea of what kinds of stories teach moral or safety lessons that can lead to great teaching moments:

- **Aesop's Fables.** These are super short stories and teach lessons every person needs to learn to become a decent human being. (If you buy a copy of Aesop's Fables, get a kid's version that offers commentary; even you might not get the point of some of the more obscure[143] lessons.)

---

143 Obscure = The meaning isn't obvious or clear. (I don't mean I don't know what this word means; that's the actual definition, lol.)

- **Snow White and the Seven Dwarves.** This one's loaded with all kinds of great fodder for safety chats—dangerous people (the queen), compassion (the huntsman who chooses not to kill Snow White), the danger of accepting gifts (the poisoned apple from the disguised queen), and the importance of having friends (the seven dwarves). This story also has some great negative lessons to discuss with your child (such as the fallacy of needing a prince to save you when you're in trouble) that can lead to very lively conversations.

- **Little Red Riding Hood.** Another oldie but goodie that covers everything from the need for situational awareness to recognizing tricky people (e.g., Red at first doesn't see that her grandmother is actually the wolf, but figures it out by paying attention to the clues—big ears, teeth, etc.).

- **Pinocchio.** Poor Pinocchio wants so desperately to be someone other than who he is. He ultimately gets his wish after he learns several important lessons along the way: Your conscience and intuition (thank you, Jiminy Cricket!) can tell you what's right from wrong, always be truthful, and that there are consequences when you make the wrong choices. This story is great for kids who lack self-esteem and want to be different than they are. It can teach them the value of appreciating who they authentically are and that with time and experience, they'll grow up to be just awesome.

- **The Little Mermaid.** Ariel not only runs away to meet up with a boy she doesn't know (egads!), she makes a deal with the obviously evil Ursula, giving up something highly personal (her voice) in exchange for something she wants (to be human).

There are also a multitude of excellent books specifically covering body safety topics that you can find on my website under the Cool Sh*t tab[144] or on any online bookstore.

Using Imagination & Role-Playing

Harness your 3- to 5-year-old child's vivid imagination by engaging him in roleplaying different body safety scenarios. Start with a short chat about a body safety issue (for example, not going somewhere with other people unless you say it's okay), and then ask your child questions like, "What would you do if you were in the front yard and someone in a car rolled down their window and asked if you wanted some candy?" Let your child fully answer, without interrupting or correcting him, until he's done answering your question.

---

144 www.cjscarlet.com/coolsht

Heroic Parenting

If he's off base and says he'd go up to the car to get the candy, don't scold or punish him. Remember this is a new concept for him and teaching him about body safety is a marathon, not a sprint. Instead, you might say, "That wouldn't be a good idea because you might put yourself in danger. What do you think could happen if you went over to his car to get the candy?" Continue gently guiding him and asking questions to help him think through the ramifications of going up to the car.

Remember, your goal is to guide your child, not scare him to death, so don't jump in when he's in mid-sentence to frantically warn him that he could be snatched and taken away from you forever!

When he gives you the "correct" answer (that he would run into the house and tell you right away), praise him and tell him how smart he is. You can even reward him with a special treat or toy (for a small child it could be as simple as one gummy bear for the correct answer).

Don't accept just a verbal answer; make him show you what he would do. Actually take him outside and then have him run up to you and tell you the story of the imaginary person in the car. If you can't do this, have your child play out the scenarios using stuffed animals or other toys, or have him draw pictures to show what he would do.

Then give him a couple more scenarios, for example: "But what if your soccer coach told you he'll give you a ride home from practice?" Correct answer: Don't get in his car unless YOU, the parent, tell him it's okay.

Or, "And what if Grandpa asked if you want to go to the store with him?" Correct answer: This one's tricky; if Grandpa is babysitting him, he's the one in charge, so it's okay. But if he's not the one in charge, your child always has to ask you first, no matter who asks him to get in their vehicle.

I hope you see what I mean here.[145]

Questions

When you introduce or reinforce body safety rules and scenarios, your child is bound to have lots of questions. That's a good thing. Yes, I know you're sick of your 4-year-old asking "Why is

---

[145] If you have questions about this, or anything else in this book for that matter, you can contact me via my website at www.cjscarlet.com.

the sky blue?" questions,[146] but you *want* your child to be curious and engaged in these body safety conversations, so be patient and keep answering until (a) she runs out of questions, or (b) she's exhausted your entire library of knowledge on the subject.

When you've run out of steam or brain cells, you can tell your curious imp that you'll talk more about it another time. In the meantime, I guarantee she'll think about what you shared with her and have more questions later. That's also a good thing.

What to Teach Your Child

Below you'll find information on the broad categories that cover what you'll want to teach your child 2 to 5. Remember, you don't have to cram all this information into one big conversation. On my website,[147] I provide a handy dandy calendar you can refer to that introduces one topic at a time over the course of one year.

Intuition

People often confuse "intuition" and "feelings" because we tend to use the terms interchangeably and because we *feel* intuitive hits in our bodies. But while intuition may present as a feeling in the body (e.g., butterflies in the stomach), it's more of a sixth sense that provokes feelings; intuition comes first, followed by feelings based on it. So, for example, you may sense intuitively that the man who's standing next to you is "creepy" and then feel nervous or unsettled around him.

Your child's intuition is her first line of defense against danger and predatory people. Listening to her intuition will also help her be more confident and increase her self-esteem. She'll gain a strong internal sense of self to guide her and help her better resist pressure from others, and she'll behave in ways that are authentic to her.

You want to foster your daughter's nascent intuitive sense and help her learn to recognize it and act on it. Understanding the concept of "intuition" is likely too advanced for your child, so you can explain it to her like this:

> "Deep inside your body you have a special sense called 'intuition.' It's your very best friend that will help you your whole life if you listen to it. Mommy and Daddy have it too;

---

146 BTW, the sky is blue because molecules in the air scatter blue light from the sun more than they scatter red light. At sunset, we see red and orange colors because the blue light has been scattered out and away from the line of sight. You're welcome.

147 www.cjscarlet.com/freebies

everyone does. Your intuition pays attention to everything and everyone around you, and it tells you when something doesn't feel good.

"It doesn't talk with a voice like you and I do. It tells you things by giving you good or bad feelings that you might feel in your tummy or your chest. Like when you feel happy, you might feel like your heart is singing. Or when you feel scared or nervous, it might make your stomach hurt or feel like it has butterflies in it. You might notice your intuition does this when you meet a new person, or when someone does something they shouldn't.

"Your intuition is veeery quiet, so when you notice it talking, you need to pay really close attention to see what it's saying. Sometimes your mind will try to talk louder than your intuition, but you must always listen to your intuition first."

Your child will likely have lots of questions for you about this. Take the time to answer them all until you feel like she understands as much as her age and maturity level allow. This is a conversation that will continue and shift over time.

Children's book author and coach Ariane de Bonvoisin offers the following words of advice for parents when they talk to their kids about intuition:[cxl]

- Start with small ways for your child to see that intuition can be fun. When she loses something, ask her, "Where does your intuition tell you it is?" Ask her how she *feels* instead of overusing the phrase, "What do you think?"

- When she brings up any feelings or insights, always respect and validate them as real and important. If not, many kids go into self-doubt and are more likely to defer to what other people want.

- If your child senses something and says, for example, "Mom, are you upset?" and you say "No" when in fact you are, you're teaching her not to trust her feelings. Always be honest with your child so she knows what she's sensing is true and right. Otherwise, she learns to shut this part of herself down.

- The best way to teach your child about intuition is to show her on a regular basis how you use it. As a parent, how well are you doing with listening to *your* intuition? Modeling this behavior for your child is the fastest way to teach her to want to do the same. Talk openly about what your intuition is telling you.

Here are five things you can do to help your child develop and learn to trust her intuition:

1. Don't force her to hug or kiss anyone if she doesn't want to.

2. Take her fears and discomfort around others seriously. The physical and emotional feeling of fear is designed to protect us from danger. When you minimize your child's fears by telling her there's nothing to be afraid of, it neither removes the fear nor calms her down. She just feels ashamed and learns to keep her fears to herself, and that runs counter to your desire to encourage her to come to you if she's in real danger. Over time, she'll get better at stuffing her feelings and her intuition will be tamped down in the process. Validate and acknowledge her fears and ask questions about them to see what's beneath the surface. Her fears may in fact be irrational (you don't want to say that, of course; that would come across as ridicule), or they may point to something you need to be concerned about.

3. Tell your child that if a particular person makes her intuition go off, she should get away from that person immediately and come tell you right away.

4. Teach her to protect herself. Rather than promising you'll protect her from all harm for all time—a promise you can't keep—promise her you'll teach her what she needs to know to take care herself… and then do so. By reading and applying what you're learning in this book, you're helping keep that promise.

5. Teach her that adults make mistakes too and that they're not always right. This takes the pressure off her to automatically obey any adults' commands that might not be in her best interest. Teach your daughter that she's not obligated to obey any adult (or child) who makes her tummy feel icky.

Boundaries

Boundaries are the invisible line we allow people to cross—or not—in our physical and emotional space. Teaching your child to set and enforce solid boundaries is the second most important thing you'll ever teach him (the first is how to trust his intuition).

You can explain boundaries to your child in this way:

"Your body and feelings are so special, and they belong only to you. I want to tell you about a way to keep your body and feelings safe. Look at your body. Do you see how your skin protects your body from things like dirt and rain and germs? Well, there's a thing called boundaries that do the same thing to protect your body and your feelings from things other people may do or say to you.

"Boundaries are like invisible fences or rules that keep some things out and other things in. A body boundary is a rule that keeps people from touching our bodies in ways we don't like. An emotional boundary is a rule that helps us when people say and do things that make us feel sad, bad, mad, or scared.

"It's my job as your parent to help you set your boundaries and teach you how to use them to stay safe. One boundary rule is that we don't let other people touch our private parts, except when mommy or daddy are cleaning you or you go to the doctor for a check-up. The way you protect your body boundary if someone else tries to touch your private parts would be to yell 'No!' and get away from them as fast as you can. Then you should come and tell me right away.

"Another boundary rule is that we don't let people say mean things that hurt our feelings. So, if someone said, 'You're stupid,' you could put up an emotional boundary by saying, 'That's not nice. Please don't talk to me like that.'

"Sometimes when you set a boundary, you might feel afraid that you'll hurt the other person's feelings or make them mad, but keeping you safe is more important than their feelings. And if they're doing something you don't like, they need to know that. If they get mad at you, get away from that person and come tell me right away."

It's your job to help your child recognize when his boundaries are being crossed and remind him to enforce them. For example, if you see someone disrespect him or hug him without permission, you need to step in right then, in front of your child, and explain what his boundaries are and that they need to respect them.

Just as your child might be afraid of hurting someone's feelings or making them mad, you too might be nervous about saying something. Get over it. The 15 seconds of discomfort you and the other person might feel are worth it to protect your kid.

I want to add a word about consent. Your child needs to know he can withdraw consent at any point, even if he initially liked what was happening. Say, for example, "I want you to know that if someone was tickling you or playing with you and it felt fun, but then it became irritating or even scary, you can tell that person to stop. If they don't stop, you need to get away from them and come tell me."

Body Words

You may think it's cute to call your daughter's vulva her "pooney" or your son's penis his "wee wee," but it makes it harder for them to tell you what happened if someone touches them inappropriately. And using pet names for body parts can make sexual contact sound super fun; not exactly what you're going for.

Thinking that using proper terms for your child's body parts is too "advanced" for her age is just another way of saying that you yourself aren't comfortable with those words. *Don't be a prude.* Here are the proper terms and their meanings (some may surprise you):

- **Vulva:** According to the Encyclopedia Britannica, the vulva is the "external female genitalia that surround the opening to the vagina; collectively these consist of the labia majora, the labia minora, clitoris, vestibule of the vagina, bulb of the vestibule, and the glands of Bartholin. All of these organs are located in front of the anus and below the mons pubis (the pad of fatty tissue at the forward junction of the pelvic bones)."[148] Don't worry, you don't have to explain all those terms; simply teaching your child what the vulva is will be sufficient for now.

- **Vagina:** The vagina is often used to refer to the entirety of a girl's genitals, but it is, in fact, just the interior part of her body that connects the vulva to the uterus. The vulva is the correct term for the external parts of her genitalia and the vagina.

- **Clitoris:** The clitoris is the small fleshy nub located just above the vagina and urethra and inside the labia. Covered by a hood of skin, it's the female version of the head of the penis. When rubbed, it causes intense sexual pleasure.[cxli]

- **Labia:** The labia are the inner and outer folds of the vulva, at either side of the vagina.

- **Urethra:** This is the tiny hole at the end of the penis or hidden between the labia (in girls) where urine comes out.

- **Penis:** C'mon, man! Surely, you know this one? Just in case, it's the male organ that hangs between a boy's legs and that he urinates and ejaculates from.

---

[148] Wow! I never knew my Lady Garden was so complicated! Some of these parts sound like locations in the *Game of Thrones!*

- **Testicles:** The testicles (also called testes) are located in the scrotum, a sac[149] of skin that hangs below the penis and between the legs.

- **Rectum.** The rectum is the section of the digestive tract above the anus.

- **Anus:** The anus is the actual opening at the end of the digestive tract where stool (poop) leaves the body.

- **Nipples:** Seriously? Figure it out.

There are tons a great children's books on bodies and body differences that can help make this conversation easier (for you). Google it.

Body Autonomy

Your child needs to know that his body is his and his alone and that *no one* has the right to touch it in an inappropriate way that's hurtful or makes him feel violated—not you, not anyone. When you teach him about boundaries, also talk to him about this.

This means he gets to have a say in what happens to his body. That doesn't mean he has the final say, though; having his diaper changed or his body washed are non-negotiable. If he objects to something you're doing that must be done, acknowledge his feelings, saying something like, "I know you feel angry because you have to get dressed now, but it's time to leave for soccer and we can't have you running around naked," or "I know it doesn't feel good when I put the rash cream on, but it's important for you to get better."

The only time your child should have to endure someone doing something painful to his body is when it's appropriate and necessary, say, to treat an injury or have a medical procedure. To teach him this, you could say, "Sometimes when you go to the doctor she may have to give you a shot that hurts for a just a second, but no one else is ever allowed to touch your body, especially your private parts, in a way that hurts you or makes you feel yucky inside."

Speaking of doctor visits, you need to explain to your child that sometimes the doctor will need to touch his private parts to ensure they're healthy. ALWAYS stay in the room with your child during any doctor's exam and for heaven's sake, keep your eyes open and not on your phone screen. If the doctor asks you to leave the room for a legitimate reason (I can't think of a good one for a child this age), be sure a nurse or assistant stays in the room with them to provide oversight.

---

149 No, I didn't accidently leave off the "k" in sac; that's how you spell it when it refers to animals or plants.

The same applies at the dentist's office (mouths are private too!). Prepare your child in advance of his first dental visit by explaining that the dentist will look at and touch the inside of his mouth.

Almost forgot—when you teach your child not to let others touch his private parts, also tell him he's not to touch other people's private parts either. This way, if someone tries to make him touch them inappropriately, your child won't go along with it because you never warned him not to. "Not touching other people" includes your child putting his hands on or down anyone's pants or up their skirt because he was told to by the other child or adult.

Saying No

One word. One simple freaking word. I swear to God if I'd known it was okay to say no to anyone who was trying to harm me, most of my sexual molestations and assaults would never have happened. But I didn't know because my parents didn't know to teach me that. Instead, I learned to make nice, to make everyone around me feel comfortable, even if it meant *I* felt uncomfortable. (My parents weren't trying to set me up; that's just the way kids, especially girls, were raised in medieval times.)

This is probably the easiest lesson you'll ever teach your child because she's a master at saying "No!" loud and often. Every parent dreads running in the "no" wall with their child, but if you teach her when and how to say it, you're giving her THE most important tool to keep predators at bay.

When to Say No

At this age, your darling will say "no" whenever and wherever she wants. The trick is to teach her when it's most important to say it. Try this: "I want you to know that if anyone makes you feel uncomfortable or scared or yucky inside, you should yell 'No!,' and run away from them. Then you should tell me or another safe person right away. Even if it's somebody you like or love, like Grandpa or your teacher or your babysitter, you can always tell them no if they do something that makes you feel bad inside."

Of course, the person may not stop just because your child tells them to. I'll cover how to teach your child to physically defend herself in Chapter 17.

How to Say No

There's a mnemonic device you can use to help your child remember what to do in a sketchy situation. Have her practice thinking, "No! Go! Tell!" Explain that this means she should yell "No! Don't touch me!" then run away from that person, and then tell somebody what happened.

Reassure her that if she isn't able to say no and leave right away, it's not her fault; it's the other person's fault for being inappropriate.

Teach your older toddler *how* to say no in a way that will ensure she'll be taken seriously by the offender. Say: "There's a good way to say no and a not-so-good way to say no. You want to make sure the other person understands that you mean no. You show people you mean no by the way you hold your body and the way you talk. You stand tall, look the person in the eyes and say 'No!' in a firm, clear voice." (Show her what this looks like and have her practice it until she says it loudly and with conviction.)

Safe Touch vs. Unsafe Touch

Because your child is so innocent and still learning about the world, she has no clue what safe and unsafe touches are, so spell it out for her: "A safe touch is a way people show they care for each other. That means hugging, kissing, and helping each other. It's like when Grandma brushes your hair or I wash your body when you take a bath. An unsafe touch is the kind you don't want because it makes you feel scared or yucky and you want it to stop right away, like if someone tickled you too much or tried to touch your private parts."

Reassure her that most touches are safe touches that feel good, but that if a safe touch that starts out feeling good begins to feel bad, she can always tell the person to stop by saying, "No! I don't like that. Stop!" Remind her that it's a family rule that no one is allowed to touch her private parts (except for her parents and the doctor, as specified above).

Please don't tell your child that you would "Kill anyone who hurt her." She'll take your words literally and might not tell if something happens because she fears the offender will die at your hands and you'll get in trouble.

Safe vs. Unsafe People

Ask your 2 to 5-year-old what a "bad guy" looks like and he'll probably describe an evil-looking villain straight out of the cartoons or superhero movies. Funny, but not helpful. He needs to know that unsafe people don't always look like "bad" people. As you've already learned, over 98 percent of the time, the bad guys are someone your child knows and maybe even loves.

Your 2 and 3-year-old likely won't understand what you mean here, so save this conversation for when he turns 4. Define "safe" and "unsafe" this way to your 4 and 5-year-old: "A 'safe' person is someone who cares about you and doesn't try to hurt or scare you. An 'unsafe' person is someone who tries to touch your private parts or hurt you or take you away. You can't always tell who's safe and unsafe just by looking at them. You have to watch them to see how they act and how they make you feel inside when you're with them. They may look nice, but if they try to make you do something that makes you uncomfortable, they aren't a safe person."

Kids need to have a circle of safe people they can go to if something bad happens or they need to talk because they have a secret or something inappropriate happened. Say this: "A safe person helps you when you have a problem that's too big for you to take care of on your own. You can go to this person to tell them if someone made you uncomfortable or afraid. Let's make a list of safe people you can go to."

Help your child list two people in the home[150] (parents, older siblings, live-in relatives, etc.) and three people outside the home (grandparents, aunts/uncles, etc.) who meet the following criteria: They're someone who listens well, your child trusts them and feels comfortable with them, and they're old enough to help your child (e.g., over 16 and able to drive a car, in the event they need to pick up your child and take him to safety).

Say, "If you don't feel comfortable talking to me about something, who else can you talk to?" or "What if something happens at daycare, the park, or church, who could you talk to?"[cxlii]

Draw an outline of your child's hand and label each digit with the name of one of his safe people. Have him color a picture of each person or paste a photo of them on the paper. If he wants to add someone to the picture who can't physically intervene in the moment, like God or Jesus or his favorite stuffed animal, have him add them to the palm of the drawing. Keep the picture in a prominent place where he'll see it often.

Good Secrets vs. Not-So-Good Secrets

Everyone (well, almost everyone) loves surprises. We also like secrets, but we need to teach our children that if someone tries to make them keep a bad secret, they must tell us right away. Trying to explain the difference between good secrets (a birthday present) and "bad" secrets (playing a "touching" game) is too advanced for this age group, so I'm going to have you explain it to your child this way:

"Secrets can be fun, like surprise parties or Christmas presents that will be shared soon. But 'not-so-good' secrets can be bad for you and make you unsafe, like when someone asks you to keep

---

[150] If you don't have two safe adults who live in the home, your child can select someone else who helps care for him in the home (grandma, aunt, sitter, etc.) or add someone to their list of safe people outside the home.

it a secret if they touch your private parts or someone asks you not to tell on them when they do something wrong, like playing with matches. Secrets about good things make you feel happy, but 'not-so-good' secrets might make you feel bad or scared."

Perps are crafty and they know that simple pleas or threats will often keep their victims silent. They may do it in a friendly way, like, "I love it when you come over to see my puppies, but if you tell anyone, they won't let you come over any more and we can't be friends." What small child doesn't want to cuddle squirming puppies and have a friend? Impress upon your child the importance of telling you *any* secrets they're told to keep. Say: "Even if the secret is really good, you need to tell me so I can make sure it's safe."

Other predators will use threats, such as "If you tell anyone, I'll hurt your mommy/daddy/pet," or "If you tell anyone what we did, I'll tell them it was your fault and you'll get in big trouble!" Threats are so effective on kids because they tend to believe everything people, especially adults, say as gospel.

As your child gets old enough to keep a secret, around age 5, use the surprises you're planning as an opportunity to have this talk with him. You can also roleplay different scenarios with your child to test his understanding, for example:

- "The kids next door are getting a kitten for Christmas. I ask you not to tell them. Is that a good secret or a not-so-good secret?"

- "The babysitter's boyfriend comes over after I leave. She knows he's not supposed to be there and asks you not to tell me. Is that a good secret or a not-so-good secret?"

- "Your teacher wants to play a touching game when you're alone with him. He touches the private parts of your body and you know he shouldn't do it, but you feel scared. He tells you not to tell anyone about his game. Is that a good secret or a not-so-good secret?"

I can't emphasize strongly enough the importance of using roleplaying scenarios, play-acting using toys, or drawings when you have body safety talks with your child. They really help to impress new concepts into his long-term memory.

Emotions & Feelings

Your child is one big bundle of emotions. Everything she thinks and feels is openly expressed to the whole flippin' world without shame or filters. Learning to recognize and name her emotions and read other people's facial expressions not only builds her emotional intelligence, it's important for recognizing when she's in an unsafe situation.

Teaching your child to recognize and name her emotions takes a bit of work. It's hard to describe "sad" or "happy" to a 3-year-old, but there are ways to teach her that are both fun and effective, such as:

- Make a habit of pointing out, in a non-judgmental way, what your child and other people might be feeling. Say something like, "You sound frustrated that you can't have a snack. What can we do instead?" or "Grandma looks really happy! What do you think?"

- When she's in the middle of a tantrum, help her name her feelings. "I can see that you're feeling angry. Let's talk about it." This validates her experience and invites her to verbalize her feelings rather than act them out. Once she settles down, talk about how angry she felt before, compared to how sorry or calm she feels now. Ask her which feeling (angry or calm) she likes better.

- During snack time, make different emotion faces and have her guess what you might be feeling. Then have her take a turn making the faces while you guess.

- While reading stories to her or watching TV, have her guess how the characters are feeling. Say, "Wow, he looks really upset. Can you make a face that shows me that feeling?"

- When you share your day with each other, talk about the different emotions you felt during the day, then ask her to tell you about times she felt those same emotions.

Resilience

Teaching your child that he's the master of his life is sooo important! Regularly remind him that seemingly "bad" things will happen outside of his control; that's a natural part of life, but how he responds is totally his choice. Over time, he'll come to understand that life isn't happy all the time, but that when life throws a curve ball, he'll find a way to deal with it until things even out again. He'll reach a point where he can take things in stride, knowing no situation lasts forever and that it will always get better.

Another aspect of resilience is learning that making mistakes is inevitable for everyone, even parents. If you're not failing at times, you're not trying hard enough. Let your son know he's not perfect *(I know, he really is, but that's our little secret)* and neither are you. Don't be afraid to tell him about mistakes you made and how you learned from them.

Heroic Parenting

When my grandtwins hit 6, I'm going to introduce a new ritual at Sunday family dinners where we all talk about our "epic fails"[151] of the week and how we dealt with them. We'll talk about how we felt about our mistakes, what we wish we'd done differently, and how we'll handle another situation like that the next time. If you choose to do this, make it light and fun; learning to laugh at ourselves and our foibles is a great lesson for kids.

One more thing. Teach your child that he'll probably feel awkward and clumsy and clueless when he first tries a new activity or plays a sport or takes a dance class. Let him know that's normal and that it'll get easier over time. This will increase his confidence and his willingness to keep trying even when he feels like a wiener when he can't hit the T-ball.

Telling vs. Tattling

At this age, your child will excitedly recount every slight done to him. Whether he's pushed by the pre-school bully on the playground or his older brother picks on him, he's going to tell you all about it and expect you to deliver swift justice.

However, because of his nascent[152] ability to differentiate between fantasy and reality and his difficulty fully expressing himself and his limited understanding of right and wrong, he may not recognize or know how to tell you if anyone does something inappropriate to him. This is why predators target children in this age range; it's so easy to get away scot-free or claim the child is lying or confused when he tells someone Uncle Joe touched him inappropriately.

Kids *love* to tattle, and it drives parents crazy because most of the time the tattler is equally guilty and there's no way to tell who started or finished the fight. Teaching your child the difference between tattling about minor disagreements and *telling* about unsafe body incidents is important. (Don't automatically ignore or minimize disputes between kids, especially when there's an age difference. There might be bullying going on or other inappropriate behavior that requires your intervention.)

Say: "I want to make sure that you know it's *always* okay to come tell me if something uncomfortable or scary or unsafe happens to you. I promise I won't be angry and you won't get in any trouble for telling me. In fact, I'll be proud of you and I'll protect you."

---

151 Explain to your child that an "epic fail" is something he did or tried to do that didn't turn out the way he wanted. Teach him that failures are a really important part of the learning process and that they should be respected and seen as positive lessons of what not to do the next time. Tell him there's no shame in failing, after all, he tried!
152 Nascent = Developing.

Bonus tip: To encourage your child to stop tattling so much and learn how to mediate his own disputes, when he runs up to you in tears you can ask: "Do you need me to hug you, just listen to you, or step in?" You'd be surprised how often the answer is one of the first two; kids often just need comfort and validation.

Using the Phone

When your child turns 4, depending on her maturity level, she's old enough to learn how to use your cell or home phone to call 911 for help. It's such a fun thing to play with your phone that she may want to do it just for fun. You'll need to emphasize the importance of calling 911 only in a real emergency.

Say: "Sometimes things happen and you may need to call the police for help, like if mommy or daddy got really sick and need help or if you're at Bailey's house and someone makes you feel scared or uncomfortable and you need me to come get you. The phone number of the police is 911. Can you say that? (Make her repeat it several times.) Let me show you how to call 911 on my cell phone."

Even with the screen lock on, your child can make an emergency call. Take out your phone and show her how to use it, as described below:[153]

For Android or iPhones: Show your daughter how to press the key to turn the phone screen on (usually on the right side of the phone). On the lock screen is the word "Emergency" at the bottom of the screen. Show her how to press the Emergency button and dial the three numbers of 911 and press Send.

For landline phones: Show your child how to press the "On" key and dial 911.

Your 5-year-old is likely old enough to memorize your cell phone number so she can call you if she needs to. You can also try to teach her your full home address, including city and state, in the event she needs to call 911. The best way to do this is to repeat the number and address in a sing-song voice (like a radio ad jingle) over and over together. Then help her cement it in her memory by asking her to repeat it on a regular basis: "What is mommy's number again? And where do we live?"

Teaching her what to say on the phone

Say: "When you call the police on 911, you'll need to tell them what kind of problem you're having. The police will ask you your name (make sure she knows her last name!) and where you

---

[153] For your own protection and so your child doesn't change all the settings on your cell phone to show up in Chinese, you should have an automatic screen lock in place.

are." Your child may not be able to tell them the address where she is. It's imperative to teach her to stay on the phone with the police until they can track her down and arrive on the scene.

Continue: "The police will also ask where you live, and you need to tell them so they can bring you home to me. They'll also ask you what my name is. I know you call me Mommy, but my real name is [name]. Can you repeat that for me?"

If your child isn't ready and all this is overwhelming or stressful for her, back off and try again in three to six months.

What to Do If Your Child Is in Danger

If Lost

It happens to most parents at some point. They're shopping with their child at the mall or grocery store, when suddenly their child is just… gone. It's a heart-stopping moment that, happily, nearly always ends with a quick reunion.

Here's what to teach your child to do if you get separated when you're out and about. Say, before you go out:

"We're going to the store and we'll get to see lots of people and cool things we'd like to look at. It's really important to stay by my side so I don't lose sight of you. Even if you see something you really want to look at, wait until I'm with you to go see it. If things get busy and you do lose sight of me, here's what I want you to do:

1. Stay *right* where you are. It'll be easier for me to find you that way.

2. Don't hide; stand somewhere I can see you.

3. Yell 'Mommy/Daddy, where are you?' as loud as you can. (Have her practice yelling this in a loud voice.)

4. If I don't find you right away, look for a woman with children and ask her to help you find me." (A woman with kids is the least likely threat and wild horses won't stop her from reuniting you with your child.)

If Kidnapped

I want you to remember that it's *highly* unlikely your child will experience a kidnapping attempt. Still, it does happen on rare occasions and you want to help your child know what to do if she's approached by a would-be abductor.

At this age, your child should never be unsupervised outside the home (or inside for that matter, unless you want to kiss that new Apple watch she's "cleaning" in the sink goodbye).

Say: "I want to make sure you know that it's a family rule that you never go anywhere, with anyone, or take a gift from someone unless you ask me or Daddy first and get our permission. Even if it's someone you know and trust, like Grandpa or Aunt Sukie. If Daddy and I aren't there to ask or we say no, you can't do it. Remember, it's a family rule. Do you understand? Tell me what I just said." (Make her paraphrase your words).

Have your child practice a special yell she can use if someone tries to force her to go with them or get into a vehicle. Say: "Let's practice a special yell you can use if anyone tries to make you go with them or get in their car or truck. I want you to yell as loud as you can, 'No! Let me go! Someone help me!'"

Practice this over and over until your child has it down cold. She'll love this because she gets to yell as loud as she can.

If your child is highly sensitive or prone to worry or anxiety, you may want to teach just the basic "family rule" of "don't go with anyone without mom/dad's permission," or you may need to wait until she's older to broach this subject.

In the monthly family meeting calendar I created just for you, I put the body safety conversation about kidnapping toward the end of the year, so you build up to it.[154]

Self-Defense

Showing your child how to fight like a rabid Tasmanian Devil can literally save her life if someone tries to pick her up or touch her inappropriately. By yelling, kicking, hitting, squirming, and even biting the offender, she may convince him to leave her alone and run.

After you've read through my "Inner Taz" techniques in Chapter 17, make your child show you how she would fight and yell, using a pillow or couch cushion she can hit and kick. Gently correct her form or encourage her to yell more loudly as needed to help her get it down pat. Make it fun! If your child is into superheroes, she already knows how to fight imaginary bad guys, so channel that imagination to help her learn this important lesson.

---

[154] You can find the planner on my website at www.cjscarlet.com/freebies.

If you want your child to take martial arts to help her learn discipline and some self-defense moves, great! Keep her in the program until she becomes proficient. And teach her my Taz moves as well because they just might save her life one day.

If You Have Concerns Your Child Has Been Victimized

I cover this topic very thoroughly in the Appendix, If Your Child Has Been Sexually Abused, so refer to this for detailed information on what to do if you suspect or learn your innocent baby has been victimized.

There are a few additional things I want to cover that are especially relevant to this age group. Here are some concerning signs to watch for in toddlers:

- Any sexual behavior or knowledge that's not appropriate for his age, maturity level, or developmental level.

- The use of new words for his private parts. You'll want to ask questions to find out where he learned them. They could have come from his daycare buddies, but they also could have come from an unsafe encounter with an older child or adult.

- "Traumatic play," in which he reenacts situations that are concerning, such as repeatedly running away from "the bad man" or engaging in inappropriate sexual behavior.

- Signs of stress, such as nightmares, sudden bedwetting, clinging, appetite changes, etc.

- Withdrawn or oppositional behavior that's out of character for him.

For Parents to Do

There's so much you can do to protect your child from danger and dangerous people. Recognize that you have that power and claim it! This whole book is designed to empower you with that knowledge so you can kick hopelessness, helplessness, and paralysis to the curb!

Here are more ways in which you can positively impact your child and teach her to protect and defend herself from harm when you're not around:

Be an Awesome Role Model

Your child looks to you, more than anyone else, as the authority on the world. Embrace the fact that, for now at least, you're the most intelligent, brilliant, knowledgeable person on the planet. As far as she's concerned, you're the bomb diggity. Yay, you!

That's great news if you're modeling positive values and behavior, and not-so-good if you're setting a bad example. If you know you could do better in these areas, it's never too late to start. Your child is worth the effort. Cut down on the drinking, ditch the drugs, and stop the "sleepovers" with rotating "aunts" or "uncles."

Remember when I wrote earlier that the words you say to your child become her inner voice? It really is true. Make sure the things you say and do are congruent with your values because your baby is watching, and history is bound by some weird universal force to repeat itself.

Speak Your Truth & Walk Your Talk

Have the crucial conversations and ask the tough questions to ensure your child knows what she needs to know to stay safe. It can be difficult and embarrassing to confront someone if they cross a physical or emotional boundary with you or your child, but it must be done. Risk that short period of embarrassment and lay down your family rules on boundaries. If you just can't do it because you're too nervous or embarrassed, find someone else who can talk to them. The "offender" may not even realize they've done something inappropriate (or they may!) and they need to know so they can stop the behavior.

Set & Enforce Clear Family Rules

The "Family Rules" must be sacrosanct and consistently applied. Rules like "everyone has the right to privacy" and "children don't take gifts or rides from people outside the family without permission" should be taught early and often.

In Chapter 18, I'll provide ideas for how to create and enforce family rules, and on my website I even provide a year-long calendar for your family meetings and tell you what topics to discuss and in what order. I know, I'm awesome, right? You're welcome![155]

Be Aware of What's Going on in Your Child's Life

Be present for your child; your attention is a gift to him and it's one of the most proactive things you can do to keep him safe. Here are some ways to parent up:

- Be a visible presence. Be the parent who's involved in your child's life and on alert for bad guys.

- Watch for unusual behavior in your child and check into it. Does he act anxious or throw tantrums after he hangs out with a particular person? Is he suddenly acting withdrawn or

---

155 You can find these under the Freebies tab on my website.

depressed? You know him better than anyone and are in a unique position to notice and look into concerning changes.

- Pay close attention when others seek out one-on-one access to your child. Don't allow it if you have concerns about that person.

- Trust your gut. If something or someone doesn't feel right, it probably isn't. Remove yourself and/or your child from that situation immediately. It may have been nothing at all or you may have thwarted a molestation or assault. You'll never know what *might* have happened, but you *will* know you took action when your gut warned you to, which is an awesome thing.

- Perform background checks on anyone who will care for your child, such as babysitters, daycare workers, coaches, and group leaders—even if they were referred by someone you trust. Don't be shy about doing this; your child's safety is more important than your embarrassment.

- Check your state and National Sex Offender Registries on a regular basis. Trust me, you'll be shocked by how many sex offenders live in your neighborhood and immediate vicinity of your home and your child's daycare!

Supervised Play

Toddlers, at least, should *never* play outside by themselves! They need close supervision to ensure they don't run into the street or become the target of predators. If you have a fenced-in backyard, your older toddler is probably safe as long as you check on her frequently.

Media Time

Be aware of what your child is watching on the TV, tablet, computer, or smartphone. Use parental controls to limit what sites she can access and keep an eye (or ear) on her to ensure she's seeing only appropriate content.

Support Your Child

Let your child know often that you support her. Tell her you'll always love her no matter what, even if she tells you something scary or bad. Let her know you have her back and will always do your very best to protect her from harm. Just as importantly, tell her you'll help her learn to protect and defend *herself* so she can feel more confident and in charge of herself and her life.

CHAPTER 13

Children 6 to 9

Kids 6 to 9 are still in that sweet spot where they actually enjoy your company and attention and want to hang out with you. With luck, they still look up to you as the person who has all the answers (even if you don't) and they aren't overly embarrassed to express affection toward you. Bask in this phase as long as you can because it will end all too soon and you'll have a double-digit midget on your hands who, seemingly overnight, thinks you're a complete buffoon.

Note: In case you haven't read the previous chapter on children ages 2 to 5 because your child isn't in that age range, I'm going to repeat some sections from that chapter here, although they will be updated to apply to children 6 to 9.

How This Age Group Learns & Processes Information

As your child's social interactions with other kids and adults increase, you and she begin to feel greater confidence in her ability to handle herself and new situations. During these next four years of her life, you can make a huge impact on her growing ability to protect and defend herself by deepening and broadening your body safety conversations.

Your 6-Year-Old

Your 6-year-old has been in school now for at least a year, so her days are filled with classes, after-school programs, homework, extracurricular activities, and hopefully lots of fun family time. As independent as she's becoming, though, she still needs you to facilitate her social interactions.

She probably has a best friend and maybe even a circle of friends at this point. If not, you'll need to teach her how to make friends and be a good friend herself (which I'll cover in Chapter 15). This is the age when bullying starts to become more common, so teaching her how to handle bullies and to not be a bully herself is important.

Your girl is mature enough now to understand cause and effect and the consequences that go with that. And she can tell you in clear language if she feels uncomfortable around a particular person or has experienced inappropriate behavior. At this age, she can easily remember and follow your family rules, although she's still learning what her boundaries are and will screw up on occasion—sometimes on purpose, just to test your willingness to enforce the rules and, seemingly, your patience!

Your 7-Year-Old

At 7, your child is entering the tough world of social expectations and experiencing the high cost of not fitting in with the "norm." As a result, he may be more sensitive than he was at 6. He's comparing himself—his appearance, his clothes, his "toys," and even you—to what other kids have. If the comparison isn't in his favor, he may feel embarrassed or ashamed, and he may respond either by trying harder to fit in or by withdrawing and hanging out with other kids on the fringes.

This is a critical time to teach him about loving, valuing, and respecting himself, and to encourage his unique identity. You can do this by telling him so directly and by praising his efforts. Even when he fails, you can praise him for trying and encourage him to keep at it until he masters whatever it is he's trying to accomplish. Your opinion of him matters to him more than anything.

In many ways, your son is still a baby and craves your affection and attention. He continues to need you to help him with his homework and reading assignments, and these interactions provide opportunities for pep talks.

Your 8-Year-Old

By 8, your child may be hyper-conscious of others' opinions of her—especially her peers (and you!). Popularity is becoming one of her most pressing concerns and she and her peers are jockeying for power and social position in the school.

"Friend drama" may be her favorite topic, and as tedious as it is to have to listen to *another* story about how Kimberly snubbed her in the hallway, these episodes provide you with great teachable moments when you can help her learn to navigate the tricky world of peer relationships. This is a great time to teach her not to compare her insides (where all her insecurities lie) with other people's outsides (where they show only the best parts of themselves).

At the same time, her personality is coming into focus. She has favorite classes and activities, and she wants you to encourage and support her as she jumps from one exciting project to the next.

Your 9-Year-Old

Clothes, music, friends, and extracurricular activities dominate your child's thoughts at this point. Demands for the latest smartphone, outfit, game console, or skateboard may hound you. Regularly talking about and strictly enforcing the family rules are necessary to keep your increasingly independent child in check.

This is a critical time for your 9-year-old. According to clinical psychologist Robin F. Goodman, for girls, self-esteem peaks at 9 and then goes into a tailspin.[156cxliii] And for boys, it's a critical time because their peers and the world in general are telling them it's not okay to show a lot of emotion. Any behavior that appears overly "sensitive" or weak or "girly" may result in severe teasing at best or a beat-down followed by a swirly[157] in the toilet at worst.

Feelings of insecurity and shame are two flapping red flags for predators on the prowl for victims, so you want to help your child increase his confidence and self-esteem as much as you can. (I'll talk about how to do this in Chapter 15.)

Of course many 9-year-olds are able to maintain a strong sense of self despite the gravitational pull of their peers and the media, but keep an eye on his behavior and self-talk for clues that his confidence is faltering.

Some kids at this age may be entering puberty. Be prepared to have the dreaded sex talk sooner than you thought you'd need to.

What's Real?

Kids in this age range may worry more about danger. During body safety conversations you need to steer them away from the hysterical media stories about stranger abductions and school shootings that dominate the news. Reassure your child that she's safe and remind her that through your regular talks, you're giving her the tools and information she needs to protect herself when you're not around.

---

156 Half of all 9-year-old girls admit that they've tried to diet because they thought they were too fat. At 9!!!!
157 A swirly is a gross and humiliating act that occurs when someone puts another person's head in the toilet bowl and flushes it, resulting in the person's hair being swirled in the water.

Heroic Parenting

Your Digital Native

Your child is almost certainly using a computer at school and probably at home as well, so you need to have your list of rules for online activity clearly laid out and reinforced on a frequent basis. Post these rules by the computer you keep in the living room or kitchen (he shouldn't have a laptop or computer in his room, for goodness sake!). Don't forget that he can access the Internet through his tablet or smartphone, if he has one.

Even youngsters engage in cyberbullying, so you'll want to talk to him about how to handle situations where he's being targeted, and just as importantly, that he should never be on the giving end. This is also the age range when your child might very well be exposed to pornography—online or through magazines—by his peers or by older kids or adults with bad intentions.

If Something Happens

Whether or not your child comes to you if something inappropriate happens to her depends in large part on how confident she is that she can trust you (a) to believe her, (b) not to freak out, and (c) not to scold or punish her for any role she played up to or during the incident (e.g., kissing a boy, going to her friend's house when she shouldn't have, etc.).

This is a good age to introduce the (figurative) "get out of jail free" card she can use to avoid any punishments for telling you when she's in trouble. For example, if your daughter was on a sleepover at her BFF's and some boys came over and were making her uncomfortable in some way, she could call you to come pick her up, without you yelling at her on the car ride home or grounding her without hearing the full story.

The fact is, you *want* your child to call you when she's in a jam. Yes, she may have made poor choices leading up to or during the incident, but she also made the highest and most mature choice to call you and that should count for something. Cancel that; it should count for *everything!* After all, she could just as easily have remained in the situation and been victimized.

Let her know that instead of a punishment, you'd like to sit down the next day to talk about peer pressure, how to handle sexual pressure from boys/girls, or whatever the situation was about. Make it a two-way conversation in which you allow her to tell you about the incident, how she felt, what led her to recognize the situation was unsafe, and how she handled it. Praise her for trusting her intuition and taking action to protect herself and for calling you. Share your advice about how to handle these kinds of scenarios and reinforce your family's values and body safety rules.

Look at it this way, you can't keep your child from having a life and there will be more slumber parties and dates. Wouldn't you rather rest soundly knowing she's empowered to call you if there's an issue rather than worry she'll stay silent and sneak around because she fears your wrath?

Having the "get out of jail free" rule in place from the time she's old enough to be out with her friends on her own will serve you greatly later, because she will likely, at some point, find herself in a dicey situation. Knowing she can call you and not be harshly judged or punished ensures she'll call you for help, which is exactly what you want.

Your Not-So-Little Monster

While girls tend to use social aggression (e.g., spreading rumors, excluding others, etc.), many boys at this age love to tussle with each other like young bucks clashing antlers. They punch each other in the arm playing "slug bug" and wrestle on the playground, and it can be normal, healthy behavior.

Until it's not. Don't be alarmed or step in if your son and his friend exchange blows over who won the game; they'll likely make up and shake hands within minutes. But if your child is assaulted in any way that isn't mutual or puts him under physical or emotional distress, it's considered bullying and it needs to be stopped.

Your child has graduated from Peppa Pig and the Paw Patrol and is watching shows and movies that may have more realistic violent content, which can lead to aggressive behavior. Keep an eye on what he's viewing on TV, video games, smartphones, tablets, and computers.

What Your Child Needs from You

Just as with toddlers, your child wants to be independent, but she still needs you to be a loving, guiding presence in her life. She'll continue to test her limits, but generally kids this age understand the rules and will follow them.

As her parent, your most important job is to act like a grown-up and give your child the love and affection and *protection* she deserves. Keeping her safe when she's under your watch is your chief concern, as is teaching her to protect and defend herself when you're not around (which you're doing by reading and applying the lessons in this book, you awesome thing, you!).

This is prime time for molding your daughter into a decent human being. Teach her responsibility by making her do chores and regularly volunteering to help others in need (hopefully with you by her side). Help her set challenging (but achievable) goals and encourage her to reach them.

Heroic Parenting

Play games and read with her and be a strong presence in her life, at home and at school. Maintain the family rules and lovingly and fairly discipline her when she messes up (which she will and that's okay; it's part of how she'll learn).

Your daughter craves your approval and, like it or not, you're a mirror who reflects back to her who she is. If that reflection is generally positive and encouraging, she'll feel loved, valued, capable, and worthy. If it's largely negative or disapproving, she'll doubt herself and her abilities, and her self-esteem and confidence will suffer. This makes her more vulnerable to predators who are looking for broken children to groom and victimize.

Parenting is *not* for wussies. If you're a single parent, you have it extra rough. I've been there, done that and it sucks, not to put too fine a point on it. There were days I thought I'd go mad and had to back away and lock myself in my room to keep from taking it out on my sons.

Please remember your problems and stresses should *never* be projected onto your child. I don't care how rotten a day—or life—you've had, it's not her fault, and unless she's assured of that, she'll build a story around your silence or disapproval or screams that puts herself smack in the middle as the source of the problem.

Nobody (except maybe the mean moms in the PTA) expects you to be perfect; just do your best. Raise your child as if she were the most precious being on earth… *because she is.*

Sex & Sexuality

Your baby isn't a baby anymore. He's a curious, developing little human and he almost certainly has heard more about sex from his peers and the media than you realize. Because he'll soon be (or already is!) approaching puberty, you'll want to start having "the talk" with him. But it shouldn't be just one talk, it should be many small conversations that take place over time as he grows more mature.

Kids at this age don't understand the emotional aspects of sexuality and most parents don't talk about this when they talk about the birds and the bees. It's important to emphasize that healthy sexual relationships are based on love and trust, and that without those, sex doesn't feel safe or truly emotionally fulfilling.

Your child's head is filled with a hairball of misconceptions about sex at this point. He may believe babies come out of the mother's belly button or that he can get a girl pregnant by kissing her. And you certainly don't want your son to grow up basing his sexual relationships on what he's learned from watching porn! Introducing him now to information about sex and his changing body will help him avoid a lot of embarrassment, mistakes, and misunderstandings in his adult relationships.

Your child's curiosity about sex continues to grow as he does. Rather than trying to squelch his natural inquisitiveness, use his questions and exploratory behaviors as opportunities to send the reassuring message that sex and sexuality aren't shameful and can be openly discussed *within the family*. Fact is, the more your child knows about his own sexuality, the less likely it is that others can exploit his lack of knowledge.

If you stumble upon your child masturbating (Jeepers, Mom! Knock already!), it'll be deeply embarrassing for you both, but please don't try to shame your child by screaming, "Oh my God, Billy! Jesus and all the angels can see you! You're going to go blind if you keep that up!" or something equally ridiculous and humiliating that could forever damage your child's sexuality.

Instead, calmly apologize (after all, you invaded *his* privacy) and quietly leave, closing the door softly behind you and tiptoeing away. In the unlikely event he tries to masturbate outside of his room or the bathroom, you'll definitely want to remind him that this is to be done in private, and look for other signs he may be being abused or has a problem that needs to be addressed in counseling. (See Concerning Behaviors below.)

Party of Two (or more)

Child's play is in full swing now. Remember, to be considered "normal," this behavior should be spontaneous; done in fun and out of curiosity; and the children must be similar in age, size, and developmental level.

As with babies and pre-K children, if you do come upon your budding gynecologist engaging in normal exploratory behaviors, calmly say something like, "I see you and Jessica are looking at each other's bodies. Remember that even though it's interesting to see what other people's bodies look like, we keep our clothes on when we're around others. Now get dressed."

When there's more than a 3-year gap in the ages of those involved, or the behavior becomes intrusive, hurtful, or age-inappropriate, you need to (a) stop the behavior immediately and separate the children, (b) ensure your child is okay, if she's the victim, (c) ensure the other child is okay, if he's the victim, (d) call the other child's parents to tell them what happened, (e) report it to the police if you think abuse has occurred, and (f) ensure both children get counseling to address what happened.

What's "Normal" & What's Not

Below is a range of sexual behaviors for this age group.

Normal, Common Behavior

- Has questions about physical development, sexual behavior, and pregnancy and birth.

- Has questions about relationships and sexual customs, personal values, and consequences of sexual behavior.

- Experiments with peers, often during "games" or roleplaying.

- Demands more privacy when dressing and using the bathroom.

- Masturbation takes place in private.

- May discover she's more attracted to individuals of the same sex.

Concerning Behavior (If your child exhibits concerning behaviors, you should seek counseling for her right away.)

- Displays excessive interest in, knowledge of, or language about sexual behaviors.

- Simulates or tries to initiate adult sexual behaviors by herself or with others.

- Has knowledge of specific sexual acts.

- Engages in sexual behavior in public or online (Internet or smartphone).

- Behaves sexually in a public place.

- Won't redirect her genital play or masturbation when asked.

Answering Your Child's Questions

Making sex a taboo topic may keep your child from coming to you when he has questions or if someone does something inappropriate to him. He's going to get his information about sex somewhere; wouldn't you rather it be you than his peers, misleading or emotionally damaging porn sites, or predatory older kids or adults? Of course you would. This way, your own personal views on the topic will be his guide.

Speaking of personal views, your child will at some point learn that not every adult relationship is heterosexual. Deal with that as you will, but I fervently hope you'll remain open-minded about it and encourage your child to as well.

Keep an eye out for opportunities to talk to your child openly about the topics of sex and sexuality. I do NOT recommend using the monthly meetings I suggest later in Chapter 18, when the whole fam[158] is present. Make them one-on-one conversations that take place in his room or when you're driving together in the car. My sons preferred to talk to me in the car because they could stare at the road and not have to look me in the eye, which was less embarrassing.

Greatest Threats at This Age

Bullying

(Refer to Chapter 7)

Digital Dangers

(Refer to Chapter 8)

No doubt you have parental controls on your child's electronic devices (phone, computer, tablet, gaming system) and he's only allowed to use them in a common family area, right? If you answered yes, good for you! If you said no, get with the program, dude!

Children in this age range are so trusting and are likely to believe that the strangers they interact with online are who they claim to be. Under no circumstances should a kid under 10 be allowed to use a chat room! These places are hotbeds for cyberbullying, sexting, and other predatory behavior. Explain that in some cases, people lie about who they are in order to exploit or abuse kids. This is a lesson you'll want to emphasize on a regular basis.

Work with your child to come up with a list of family rules for online behavior (that are posted right next to the family computer and taped to the back of his tablet for quick reference). Also make a list of sites he's allowed to use and help him create his profiles for each one. Work with him to choose good (and appropriate) usernames and passwords that you write down and keep so you can check in on occasion to ensure he's making good choices and isn't being harassed by creepers.

Pornography

(Refer to Chapter 8)

---

158 Fam = Family.

Molestation & Sexual Assault

(Refer to Chapter 9)

Your child in this age range is now able to understand what sexual abuse is beyond "touching someone on their private parts." You can explain that some people choose to do bad things to children and that it's never the children's fault. Tell him that this includes touching his genitals or his body in any way that makes him feel uncomfortable, scared, or yucky. That way, if his coach rubs his shoulders in a creepy way, your son will now that it's not okay even though it didn't involve his private parts. Also tell him he shouldn't touch anyone else in those ways, even if an adult tells him to.

It's important to emphasize that while adults are often in charge, it doesn't mean they should be obeyed if their behavior—say it with me—makes your child feel uncomfortable, scared, or yucky.

Kidnapping

(Refer to Chapter 10)

Strangers

(Refer to Chapter 2)

Siblings, Peers & Older Kids

(Refer to Chapter 3)

Partners, Stepparents & Non-Custodial Parents

(Refer to Chapter 4)

Relatives

(Refer to Chapter 4)

Babysitters & Other Caregivers

(Refer to Chapter 5)

Other Adults

(Refer to Chapter 6)

A Word about Sleepovers for This Age Group

Sleepovers or slumber parties are a rite of passage for kids. While they may be exciting and super fun, they can also result in anxiety and homesickness in kids who aren't ready. So, what's the right age to allow your child to attend or host a sleepover?

Most experts advise parents to wait until their child is at least 10 to ensure he's emotionally and socially mature enough to handle being away from home (and perhaps away from you for the first time). I myself was 9 when I went to my first slumber party and I didn't miss my family even one little bit. I had a blast!

If you believe your child *is* emotionally and socially mature enough to have a sleepover at 8 or 9, then go for it, but make sure you do your homework first:

- Consider being the host for your child's first sleepover so you can get to know the other kids and their parents (and each time a new child is introduced into the mix). That way you can run what you learn about them through conversation and observation against what your gut is telling you.

- When you invite another child over, notice how curious his parents are about you and your home. Do they want to meet you first? Do they ask questions about who will be present in the home (e.g., adults, older kids, etc.)? Do they want to exchange contact info? If they don't ask these kinds of questions when their child is going to stay at your house, then they may be lax about other household rules, so while you may be willing to host their child, you might not choose to let your son stay at theirs.

- Before letting your child play or stay overnight in a friend's home, *always* insist on meeting the other kid's parents *at their home* (so you can observe the family dynamics and the home for safety concerns) and ask the questions from the last bullet point (above) of anyone whose home your child will be staying—or even playing—in. Also ask if they have guns in the home and how and where they're stored and locked. If the other parents act too casually when answering questions or seem offended, think long and hard about whether you want to expose your child to their home and family.

- Talk to the other parents about what kinds of activities the kids will enjoy and where they'll be sleeping. If you have questions about an activity (e.g., the kinds of video games they'll be playing) or don't want your child to be able to use their family's computer, tell them so.

- If the kids will be taken to a movie or dinner, ensure the family has enough child safety seats and that an adult will be driving and present at all times.

- Tell the other parents what you want to happen if your child misbehaves. For example, say, "If Trevor misbehaves, please call me right away and let me handle it, no matter how late it is."

- Once your child is back home and has recovered from his fun, do a debrief to find out how it went. After he's shared all the cool things they did, you can ask for more details, such as what the parents were like and who came in and out of the home while he was there—info that might determine whether he'll be allowed to stay there again.

Make it a family rule that your child can't participate in sleepovers until he's [insert age here] years old or until he feels ready, shows competence in chores, is no longer afraid of the dark or of nighttime bedwetting accidents, etc. Or it may even be a family rule that sleepovers aren't allowed at all. I believe sleepovers are fun activities and a rite of passage, but you're the parent here; it's your choice.

Discussing Body Safety

Talking to kids in this age range can still feel awkward, but it's less tricky than talking to younger children because your 6 to 9-year-old can more readily understand and remember what you teach her about body safety issues.

Again, the point of this book is to teach you how to talk to your kid about danger without scaring her to death. You don't have to give her a bunch of scary stats or terrifying stories about stranger abductions that will freak her out and make her anxious. Keep your ongoing conversations light.

When to Talk to Your Child About Body Safety Issues

Choose a time to talk to your child when you're both comfortable and relaxed, and not stressed or under a time constraint.

Consider using the following times to have safety conversations with your child:

- **Changing clothes.** At this age, your child may or may not still be changing his clothes in front of you. If he does, occasionally remind him that his body is for him alone and that no one is allowed to touch his private parts (except the doctor, with you there).

- **When hugging.** Occasionally say something like, "You're getting so big and your body's growing so strong! Around this time a lot of kids notice their bodies starting to change in strange ways. Remember that I'm here to talk to if you have questions about any changes you may be experiencing." He'll probably roll his eyes and make a disgusted noise, but trust me, he'll be more likely to take you up on it later than if you don't offer at all.

- **Bedtime/storytime.** Your child likely still enjoys sharing bedtime rituals with you when you read together or share stories. Highlight the moral lessons and any safety themes the stories hold. Ask open-ended questions like, "What would you do if that happened to you?" and use your child's answer for further discussion. Keep it light. (Again, I don't recommend talking about overly scary danger topics just before bed.)

- **Leaving the house.** Go over your safety rules, especially if he's going somewhere without you (e.g., "Remember to stick to our family rules" (about body safety, not getting in people's cars, etc.).

- **Over a treat.** While having a chat over a snack, answer any questions or concerns he may have around body safety and his body in general. This could include asking questions like, "How safe do you feel at school?" followed by, "Are there any bullies at your school?" and "Has that kid ever picked on you?"

How to Teach Your Child About Body Safety Issues

Using Stories

Hopefully you child is an avid reader or at least likes having you read to her. Books and movies almost always contain moral and safety lessons that you can talk about together. Here are a few to get you started:

- **The Harry Potter series by J. K. Rowling.** What's not to love about Harry's story? He's an abused and maligned orphan *and* a wizard with all kinds of cool magical powers that capture kids' imaginations. Harry is bullied, encounters scads of evil people, and is constantly challenged with tough moral choices.

- **Any superhero movie** (with the exception of Guardians of the Galaxy and Dead Pool movies, which are waaay too graphic and mature for this age group, albeit[159] hilarious!). Kids of all ages love superheroes and the battles between good and evil.

---

159 Albeit = Although.

- **Frozen.** This box office smash teaches kids about self-control, making sacrifices for those we love, and how our actions affect others. Anna is very naïve and a bit of a flibbertigibbet[160] who immediately trusts and falls for a handsome stranger who's got more on his mind than love (riches, the answer is riches). All of it's bound to lead to a very lively conversation with your child.

- **The Karate Kid** (any version, but I like the 1984 original version best—Mr. Miyagi rocks!). Dealing with bullies is the big theme here, but there's so much more this movie imparts, including the power of perseverance, discipline, and hard work; and that when you work to improve yourself, the trials are worth the effort because you become a better person.

- **The Lion King** (the 2019 animated version is *incredible!*). Like many Disney movies, this film features themes of innocence, the death of a loved one, innocence lost, overcoming obstacles and the machinations of evil people, and conquering challenges. It's worth watching just for the "circle of life" lesson alone.

There are so many excellent books specifically covering body safety topics that you can find on my website[161] or any online bookstore. I'll also be publishing a series of age-appropriate children's books you can use to teach the body safety topics I address here.

Using Imagination & Role Play

Cement the body safety and moral lessons you're teaching your child by using roleplay. After talking about a body safety issue (for example, not letting others cross our physical or emotional boundaries), say, "Sometimes things happen that we just don't understand, but that we know don't feel right. So, if you were playing at Maria's house and her big brother tried to touch your private parts, what would you do?" Let your child talk, without interrupting or correcting her, until she's done answering your question.

If she gets the answer wrong, don't scold or punish her. Instead, say, "We never let anyone touch our private parts EVER, except the doctor to keep you healthy, when I'm there with you. Remember? What could you say and do to get away from him?" Keep gently guiding her and asking questions to help her think through the ramifications of the actions she could take.

---

160 Flibbertigibbet = Flighty and a bit air-headed.
161 www.cjscarlet.com/coolsht

When she gives the correct answer, praise her and offer her a reward, which could be as simple as a hug or a high-five. As you would do with a toddler, don't accept just a verbal answer; make her show you what she would say and do (shouting "No! Leave me alone!" and running away and telling you what happened). She's still young enough to get into the role.

Give her a couple more scenarios (e.g., "What if a kid at school tried to show you pictures of people doing inappropriate things?" Or, better yet, teach her what the word "pornography" means and use that term instead.). Correct answer: "I would tell her 'No! That's gross,' and walk away."

Or, "And what if that same kid sent you a link online to pornographic pictures?" Correct answer: "I wouldn't open it and I'd come tell you right away." Or, if she opened it without realizing in advance what it was, the answer would be: "I would close the link and come tell you right away."

You want to emphasize that she's NOT to delete the link or email containing the images because you'll want to investigate to see who sent them and print out a copy of the online exchange to show the police when you report it. And you should always report it if someone sends inappropriate content to your child!

An exception would be if the link came from a friend who's a peer, in which case you may instead decide to tell that child's parents and let them handle it. If you have *any* concern that the other child might be the victim of abuse or is a predator, then you DO want to report it to the police rather than the other child's parents.

Questions

Your child is bound to have lots of questions about his body and body safety issues at this age, and not only when you're having a planned conversation about it. Be patient and keep answering until (a) he runs out of questions, or (b) he's exhausted your entire library of knowledge on the subject, in which case, you've got homework to do! Tell him he can come to you anytime with more questions. The two of you can always hop online to look up the answer to any questions you don't know how to handle.

What to Teach Your Child

Below, you'll find information on the broad categories that cover what you'll want to teach your child. Remember, you don't have to cram all this information into one big conversation. On my website,[162] I provide a calendar you can refer to that introduces one topic at a time over the course of a year.

Intuition

Your child's intuition is her first line of defense against danger and predatory people. And more than that, listening to her intuition will help her be more confident and increase her self-esteem, giving her a strong internal sense of self that will guide her and help her better resist pressure from others to behave in ways that aren't authentic to her.

You want to foster her intuitive sense and help her learn to recognize it and act on it. KidPower.org suggests having the following conversation with you child in this age group:[cxliv]

Say, "Have you ever had an 'uh-oh!' feeling that told you that something isn't right? You might notice this feeling as butterflies in your tummy, a shiver along your arms, or a big worry in your head. Your 'uh-oh!' feelings are a way your body has of telling you to be careful and to go get help from your adults."

Ask your child: "Where do you feel 'uh-oh' feelings in your body? Does this feel like a lump in your throat? Or a sinking feeling in the bottom of your stomach? A creepy feeling on the back of your neck? A thought that keeps coming back to bother you?"

Help your child identify in her own body where the "uh-oh!" feeling shows up—it can be different for everyone!

Your child will likely have lots of questions for you about this. Take the time to answer them all until you feel like she understands as much as her age and maturity level allow. This is a conversation that will continue and shift over time.

Here are five things you can do to help your child develop and learn to trust her intuition:

1. Don't force her to hug or kiss anyone if she doesn't want to.
2. Take her fears and discomfort around others seriously. The physical and emotional feeling of fear is designed to protect us from danger. When you minimize your child's fears by telling her there's nothing to be afraid of, it neither removes the fear nor calms her down. She just feels ashamed and learns to keep her fears to herself, and that runs counter to your

---

162 www.cjscarlet.com/freebies

desire to encourage her to come to you if she's in real danger. Over time, she'll get better at stuffing her feelings and her intuition will be tamped down in the process. Validate and acknowledge her fears and ask questions about them to see what's beneath the surface. Her fears may in fact be irrational (you don't want to say that, of course; that would come across as ridicule), or they may point to something you need to be concerned about.

3. Tell your child that if a particular person makes her intuition go off, she should get away from that person immediately and come tell you right away.

4. Teach her to protect herself. Rather than promising you'll protect her from all harm for all time—a promise you can't keep—promise her you'll teach her what she needs to know to take care herself... and then do so. By reading and applying what you're learning in this book, you're helping keep that promise.

5. Teach her that adults make mistakes too and that they're not always right. This takes the pressure off her to automatically obey any adults' commands that might not be in her best interest. Teach your daughter that she's not obligated to obey any adult (or child) who gives her that "uh-oh" feeling.

Boundaries

Boundaries are the invisible line we allow people to cross—or not—in our physical and emotional space. Teaching your child to set and enforce solid boundaries is the second most important thing you'll ever teach him (the first is trusting his intuition).

You can explain boundaries to your child in this way:

"Your body and feelings are so special, and they belong only to you. I want to tell you about a way to keep your body and feelings safe. Look at your body. Do you see how your skin protects your body from things like dirt and rain and germs? Well, there's a thing called boundaries that do the same thing to protect your body and your feelings from things other people may do or say to you.

"Boundaries are like invisible fences or rules that keep some things out and other things in. A body boundary is a rule that keeps people from touching our bodies in ways we don't like or feel comfortable with. An emotional boundary is a rule that helps us when people say and do things that make us feel sad, bad, mad, or scared.

"It's my job as your parent to help you set your boundaries and teach you how to use them to stay safe. One boundary rule is that we don't let other people touch our private parts, except when we go to the doctor for a check-up. The way you protect your body boundary if someone else tried to touch your private parts would be to yell 'No!' and get away from them as fast as you can. Then you should come and tell me right away.

"Another boundary rule is that we don't let people say mean things that hurt our feelings. So, if someone said, 'You're ugly,' you could protect your emotional boundary by saying, 'That's not nice. Please don't talk to me like that.'

"Sometimes when we set a boundary, we might feel afraid that we'll hurt the other person's feelings or make them mad, but keeping you safe is more important than their feelings. And if they're doing something you don't like, they need to know that. If they get mad at you, get away from that person and come and tell me right away."

When you teach your child not to let others touch his private parts, you also need to teach him that he's not to touch other people's private parts either. That way, if someone tries to make him touch them inappropriately, your child won't go along with it because you never warned him not to.

It's your job to help your child recognize when his boundaries are being crossed and remind him to enforce them. For example, if you see someone disrespect him or hug him without permission, you need to step in right then, in front of your child, and explain what his boundaries are and that they need to respect them.

Just as your child might be afraid of hurting someone's feelings or making them angry, you too might be nervous about saying something. *Get over it.* The 15 seconds of discomfort you and the other person might feel are worth it to protect your kid.

I want to say a word about consent. Your child needs to know he can withdraw consent at any point, even if he initially liked what was happening. Say: "I want you to know that if someone was tickling you or playing with you and it felt fun, but then it became irritating or even frightening, you can tell that person to stop. If they don't stop, you need to tell them, 'No! I don't like that!' and get away from them and come tell me."

Body Words

If you haven't yet taught your child the actual names of his private parts, go back and read the section on Body Words in the previous chapter. Your child isn't a baby and shouldn't be using baby words for her body parts.

I'm going to add a few more definitions to your repertoire:

- **Pornography:** Tell your child that pornography consists of pictures and videos of people showing their private parts or doing sexual things to themselves or other people. You don't have to get explicit at this age, unless your child has seen a pornographic image(s) and has questions or needs you to put it into perspective.

- **Puberty:** Puberty is the physical process a child's body goes through as it matures into an adult body capable of sexual reproduction. During puberty, hormonal signals are sent from the brain to the gonads: which are the ovaries in a girl and the testes in a boy, triggering the ability to sexually reproduce.[cxlv] This means your baby boy, who generally starts puberty between 9 and 13, is capable of impregnating someone else's baby girl. And this leads us to…

- **Menstruation:** Menstruation is the 2 to 7-day "period" when a girl or woman has her menstrual flow, when blood and tissue leave her body through her vagina. Each month, blood and tissue build up in the uterus to prepare for a fertilized egg in case a woman becomes pregnant.[cxlvi] When your daughter starts her period, generally between 8 and 13, *she's now physically capable of becoming pregnant.*[163] Yes, I said 8.[164]

Body Autonomy

The media and advertisers think it's trendy to make little kids look and act sexy. Just flip through any teen magazine or Abercrombie & Fitch catalog (which exploits boys as well as girls in its photo shoots). They sell *thongs* for 5 and 6-year-old little girls, for goodness sake! Of course, little girls want to be like big girls, and seeing these kinds of images leads them to grow up thinking that's how they're supposed to look too. And boys grow up learning that they're supposed to desire and seduce those little thong-wearing nymphs.

Kids whose bodies are hyper-sexualized or whose bodily integrity is repeatedly violated—girl or boy—are less likely to challenge predators when they attempt to molest or assault them. You need to continue to reinforce that your child's body is his and his alone and that *no one* has the right to touch or photograph it in any way that's scary, hurtful, or makes him feel violated—not you, not anyone. When you teach him about boundaries, also talk to him about this.

---

163 Betcha didn't think you'd have to worry about THAT for a while! WRONG! Welcome to adolescence!
164 Remember to breathe.

Heroic Parenting

Saying No

I said it in the last chapter: if I'd known it was okay to say no to anyone who was trying to harm me, most of my sexual molestations and assaults would never have happened. But I didn't know because my parents didn't know to teach me that. Instead, I learned to make nice and to make everyone around me feel comfortable, even if it meant *I* felt uncomfortable.

Please, please, PLEASE teach your child that it's okay to say no to anyone—child or adult, coach or priest, man or woman—who tries to do *anything* that makes her even the least little bit uncomfortable. Give her the language to do this.

Here are some polite but firm responses to boundary violations:

- "You're standing too close. Could you please move back a bit?"
- "Excuse me, but I don't like that."
- "No, thank you."
- "I don't want to do that."
- "Stop that!"
- "No!" (Enough said.)

A Word about Lying

Every parent hammers it into their kids' heads never to lie, but there's one caveat to that rule and it's an important one: if your child is in a situation where his boundaries are being violated, it's *perfectly okay* for him to lie.

Tell your child: "If you're with someone who's making you feel uncomfortable or scared, or who's trying to do something inappropriate, you have my permission to tell a lie to get away from them. For example, you could say, 'I have to go home now because my mom is waiting for me,' or 'I have to go to the bathroom,' and then run away as soon as you leave the room."

Promises are another way predators try to control children. Tell your child it's okay to break a promise if someone breaks a body safety rule.

Here are some other excuses you child can use to avoid a bad situation (if, for example, someone is trying to show him pornography or take drugs):

- "I have to go home and do my homework now."
- "My mom is expecting me at home right now."
- "I have to go to soccer practice now."
- "My parents would kill me."
- "I don't like that."
- "I'm not going to do that."
- "No. "
- "Stop!"
- "Get away!"
- "Help!"

Safe Touch vs. Unsafe Touch

Sexuality and sexual touch can be confusing at times even for adults, but even more so for kids, especially once they start puberty. Their hormones are raging and their bodies are doing freaky things that they have no control over.

If someone touches your child sexually, there's a chance his body will experience arousal, even if his mind and intuition object. This may cause him to feel guilty if he's molested or assaulted because he figures he must have wanted it to happen.

You can help him by explaining that most touches are safe and feel good, but that if a touch that started out feeling good begins to feel bad, he can always tell the person to stop by saying, "No! I don't like that. Stop!" Remind him that it's a family rule that *no one* is allowed to touch his private parts or do anything sexually inappropriate with him.

Time for another definition!

Sexually inappropriate behavior includes:

- Anything anyone does that involves touching his private parts (under or over his clothes).
- Looking at or photographing the private parts of his body.

- Making him touch or look at the private parts of *their* body.
- Showing him pornography.

Ask your child to repeat what you've just told him to ensure he understands what you mean. You don't want to leave any loopholes here that a predator could exploit.

Safe vs. Unsafe People

Define "safe" and "unsafe" people for your child.

Safe people are people she can go to if:

- Someone tries to be inappropriate with her.
- Someone threatens or harms her.
- She has a secret she needs to share.
- She needs help and/or protection.

Unsafe people include anyone who:

- Triggers her intuition, meaning they make her feel uncomfortable, scared, confused, or violated.
- Tries to do anything inappropriate or make *her* do anything inappropriate.
- Tries to lure her into their vehicle or home by offering her gifts or money, threatening to hurt her, calling her names, or telling her that you'll be angry with her or not love her anymore if she doesn't comply with his demands.
- Is on Mom or Dad's "no-fly" list, meaning she's not allowed to be around them because you said so, or
- She knows is NOT to be trusted (because other kids or people have identified them as predators; for example, the gymnastics coach who everyone knows is a pervert). Tell her to always come to you if anyone warns her to avoid a certain person.

Help her create her list of safe people that includes two people in the home (if available) and three or more people outside the home. Tell her that the people she chooses must be human adults (not Jesus, God, Fluffy, or her favorite superhero) who are old enough to drive a car in case they need to come get her and take her to a safe place. Her safe people could include you, your partner, her grandparents, other relatives, a favorite teacher or coach, etc.

Draw a circle and put the names of her safe people inside the circle. Then ask her to name the "unsafe" people she wants to put outside the circle. Gently and carefully ask her about each person she put outside the circle to find out why she doesn't trust them and considers them unsafe. Pay close attention for clues that these people may pose a threat to her.

Let the people you and your child choose as safe people know they've been chosen and talk to them about what that means. Make sure they're okay with being on the list.

Teach her the tricks "bad people" (the word "predators" may be too scary for her) use to groom children. She's old enough to understand and remember them now. You can say to her, "If someone touches your private parts, it's never your fault. Bad people just say that to trick you; don't believe them."

If the unsafe person is someone she knows, likes, loves, or trusts, she may not want to tell on him for fear he'll get in trouble or that you'll be upset with him. Say, "I know you feel scared about what's going to happen to your coach/step-grandparent/family friend, but when people are inappropriate with a child, they need help so they don't hurt any other children."

Good Secrets vs. Not-So-Good Secrets

Teaching your 6 to 9-year-old the difference between good secrets versus not-so-good secrets is an easier task now that he has more self-control and can actually *keep* a secret. Although he's older now, the emphasis is still on encouraging him to always tell if something bad or hinky[165] happens to him. The language to use is almost the same as it was with the younger set:

"I want to talk to you about good secrets and not-so-good secrets. Do you know the difference?" Let the child guess, and praise or gently correct as needed. Continue, "Good secrets are surprises that are good for you and are fun, like surprise parties or Christmas presents that will be shared soon. But not-so-good secrets are bad for you and make you unsafe, like when someone asks you to keep it a secret if they touch your private parts or someone asks you not to tell on them when they do something wrong, like looking at pornography. Good secrets make you feel happy, but not-so-good secrets might make you feel bad or scared." Ask the child to repeat what you've shared to ensure he gets it.

---

165 Hinky = Weird or out of the ordinary.

Heroic Parenting

Perps love to use lures to groom their targets and often couch them as "fun secrets" that they warn children not to share with anyone, or face consequences that range from them no longer being "friends" to the perp threatening to hurt the victim's family or pets. Impress upon your child the importance of telling you *any* secrets he's told to keep, unless it's a surprise for you, the parent, from someone you and your child trust. Say: "Even if the secret is really good or really scary, you need to tell me so I can make sure it's safe. Remember, if someone says DON'T tell, you MUST tell!"

Roleplay different scenarios with your child to test his understanding, for example:

- "The kids next door are getting a kitten for Christmas. I ask you not to tell them. Is that a good secret or a not-so-good secret?"

- "The babysitter's boyfriend comes over after I leave. She knows he's not supposed to be there and asks you not to tell me. Is that a good secret or a not-so-good secret?"

- "Your teacher wants to play a touching game when you're alone with him. He touches the private parts of your body and you know he shouldn't do it, but you feel scared. He tells you not to tell anyone about his game. Is that a good secret or a not-so-good secret?"

I can't emphasize strongly enough the importance of using roleplaying scenarios, play-acting using toys, or drawings when you have body safety talks with your child. They really help to impress new concepts into his long-term memory.

Emotions & Feelings

Your child is one big bundle of emotions. Everything she thinks and feels is openly expressed to the whole world without shame or filters. Learning to recognize and name her emotions and read other people's facial expressions not only builds her emotional intelligence, it's important to recognizing when she's in an unsafe situation.

Make a habit of pointing out, in a non-judgmental way, what your child and other people might be feeling. Say something like: "You sound frustrated that you can't go over to Nathan's. What can we do instead?" or "Grampa seems really sad. What do you think?"

While reading stories to her or watching TV, have her guess how the characters are feeling. Say: "Wow, he's really emotional. What do you think he's feeling?"

When you share your day with each other, talk about the different emotions you felt during the day, then ask her to tell you about times she felt those same emotions.

CJ Scarlet

Resilience

Teaching your child that he's the master of his life is sooo important! Regularly remind him that seemingly "bad" things will happen outside of his control; that's a natural part of life. But how he responds is totally his choice. Over time, he'll come to understand that life isn't happy all the time, but that when life throws a curve ball, he'll find a way to deal with it until things get better again. He'll reach a point where he can take things in stride, knowing no situation lasts forever and that it will always get better.

Obviously, this is a complicated lesson for a child to learn. It gets much easier if you tell him the following story, which comes from an ancient eastern tale about the value of pragmatism:

Long ago in a small village, there lived a farmer and his son. One day, the farmer's best horse broke through the fence and ran away. His neighbors came to visit and offer their condolences for his loss.

"Such bad luck!" they said sympathetically.

"Perhaps," replied the farmer. His neighbors were puzzled by his response.

The next day, the horse came back, and with it were two new wild horses.

The neighbors, hearing the news, visited the farmer again. "Wow, such good luck you have!"

"Perhaps," said the farmer.

That day, the farmer's son was trying to ride one of the wild horses when he fell and broke his leg.

"Oh, what bad luck!" the neighbors said.

"Perhaps," the farmer replied.

The following day, the army marched through the village on the way to war, making all the young men in the village join them. They noticed the farmer's son's broken leg and didn't take him.

"Such good luck!" said the neighbors.

"Perhaps," said the farmer.

I *love* this story! It holds such a great lesson and it's easy for children to grasp. Later, when your child is bemoaning the latest drama, you can gently remind him of the farmer's response to difficulty.

Heroic Parenting

Another aspect of resilience is learning that making mistakes is inevitable for everyone, even parents. If you're not failing at times, you're not trying hard enough. Let him know he's not perfect and neither are you. Don't be afraid to tell him about mistakes you've made and how you learned from them.

One more thing, teach your child that he'll probably feel awkward and clumsy and clueless when he first tries a new activity or plays a sport or takes a dance class. Let him know that's normal and that it'll get easier over time. This will increase his confidence and his willingness to keep trying even when he feels like a dork when he can't hit the baseball.

Telling vs. Tattling

Teaching your child the difference between tattling about minor disagreements and *telling* about unsafe body situations is important. (Don't automatically ignore or minimize disputes between kids, especially when there's an age difference; there might be bullying going or other inappropriate behavior that requires your intervention.)

Say: "I want to make sure that you know it's *always* okay to come tell me if something uncomfortable or scary or unsafe happens to you. I promise I won't be angry, and you won't get in any trouble for telling me. In fact, I'll be proud of you."

Remember, if you want to encourage your child to stop tattling so much and learn how to mediate his own disputes, when he runs up to you in tears, you can ask: "Do you need me to hug you, just listen to you, or step in?" You'd be surprised how often the answer is one of the first two; kids often just need comfort and validation.

Code Words

Your child is old enough now to understand the concept of "code words" and remember them. A code word, for the uninitiated, is a simple word that's easy to remember (like "octopus" or "meatball") that only you, your child, and another trusted adult know and can use in different situations, such as when you need your best friend to pick up your child from dance class, for example. That way, if anyone tries to convince your child to go with him—whether she knows him or not—if he doesn't know the code word, your child knows not to go with him.

Your child can also use the code word if something inappropriate is happening right in front of you that you can't see. For example, if she's sitting on someone's lap and they're rubbing their erection against her, your child could say, "Mommy, I want a meatball." The incongruity of her statement will, hopefully, trigger your memory of the code word and prompt you to rescue her.

Another example when the code word can help your child out of a jam: If she's at her friend's house and something inappropriate happens, she can call you and say the code word so you'll know to come get her right away. You can turn around and call her friend's parent and tell them you need to pick up your daughter because there's a family emergency. That way it's not up to your child to have to tell her friend that she wants to leave, which she might be afraid or embarrassed to do.

We've already established that predators are crafty as all get out and won't hesitate to lie to a child, telling her that her mother has been in an accident and sent him to pick her up and take her to the hospital. You need to question your kid on occasion to see if she remembers the code word and emphasize how important it is that she never tell anyone the word—not even her very best friend or her non-custodial parent.

Say: "What's our code word again? Good. And what do we do with our code word? Not share it with anyone *ever*. That's right! And what if someone comes up to you at school or on the street or anywhere else and they don't know the code word? That's right! You never EVER go with them! You run and tell a safe adult. And what if they DO know the code word? That's right, when someone comes to take you home and they first tell you the code word, you know I must have shared it with them and that they're a safe person. Now, remember, you must never tell anyone, not your very best friend or even an adult what the code word is. They must tell it to *you!* Good job!"

Once a particular code word has been used one time, you need to choose a new one and work with your child to memorize it. Use roleplaying scenarios to test her commitment to waiting for someone to tell her the code word.

Using the Phone

Your child is old enough to use a cell phone and landline phone at this point. You'll still need to remind him that he's to call 911 *only* when there's an emergency. Say, "Sometimes things happen, and you may need to call the police for help, like if Dad or I got really sick and needed help, or someone touched your private parts or tried to take you away. The phone number of the police is 911. (Make him repeat it several times.) Let me show you how to call 911 on my cell phone."

For your own protection and so your child doesn't mess with your phone settings, you should have an automatic screen lock in place. Even with the screen lock on, your child can still make an emergency call.

For Android or iPhones: Show your son how to press the key to turn the phone screen on (usually on the right side of the phone). On the lock screen, he can find the word "Emergency" at the bottom of the screen. Show him how to press the "Emergency" button and dial the three numbers of 911 and press "Send."

For landline phones: Show your child how to press the "On" key and dial 911.

Your 6 to 7-year-old is probably old enough to memorize your cell phone number so he can call you if he needs to; your 8 to 9-year-old certainly is old enough. Also make sure he knows your full home address, including city and state, in the event he needs to call 911. The best way to do this is to repeat the number and address in a sing-song voice (like a radio ad jingle) over and over together. Then help him cement it in his memory by asking him to repeat it on a regular basis: "What is my number again? And where do we live?"

Teaching him what to say on the phone

Say: "When you call the police on 911, the first question they're going to ask you is if you need the police, the fire department, or an ambulance. Tell them you need the police and that it's an emergency. The police will ask you your name and where you are." Your child might not be able to tell them the address where he is. It's imperative to teach him to stay on the phone with the police until they can track him down and arrive on the scene.

Continue: "The police will also ask the names of your parents and where you live; you need to tell them so they can bring you home to me."

If your son can memorize all this information, add in where you and your partner work and in what town. Say: "If it's daytime, the police may ask you where Mommy and I work. We work at…" Make him repeat that info until you're sure he has it down pat. Give pop quizzes on occasion to test his memory. If your child isn't ready and all this is overwhelming or stressful for him, back off and try again in three to six months.

What to Do If Your Child Is in Danger

If Lost

It isn't just toddlers who wander off and get lost. Kids in the 6 to 9 age group are slippery little suckers too. And let's admit it, we don't watch them quite as hypervigilantly as we did when they were little. I've seen oblivious moms spend inordinate amounts of time in the store dressing room while their children slumped in a chair and played handheld games, and I've seen dads who were so caught up in the game on the monster TV screen at Best Buy who wouldn't know their kid had wandered off if she had a screaming siren attached to her head.

Here's what to teach your child before you go out. Say: "If things get busy and we lose sight of each other, here's what I want you to do: (1) Stay *right* where you are. It'll be easier for me to find you that way. (2) Don't hide; stand somewhere I can see you. (3) Yell 'Mom/Dad, where are you?' as loud as you can. (4) If I don't find you right away, go up to the check-out counter (show her where it is) and ask the clerk to page me (explain what "paging" means[166]). If you don't see a store clerk or can't find your way to the counter, you can ask a woman, preferably one with kids, to help you find the check-out counter."

Continue, "Under NO circumstances are you to leave the store or go anywhere with anyone else. That includes the dressing room, the bathroom, or anywhere else someone might try to take you. Stay right by the check-out counter until I come get you. Are we clear?" Make her repeat what you said until you're certain she understands.

While your child is staying in place or making her way to the check-out counter, you should notify the store manager or security officer that she's missing. Ask the manager to activate the "Code Adam" (which signals all store personnel to lock down all exits). If they don't have that policy, just tell him to lock down the store's exits until your child is found. If you don't locate your child within a few minutes, call the police to come help search for her.

Thwarting a Kidnapper

We've established that it's highly unlikely your child will experience a kidnapping attempt, but it's not impossible, so let's talk about what he can do to thwart would-be abductors. By 6, your child may be playing outside in your front yard, unsupervised, with his friends.

I personally believe that 6 is too young for a child to be running around the neighborhood unsupervised, but that's your call.[167] As he gets older and more mature, he gets more freedom of movement; that's the natural order of things. By 9, he's certainly old enough to explore the neighborhood and walk to his friends' houses (close by), but there should be strict family rules about where and how he wanders, as well as enforced consequences for not following those rules.

---

166 Paging means the clerk gets on the loudspeaker and makes an announcement that there's a lost child in the store and where to find him/her.

167 When I was 6, my sibs and I used to run all over the neighborhood and beyond, coming home only for meals. The world wasn't any safer then but my parents didn't know that, or they figured we'd handle whatever came up, or they were secretly hoping we'd be adopted by gypsies; I'm not sure which. There were six of us, so the last option seems most likely. However, if you let your 6-year-old wander that freely today, you're likely to get a visit from Child Protective Services because your nosy neighbor Nancy called them to report you for neglect. If you believe, as I do, that kids should have a bit more freedom to roam and play, consider reading *Free Range Kids* by Lenore Skenazy.

The family rules might include:

- "Only leave the yard to go play somewhere else with my permission. If you don't have permission, you don't leave the yard. Understand?"

- "If you get my permission to play in the neighborhood, you have to stay between [insert boundary here] and [other boundary]." For example, "You can't go past Julian's house and the Reynolds' yard."

- "If you're playing around the neighborhood, have at least one friend with you at all times."

- "Whether you're playing in the yard or around the neighborhood, if anyone tries to convince you to go with them, scream 'No! Leave me alone!' and run home or to a safe neighbor's house." I recommend actually getting to know your neighbors and creating a kind of neighborhood watch that identifies "safe" houses kids can go to if they need help. Good safe houses are those where someone's usually home and you've met and trust them enough to let your child go into their house if he needs to get away from someone.

- "If you're approached by someone in a vehicle who tries to get you to come to them or get in their vehicle, yell for help and run or ride your bike in the opposite direction that the car's facing and go home, into a safe person's house, into a store, or someplace where there are lots of people."

- "Never accept a gift or favor of any kind from anyone unless you ask me or your dad first and get our permission."

- "Don't leave school (or gymnastics, soccer, etc.) with anyone but me and Dad unless they tell you we asked them to pick you up AND they know the code word." Ask, "What's the code word again?"

Of course, you aren't going to jam these rules down your kid's throat every time he asks to go play with his friends. That would be overkill. Save the "Family Rules" talks for the monthly family meetings. You *should* say, "Thanks for checking with me. You can go play with Jamal, but remember to stick to the family rules. K?"

Teach your child that if someone actually grabs him or tries to force him to go with them, he should yell "Stop! No! You're not my Dad/Mom!" all while physically resisting in any way he can (e.g., kicking, biting, pulling away, grabbing and holding onto a pole, etc.).

You can also teach your child how to escape if he's snatched and forced into a predator's car. Author Steve Kovacs[168] offers the following advice:

"If an abductor manages to force a child into a car, there is usually an opportunity of one to several hours before the abductor hurts the child. There is time to escape. Emphasize that your child must remain calm. That is actually not as difficult for your kids to do as you might think, but you must tell them to be calm. Then teach your children these moves and practice them:

"Reach for the door and try to get out immediately. No hesitation, go right for an immediate escape—preferably on the other side of the car from where the abductor is standing (or sitting, if they've followed the child into the car). In a four-door car, the child can jump in the backseat and try the rear door quickly. Be aware that in newer cars the child safety locks may be engaged.

"If the child is placed in a trunk, tell them not to panic. Vehicles, starting from 2002 models, have a glow-in-the-dark trunk-release lever that can be pulled down and the trunk will open. [Important: They should make every effort to get out of the trunk before the car starts moving.] Show your child the trunk release in your own car so they know what they're looking for.

"An abductor may have an older car, however, or may have removed the safety lever in their trunk, so if they can't find the one in the abductor's car, tell them they should then look for a panel in the trunk that comes out easily when you pull on it. Tear out all the wires that can be seen, most of which are tail-lights and brake-lights. Police might then pull the abductor over.

"Tail-lights are often attached with easily-broken plastic connectors, so, it may be possible for your child to kick them out. If they are able to do so, they can wave at passing motorists who are more than likely going to call 911. If the car stops for any reason, tell them to start screaming and yelling."

Self-Defense

Showing your child how to fight like a rabid Tasmanian Devil (which, again, I teach in Chapter 17) can literally save her life if someone tries to pick her up or touch her inappropriately.

---

168 From his book *Protect Your Kids! The Simple Keys to Children's Safety and Survival.*

By yelling, kicking, hitting, squirming, and biting the offender, she may convince her aggressor to leave her alone and run.

Consider starting martial arts training or taking a series of self-defense classes together to empower her to protect and defend herself. Know that just a few classes won't cut it; it can take years of training in these programs to become proficient. That's why teaching her the Taz moves I suggest, which don't require formal training, are so important. Reading Chapter 17 will also help YOU to protect your own precious body from predators—another big plus!

Personal security apps & devices

You can further protect your child by having her wear a personal security device or keeping a special app on her cell phone, if she carries one already. I address personal security on my website under the Freebies tab.

If You Have Concerns Your Child Has Been Victimized

I cover this topic very thoroughly in the chapters on Bullying, Digital Dangers, and Sexual Molestations and Assault, and in the Appendix, so refer to these sections for detailed information on what to do if you suspect or learn your child has been victimized.

For Parents to Do

YOU are an heroic parent! Yes, you! Just the fact that you're reading this book shows you care about your child's safety and are committed to protecting her and teaching her to protect and defend herself in your absence.

Both you and your child will feel more confident, self-assured, and powerful because YOU took action. You rock!

Here are more ways you can positively impact your child and help her protect her miniature bod from predators:

Be an Awesome Role Model

You're still the smartest, and possibly the coolest, person on the planet, according to your 6 to 9-year-old. That won't last much longer, so milk that belief for all it's worth while you can. Again, that's great news if you're modeling positive values and behavior, but not so good if you're a jerk. Do what you need to do to model positive behavior. If that means getting into AA or staying home at night rather than going on the prowl, then do it.

Your kid is watching everything you do and will often follow in your footsteps, however staggered they may be. Make sure those footsteps are leading in a positive direction and not going in circles or backward.

Remember when I wrote earlier that the words you say to your child become her inner voice? It really is true. Make sure the things you say and do are congruent with your (positive) values because your baby is watching, and history is bound by some weird universal force to repeat itself.

Speak Your Truth & Walk Your Talk

Have the crucial conversations and ask the tough questions to ensure your child knows what she needs to know to stay safe. When you're willing to talk openly about body safety issues, you signal to your child that it's safe for her to do so as well, and she's more likely to come to you with questions and concerns.

Your willingness to speak your truth and walk your talk gives your child permission to do the same. To paraphrase Henry David Thoreau, most people live lives of quiet desperation and they have no clue who they are or what their purpose is on this planet. When you model for your child how to live from a place of integrity and authenticity, you're giving her one of the greatest gifts a child could receive—a deep knowledge and acceptance of her *Self*—body, mind, and soul. It's a beautiful thing.

Set & Enforce Clear Family Rules

The "family rules" must be sacrosanct and consistently applied. Rules like "no one touches our private parts" and "only go on approved social media sites" should be strictly enforced and backed up by reasonable but meaningful consequences.

Be Aware of What's Going on in Your Child's Life

Be present for your child; he craves your attention and it's one of the most proactive things you can do to keep him safe. Here are some ways to parent up:

- Be a visible presence. Be a parent who's interested and involved in your child's life and on alert for bad guys.

- Watch for unusual behavior in your child and check into it. Does he act anxious or sullen after he hangs out with a particular person? Is he suddenly acting withdrawn or depressed? You know him better than anyone and are in a unique position to notice concerning changes.

- Pay close attention when others seek out one-to-one access to your child. Don't allow it if you have concerns about that person.

- Trust your gut. If someone or something doesn't feel right, it probably isn't. Remove yourself and/or your child from that situation immediately. It may have been nothing at all or you may have thwarted a molestation or assault. You'll never know what *might* have happened, but you *will* know you took action when your gut warned you to, which is a great thing.

- Perform a background check on anyone who will care for your child, such as sitters, coaches, and group leaders—even if they were referred by someone you trust. Don't be shy about doing this; your child's safety is more important than your embarrassment.

- Check the state and national sex offender registries on a regular basis. Prepare to be appalled by how many sex offenders live in your neighborhood and immediate vicinity of your home and your child's school!

Provide Supervision

Yes, your child is old enough now to walk to a friend's house a few doors down (or blocks, for older kids), as long as you're confident he understands and will obey the family rules and knows what to do if he encounters a dangerous person along the way.

I would add another rule: that he's absotively posolutely[169] *required* to call you as soon as he arrives at the friend's house. Immediately. No exceptions. If you know it takes him five minutes to get there and he doesn't call within 10, go get him and bring him home.

He won't be happy about it and that's the point. He probably won't have a phone at this point, so tell him to use his friend's house phone or his mom's cell phone to call. That way, if something bad does happen and he doesn't make it to his friend's house, you'll only be a few minutes behind him. And, it's a good way to get him to memorize your number in case of emergency.

When I was a kid, I used to dilly-dally on the way home from school, stopping to play on the playground, climb trees, and run around with my friends. Those are all fun, healthy activities, but you should make it a family rule that your child has to come straight home from school and check in before doing any of these. Let him know that if he doesn't come straight home within X minutes, there will be a consequence (for example, he won't be able to play with his friends after

---

[169] Yes, I know I mixed up those words; it was intentional.

he's done his homework). Again, if something happens and he's not home within the expected timeframe, you'll know within minutes to begin looking for him.

If your child walks to school, decide with him in advance what route he'll take and have him stick to it. Some safety experts suggest having your child regularly alter his route to throw off would-be abductors, but that's silly; he's a kid, not a secret agent. Walk the route with him, pointing out safe places he can run to in an emergency, until he's comfortable walking it by himself. You can make it a rule that he only walks to school with a friend or group.

Media Time

Your child now regularly uses the family computer (which is kept in a common room; please don't give her a laptop of her own yet!) or tablet, and is on the Internet doing her homework and chatting with friends through social media.

With the parental controls you've placed on every electronic device she has access to (even the ones you don't allow her to use but that she can get her sly little hands on), you can feel fairly secure that she won't see inappropriate content. Still, keep an eye on what she's viewing and the online chats she's having to ensure she's making good choices and not exposing herself to potentially unsafe people or conversations.

Be aware of what your child's watching on the TV and gaming console. Violent and sexual situations can appear even in seemingly "childish" shows.

Support Your Child

Let your child know often that you support her. Tell her you'll always love her no matter what, even if she tells you something scary or bad. Let her know you've got her back and will always do your very best to protect her from harm. Just as importantly, tell her you'll help her learn to protect and defend *herself* so she can feel more confident and in charge of herself and her life.

CHAPTER 14

Children with Disabilities

Why I Wrote This Chapter

As I shared with people over the past year that I was writing this book, I had a number of them come up to me and beg me to include a chapter on how to protect children with disabilities. The first couple of times this happened, I thought it was a good idea but brushed it off because I had no expertise in this area. But after the fifth time a worried mom approached me, I decided I had to find a way to meet the demand for information from these desperate parents.

Then I learned that:

- People (not necessarily just children) with any kind of physical, mental, developmental, or emotional disability are far more likely to be the victims of sexual assault—up to *7 times more likely*, according to unpublished US Department of Justice (USDOJ) data obtained by NPR.[cxlvii] In NPR's report, they noted that this estimate is most likely an undercount because the USDOJ data didn't count people living in group homes or state institutions, and because many victims with disabilities can't communicate what happened to them.[cxlviii]

- More than *90 percent* of people with intellectual disabilities will experience some form of sexual abuse and 49 percent will experience *10 or more abusive incidents*.[cxlix]

- Nearly 100 percent of predators who abuse people with disabilities are known to the victim.[cl]

- The abusers are often caregivers upon whom the victims are dependent. Research shows that caregivers and developmental disability service providers represent the largest number of identified perpetrators against their charges.[cli]

- Children with disabilities are two to three times more likely to be bullied than those without disabilities.[clii] One study reported that 60 percent of students with disabilities are regularly bullied compared with 25 percent of all students.[cliii]

I was distraught and horrified. It was clear I had to write about violence against children living with disabilities in order to give parents the information they need to protect this incredibly vulnerable population of kids.

I really am not an expert in this area, so I'm bound to make mistakes and say something insensitive or inaccurate at some point in this chapter. When I screw up, please forgive me and don't send hate mail. Rather, gently correct me so I'll be more "woke" in the future. I'll do the very best I can to help you protect your dear child.

IMPORTANT NOTE!!! If your child is between the ages of 2 to 9, or is older but developmentally, intellectually, or socially less mature, please be sure to read both Chapter 12 and Chapter 13 (on children 2 to 5 and 6 to 9) for information on what and how to teach them about danger. I will repeat some of the info from those two chapters here because I want to ensure those who skip around this book get the information they need.

Now, let's get started by being clear on what we're talking about here.

Definitions

Disability

A physical, intellectual, developmental, medical, learning, or other condition that substantially limits one or more major life activities.

Child with a Disability

A child who's been diagnosed with an intellectual disability, hearing impairment, speech or language impairment, visual impairment, serious emotional disturbances, orthopedic impairment, autism, traumatic brain injury, other health impairments, or specific learning disability and who, because of the condition, needs special education and related resources.[cliv]

Specific Learning Disabilities (SLD)

The umbrella term "SLD" covers a specific group of learning challenges which affect a child's ability to read, write, listen, speak, reason, or do math. This includes dyslexia, dysgraphia, auditory processing disorder, and nonverbal learning disabilities. SLD is the most common category used under the Individuals with Disabilities Education Act (IDEA), covering about one-third of students who qualified as disabled under that act.[clv]

Physical Disabilities

Conditions that are attributed to a congenital or physical cause that impact the ability to perform physical activities, such as mobility.

Medical Disabilities

This includes conditions affecting one or more of the body's systems, including the respiratory, immunological, neurological, and circulatory systems.[clvi] Included in this category are illnesses, such as cancer, lupus, and HIV+/AIDS.

Intellectual Disabilities

Kids with this type of disability have below-average intellectual abilities. They may also have poor communication, self-care, and social skills. Down Syndrome is one example of an intellectual disability.[clvii]

Speech & Language Disabilities

Speech and language disabilities may result from hearing loss, cerebral palsy, learning disabilities, and/or physical conditions. There may be a range of difficulties, from problems with articulation or voice strength to the complete absence of voice. Included are difficulties in projection; fluency problems, such as stuttering and stammering; and in articulating particular words or terms.[clviii]

Learning Disabilities

Learning disabilities are neurologically-based and may interfere with learning and using skills like listening, speaking, reading, writing, reasoning, or math. These kids may be highly intelligent, but their learning difficulties may lead to poor academic performance.[clix]

Developmental Disabilities

This includes a diverse group of chronic conditions that are due to mental or physical impairments that arise before adulthood. Developmental disabilities cause individuals living with them many difficulties in certain areas of life, especially in language, mobility, learning, self-help, and independent living.[clx] Some examples of more common developmental disabilities include attention deficit hyperactivity disorder (ADHD), autism spectrum disorders, cerebral palsy, intellectual disabilities, and vision impairment.[clxi]

Development Delay

Development delay involves children under the age of 6 who are less developed mentally or physically than is normal for their age. These children may have specific disabilities that have not yet been identified.

Cognitive Disabilities

This category includes limitations in mental functioning and in skills such as communicating, taking care of oneself, and social skills.

Psychiatric Disabilities

Psychiatric disabilities refer to a wide range of behavioral and/or psychological problems characterized by anxiety, mood swings, depression, or compromised assessment of reality. These behaviors persist over time and aren't in response to a particular event.[170][clxii]

Disability Harassment

Disability-related harassment is intimidation or abusive behavior toward a student based on their disability that creates a hostile environment by interfering with or denying a student's participation in or receipt of benefits, services, or opportunities in the institution's program.[clxiii] This can occur in any location connected with the school, including classrooms, the cafeteria, hallways, the playground, athletic fields, or school buses. It also can occur during school-sponsored events.[clxiv]

Disability-related harassment also includes repeated or one-off conduct against the family, friends, and associates of a disabled person (such as bullying or hate crimes) because of their connection with that person.

Disability harassment is illegal under section 504 of the Rehabilitation Act of 1973 and Title II of the Americans with Disabilities Act of 1990.[clxv]

---

[170] I guess this definition doesn't include post-traumatic stress disorders, which are related to particular events, but they too are considered psychiatric disabilities.

Individuals with Disabilities Education Act (IDEA)

IDEA requires public schools to provide special education and related services to eligible students. Not every child who struggles in school qualifies. To be covered, a child's school performance must be "adversely affected" by a qualified disability.[clxvi]

According to Understood.org, the primary purposes of IDEA are to:[clxvii]

- Provide free, appropriate public education to children with disabilities. IDEA requires schools to identify and evaluate students suspected of having disabilities, at no cost to their families, through a process called Child Find. Once kids are found to have a qualifying disability, schools must provide them with special education and related services (such as speech therapy and counseling) to meet their unique needs and help them make progress in school.

- Give parents (or legal guardians) a voice in their child's education. Under IDEA, you have a say in the decisions the school makes about your child. At every point in the process, the law gives you specific rights and protections, called procedural safeguards. For example, one safeguard is that the school must get your consent before providing services to your child.

IDEA covers kids from birth through high school graduation or age 21 (whichever comes first). It provides early intervention services up to age 3, and special education for older kids in public school, including charter schools.

Individualized Education Program (IEP)

An IEP is a written statement of the educational program designed to meet a child's individual needs. Every child who receives special education services must have an IEP.[clxviii]

Section 504

Section 504 is an anti-discrimination, civil rights statute that requires that the needs of students with disabilities be met in the same way as those of non-disabled students.

How Children Living with Disabilities Learn & Processes Information

For any child, grade school is overwhelming and fraught with drama, violence, and murky social swamps. For children living with disabilities, it's all that AND they have to manage very real physical, mental, intellectual, or emotional conditions that challenge their ability to fit in with their peers.

How children with disabilities learn and process information is so personal to each child that I won't attempt to generalize here. My purpose in this chapter is to teach you what you need to know to protect your child with a disability and how to teach her to protect and defend herself when you're not around—all in a way that's appropriate for her developmental and maturity level.

Let's face it, living with a disability puts a big fat target on your child's back that bullies and predators may try to exploit.

My job is to help you turn that target into a shield.

Sex & Sexuality

Many people never consider that people with disabilities, especially severe physical disabilities, desire love and intimacy just like everyone else. Like any child, your youngster with a disability is a sexual being and will have sexual thoughts and desires as he grows older. The sections on Sex & Sexuality in Chapters 12 and 13 apply to this population as well, and I hope you'll read them.

Because children with disabilities are at such extreme risk of being sexually abused, it's imperative that you talk to your child about sex and safe versus unsafe touch, at his maturity and developmental level, of course.[171]

Sexual Development

According to StopItNow.org, "All children, even those with severe disabilities, need to understand basic concepts like the differences between boys and girls, accurate names for all body parts, and where babies come from. When parents present this information in a matter of fact way, children learn that it is okay to talk with parents about their questions. Adapt how you present this information to your child by using tools including roleplaying, structured play with dolls, books and videos, etc."[clxix]

Your child needs you to prepare him for the physical changes he'll experience when he goes through puberty. If you're unsure when these changes might occur in your child, talk to his pediatrician for guidance and advice.

---

[171] StopItNow.org has a whole library of incredible tip sheets on protecting children from sexual abuse and teaching them healthy behaviors. They even have one specifically on the sexual development of children with disabilities, which I reference in the Resources section of my website at www.cjscarlet.com/resources.

Like any child, your child with a disability may be curious about his body and those of his peers and may engage in innocent child's play with others. Please read Chapters 12 and 13 for more information about how to deal with that and what behaviors you should be concerned about.

Greatest Threats to These Children

Please be sure to read each referenced chapter for additional information on the threats and predators your child may encounter. Also read Chapter 12 on children 2 to 5 and Chapter 13 on children 6 to 9 for ideas on what to teach your child in these age or developmental level groups. When I can, I'll add information below to each threat that's pertinent to children with disabilities.

Bullying

(Refer to Chapter 7)

It's well known that bullies tend to target children who are more physically, mentally, socially, or emotionally vulnerable. Kids with disabilities make perfect targets not only because they tend to look or act differently than the so-called average child, but because they often can't fight back.

Even kids whose disabilities are hidden, meaning they're not obvious, are at risk. For example, there have been cases where bullies have exposed children with severe allergies to the very things they're allergic to, which can not only cause a serious health crisis, it could literally mean life or death!

Bullies don't like to be challenged; it threatens the illusion of their authority and makes them look bad (as if picking on a kid in a wheelchair doesn't already make them look like complete nimrods!). They choose victims who are unlikely or unable to verbally or physically resist them. And when the victim has a condition that causes him to behave impulsively and reactively, such as ADHD, the bully knows she can easily get a rise out of him and maybe even get *him* in trouble when he acts out in response. Double fun.

Victims may understand that their disability, which they can't control, makes them a great target, or they may not understand why they're being bullied at all. Some bullies pretend to be nice to their victims to set them up for a fall and the victims may welcome the attention, believing it's friendly. When/if they discover that the joke's on them, they naturally feel betrayed and confused.

What to Teach Your Child about Bullying

Talking to your child with a disability about bullying from the time she's a tiny tot will prepare her for what she may face as she gets older. Helping her devise a plan now for how to deal with it is really important. Knowing what her options are and that she has a choice about how she responds will give her a sense of control over her own destiny, which is a confidence-builder.

She's going to be teased by other kids at some point, that's a given. Teach her what bullying is and the difference between benign teasing, which is friendly and not meant to be hurtful, and bullying, which *is* meant to be destructive and hurtful.

Say: "Sometimes other kids like to tease each other by saying things like 'Nice job, Grace,' when you trip, or 'OMG, that was so stupid!' when you say something silly. They might laugh, but they're laughing at what you did, not at you personally. If they tease you, be a good sport and laugh at yourself too. But sometimes there are kids who think it's funny to pick on other kids. They might say something really mean to you or even try to push you around. It's not funny and it isn't okay."

Teach her that bullies like to pick on kids who will either get upset or cry, or kids who'll get angry and act out, which gets the victim herself in trouble.

If your child has behavioral issues, such as ADHD, that cause her to act impulsively, say: "You know how sometimes you like to talk a lot or how you sometimes get worked up when you're upset?" Or, if she has a condition like autism, say: "You know how you don't like to be touched or have someone get in your space?" If she has a physical disability, you could say: "There are some kids who like to pick on other kids who use braces/crutches/a wheelchair. Well, some bullies like to be mean to kids who feel/look like you do. They don't have the courage or inner strength that you do. I'm going to teach you how to use that courage and inner strength to stop bullies."

Strategies to Stop Bullying

Help your child come up with several ways she could react to a bully by roleplaying different scenarios. Say: "Let's think about different situations when a bully might try to do or say something mean," and then come up with ways she could respond. For example, "What would you do if a bully said you were stupid because you didn't answer a question correctly in class?"

Then let her come up with her own answers. If she falters, help prompt her by brainstorming a variety of responses, including:

- Avoiding places where the bully is. (You or she may have to ask the school to move her locker or put her in a different class.)

- Ignoring the bully.

- Getting away from him, if she can.

- Asking for help from other kids around her, pointing to a particular child and saying: "Go get a teacher."

- Agreeing with him: "You're right. I am clumsy sometimes."

- Using humor to defuse the situation: "Does this wheelchair make my butt look big?"

- Using sarcasm: "Really? I didn't notice that I walk differently."

- Calling him on it: "Why would you say that? That's mean."

- Telling a teacher or other trusted adult (and you) when there's an incident: "Who could you tell if someone was pushing you on the bus?"

When Your Child's Reaction May Escalate the Bullying or He Initiates It

Bullies love to pick on kids who have disabilities that lead them to behave erratically or act out when provoked because it's "fun" to set them off and get them in trouble. It's not easy to teach a reactive child to regulate his emotions and behavior, but you might be surprised by how far pro-active conversations about this and roleplaying different scenarios will go toward helping him be calmer and more easy-going.

I'm not an expert on exactly how to do this, so I'll leave it to you to do the research on how to work with your child to regulate his emotions. What I *can* do is offer some tips and questions you can ask him that will help him think through his options and reactions, which will hopefully help during any future incidents.

Ask: "Tell me what you were doing just before Johnny started bullying you." And then, "What could you do differently next time so something like this doesn't happen (e.g., avoiding the bully, asking the teacher for help, etc.)?"

Help your child learn to recognize how *his* actions (talking too loudly, acting out, being too affectionate with others) might draw negative attention while emphasizing that he's not to blame for the bullying; any incidents that occur are the choice and fault of the bully, not your child's.

Together, make a list of other ways your child could behave (e.g., waiting his turn, giving compliments instead of hugs, etc.) and use roleplaying scenarios, taking turns being the bully and the victim to increase his confidence.

If you have a child whose behavior is disruptive, don't automatically assume he started the incident. Kids with behavior issues can get a bad rep that follows them from teacher to teacher, and they may automatically assume your child is the cause or equal participant in every incident. Give your child a chance to explain what happened and validate his feelings, if not his reaction to the situation.

If your child *did* start the incident, don't feel like a bad parent and wallow in it. Pour your energy into working with your child to help him find better ways of interacting with others. Work with the school to come up with consequences that are fair and appropriate for him.[172]

Counseling or behavioral therapy may help him learn to regulate his emotions more effectively, so do consider it. I don't know whether this kind of help is available for free through your child's IEP, but it's worth looking into.

What to Do If Your Child Has Been Bullied

If you learn that your child's been bullied, it's important to take action to protect her and keep it from happening again. If it happens at school, on the bus, or at a school-sponsored activity, she's protected under IDEA and her school is required to take swift action to ensure she's protected from the bully and given any accommodations she needs to address the problem.

If the abuse is relatively mild, consider calling the offender's parents to let them know what happened, but only after you've calmed down! If you do call them, don't jump down their throats and don't talk trash about their kid, which will almost certainly put them on the defensive, even if their "angel" is a total wanker. Instead, dispassionately explain what happened and ask for their help to stop it. For younger children, it may help to plan a fun playdate where the two kids can get to know each other better and maybe even become allies. Don't push it though if you think it won't help.

If the bullying goes beyond taunting and name-calling into the realm of threats of violence or actual violence, go straight to the school principal, superintendent, and/or school board and ask them to investigate the incident and take action to stop the abuse. If they don't do this right away, they may be in violation of state or federal laws.

It'll be helpful if you prepare a written timeline of the incident(s) that explains the facts as you know them, including who was involved and witnessed the incident; when it happened; what

---

[172] Check out my handout on What to Do If Your Child is the Bully that can be found on my website at www.cjscarlet.com/freebies.

occurred before, during, and after the incident; where it happened; why it happened; and how it happened.[173]

And this is important: Keep detailed records of all communications you have with school officials, teachers, guidance counselors, etc., including whom you talked to, when you talked to them, what was said and promised, and what was actually done. Ask them to tell you when action is taken. While the school may not be able to tell you what sanctions it imposed against the bully, they have to tell you what changes are being implemented to protect your child.

If the school doesn't address the problem and protect your child, you can file a formal complaint with the US Department of Education Office for Civil Rights.[174]

Know that you MUST file your complaint within 180 days of the incident! If that deadline has passed and/or you feel your child is being denied free appropriate public education in violation of the Americans with Disability Act, you can file a request for an impartial hearing with your state's Department of Education within two years of the incident.

You can also get legal advice from an attorney who specializes in disability harassment cases. Legal action usually isn't unnecessary; just the threat is often enough to spur a school system into action. Bullying isn't yet illegal in the US, but bullying or harassing a child with a disability *IS*.

Working with Your Child's School & Teachers

If you're concerned that your child is at risk of being bullied, talk to his school's administrators and teachers to implement activities that encourage peer relationships and help cultivate empathy.

Strategies may include:[175]

- Helping students come up with fun activities to do that include everyone in the class or school. For example, some schools have created programs that have students with disabilities and non-disabled students eat lunch together, when they talk and share, so no one feels left out and isolated.

- Teaching students up-front about the kinds of support their peers with disabilities need.

- Creating a buddy system for children with disabilities.

---

173 I offer a guide on my website to help you capture this information. Go to www.cjscarlet.com/freebies.
174 Go to www.ed.gov/about/offices/list/ocr/complaintprocess.html.
175 From www.StopBullying.gov.

- Helping students come up with adaptive strategies to use in the classroom so they understand the needs of children with disabilities and can assist them when help is needed.

- Conducting team-based learning activities and rotating student groupings so everyone gets to interact with everyone else. One school requires its clubs to rotate the leadership roles so every student in each club gets the chance to run the group.

- Rewarding positive, helpful, inclusive behavior.

Tell your child's school officials and teachers that because of the increased risk he faces, you'll be closely monitoring things and want to be notified immediately if there are any incidents involving your child. Also request a special IEP or Section 504 meeting where you ask for anti-bullying and social skills training to be included in his IEP.

Teach Your Child How to Make & Keep Friends

In Chapter 15, I'll help you teach your child how to make friends and be a good friend. Check it out!

Digital Dangers

(Refer to Chapter 8)

The Internet and social media can help your child be more social and independent, but they could also put her at greater risk of being cyberbullied. Disinhibited by the anonymity the Internet provides, kids who would never dream of physically bullying a child with a disability could become her tormentors online.

Even peers who are sympathetic to your child may go along with the crowd and say hateful things to or about her in order to fit in. They might feel terrible when they do this, but not nearly as bad as your kid feels when people she thought were her friends suddenly turn on her online.

Pornography

(Refer to Chapter 8 on Digital Dangers)

Molestation & Sexual Assault

(Refer to Chapter 9)

Everything I wrote in Chapter 9 on child sexual molestation and sexual assault applies to your child with a disability, so I won't repeat myself here. But I would like to take a minute to address the importance of teaching your child with a disability about sex and human sexuality (in an age-appropriate way, of course) in order to protect her from abuse and assault.

According to a report conducted in 2013,[176] one of the main reasons children with disabilities are at such high risk of being sexually assaulted is their lack of basic knowledge about sexual health and relationships.

The report says, "This practice can be traced to a desire to shield children with disabilities from the realities of life as well as a belief *that people with disabilities are asexual* [emphasis mine]. As a result, sexual education is rarely provided in special education classrooms and, when it is, it is not tailored to the needs of children with disabilities. Moreover, family members may have personal anxieties about their children having sex and therefore will not raise such issues with them or the schools. As such, children with disabilities are not taught about their bodies, do not learn to distinguish good touches and bad touches, and are never given a framework for healthy relationships. Without such fundamental lessons, children with disabilities have no language to describe what has happened to them when they are abused."[clxx]

I don't know about you, but my jaw dropped as I read that. Teaching your child about body safety, sexual health, and healthy relationships is such an easy and effective way to protect her from predators.

So do it.

Read or re-read Chapters 12 and 13 on how to talk to children 2 to 5 and 6 to 9 about body safety, body words, and sexual health issues. Then, summon your parenting wizard powers and have those conversations with her from the time she's able to understand.

Talk to Your Child

Your child with a disability is at an elevated risk of being sexually abused and because of that, you need to prepare and protect him by teaching him what "unsafe touch" is. And make sure you do the "safe people" exercise with him in which you draw a circle and put the names of his safe people on the inside, and the names of unsafe people on the outside. Ask questions about the people he chooses to add to the outside of the circle to determine why they make him feel unsafe. Use this information to protect your child from those people.

---

176 Conducted by Vera's Center on Victimization and Safety and the Ms. Foundation for Women.

Talk to Your Child's Caregivers

Your child's caregivers may be his greatest threat. Make sure you're 100 percent comfortable with them and that your intuition gives you a thumbs-up. Vet them thoroughly according to the guidelines I laid out in Chapter 5 and then make them your allies by talking to them about your family rules regarding privacy and safe touch (which I cover below). Ask for their feedback on areas of concern regarding your child and get their input on how to best safeguard him.

Refer to StopItNow.org's website for more fantastic information on how to address sexuality and sexual abuse involving children with disabilities. The site also has a tip sheet on "How to Protect Your Child from Sexual Abuse in Program Settings."[177]

Kidnapping

(Refer to Chapter 10)

When researching information about abductions of children with disabilities, I found articles stating that they're at a "significantly increased risk" of being kidnapped, but none of them explained why or referenced their sources. Please read Chapter 10 for information about how to protect your child from would-be abductors.

Strangers

(Refer to Chapter 2)

Although caregivers known to your child present the greatest risk of abuse, your child with a disability may be especially vulnerable to manipulation by strangers because of social or intellectual deficits.

Siblings, Peers & Older Kids

(Refer to Chapter 3)

Partners, Non-Custodial Parents & Relatives

(Refer to Chapter 4)

Babysitters & Other Caregivers

(Refer to Chapter 5)

---

[177] This article can be found here: https://www.stopitnow.org/ohc-content/tip-sheet-how-to-protect-your-child-from-sexual-abuse-in-program-settings.

As I mentioned in the introduction to this chapter, children with disabilities are most often abused or assaulted by the people who take care of them (family members and paid caregivers).

Teach your child from the time he's little how to identify when something inappropriate is happening, how to say "No!" to caregivers and others, and that he should always tell you if something or someone makes him feel uncomfortable, scared, or violated.

Daycare & Pre-School, After-School Program

(Refer to Chapter 5)

Other Adults

(Refer to Chapter 6)

Discussing Body Safety

We've established the importance of teaching your child with a disability about body safety issues, including sex and human sexuality. You know your child better than anyone else and only you can decide when your child's ready to learn these important subjects. My advice is to start as early as you can, given her ability to understand what you're saying.

Remember, this isn't about having one overwhelming safety talk with your child where you tell her everything there is to know about danger and walk away thinking you've done your job and now she's safe. Rather, you'll want to introduce body safety topics in tiny doses over time, throughout your child's life.

Approach the subject of body safety matter-of-factly: "It's time we went over the rules about body safety" or "I want to have a talk about body safety today." You can stop at any point if you think your child can't understand you or is getting overwhelmed. You can always try again when she's a little older.

Don't worry if you don't get it perfect or get flustered; you're going to make this part of your routine and you'll get better at it over time. In Chapter 18 I'll help you learn how to incorporate safety talks into your daily conversations and the monthly family meetings I recommend. The point of making it an ongoing conversation that you start early on is to make it into a habit for both you and your child that will still work even when she's a rebellious teenager.

When to Teach Him About Body Safety Issues

If you want your child to pay attention to you when you talk to him about body safety issues, choose a time when you're both comfortable and relaxed. Trying to talk when either of you are stressed or cranky is a bad idea.

Consider using the following times to have body safety conversations with your child:

- **Changing clothes or diapers.** When your child is changing clothes or you're changing his diaper, you can make it a habit to (occasionally) say something like, "Time to cover up! Your private parts are just for you, right? Remember, no one else should look at or touch your privates except [mommy/daddy/caregiver, etc.] when you need to get clean, or the doctor when you need help to stay healthy.

- **Bath time.** This is a great time to talk to your child about his body parts, using the correct terminology that I covered in Chapter 12 on Body Words.

- **Bedtime/storytime.** Tell or read stories to your child and talk about them afterward to highlight the moral lessons and any safety themes (e.g., the debatable wisdom of Goldilocks going into a strange house). Ask open-ended questions like, "What should you do if that happened to you?" and use your child's answer for further discussion. Keep it light. I do NOT recommend talking about danger topics just before bed.

- **Over a treat.** Create a fun routine, like having a chat over hot cocoa or milk and cookies, when you talk about any questions or concerns he may have around body safety. This could include asking questions like, "How safe do you feel at school?" followed by, "Are there any bullies at your school?" and "Has that kid ever picked on you?"

- **Before any new situation.** Before your child starts a new activity or goes somewhere where he'll be interacting with new people (e.g., daycare, school, etc.), talk to him about what he might experience and whom he might meet. Make it a fun conversation by wondering together what adventures he'll have. Introduce the most important body safety issues, such as remembering to trust his intuition and telling people "no" to hugs. Encourage him to ask questions.

How to Teach Your Child About Body Safety Issues

Using Stories

Refer to Chapters 12 and 13 for a list of stories and movies you can read or watch together that teach moral or safety lessons and are appropriate to your child's developmental level.

Using Imagination & Roleplaying

Harness your verbal child's imagination to engage in roleplaying scenarios, as described in Chapters 12 and 13.

Questions

When you introduce or reinforce body safety rules and scenarios, your child's bound to have lots of questions. If she doesn't ask questions or isn't verbal, you can say: "Here are some questions you might be thinking of that I want to answer."

What to Teach Your Child

Boundaries

Children with disabilities are often "manhandled" by caregivers who need to dress, bathe, change, or move them. Even so, it's important that your child learns to have good physical and emotional boundaries and to recognize if they're violated.

You yourself should always ask permission before touching him and tell him what you're about to do (dress or bathe him, for example). If it's something you have to do regardless of his wishes, say this instead: "I'm going to give you a bath now," rather than asking for permission. Ask your child's other caregivers to also show respect for his boundaries.

Saying No

Teach your child with a verbal disability a variety of ways she can say no that don't require verbal skills. These can include shaking her head, stomping her feet, flailing her arms, or slapping at the offender to get him to stop.

Safe vs. Unsafe Touch

Depending on the type of disability your child has and her need for help from caregivers, this can be a tough concept to grasp. If she needs help with things like bathing or going to the bathroom, explain to her that it's okay for her caregivers to undress her or pull down her pants, wash or wipe her vulva and bottom, and help her get dressed again.

Tell her it's *not* okay for them to touch her private parts outside of this (unless there are other intimate functions she needs help with that I'm not familiar with) or to touch her in any way that makes her feel uncomfortable, scared, or confused.

Talk to the people who provide care for your child about ways to effectively care for her while meeting her needs for privacy and appropriate touch. Agree on appropriate rules to reduce her vulnerability to harm or abuse.

Sharing your family rules on boundaries, privacy, and safe touch will help guide the caregivers' efforts to provide only the level of personal care she requires.

Safe vs. Unsafe People

Draw a circle and put the names of her safe people inside the circle. Then ask her to name the "unsafe" people she wants to put outside the circle. Gently and carefully ask her about each person she put outside the circle to find out why she doesn't trust them and considers them unsafe. Pay close attention for clues that these people may pose a threat to her.

Let the people you and your child choose as safe people know they've been chosen and that your child may want to come to them to talk about body safety issues or concerns. Make sure they're okay with being on the list.

Telling

Children with disabilities are not only less likely to disclose abuse, they're less likely to be taken seriously when they do. Some reasons your child might not disclose abuse include:

- A physical or intellectual limitation that inhibits his ability to tell.

- He believes he brought it on himself or he has feelings of unworthiness because of his disability.

- He feels powerless to stop the abuse.

- He doesn't want to alienate the abuser or get her in trouble.

- He's afraid he won't find another friend.

- He's dependent on the abuser for his welfare.

- He loves or admires the abuser.

Reassure your child that it's okay and important to tell you if anything inappropriate, scary, or confusing happens to him.

Code Words

Whether you should teach your child to use a code word depends on her ability to understand the concept and remember what the code word is and how to use it. Refer to Chapter 13 for more about code words and how to use them.

What to Do If They're in Danger

If Lost

Kids with autism spectrum disorder (ASD) or intellectual disabilities are particularly likely to wander away from their caregivers, and their difficulty appreciating safety concerns and communicating with others can make it harder to find them. Children with ASD are often drawn toward hazards (e.g., bodies of water, roads and highways, heavy machinery, etc.), which makes it even more important to find them quickly.

Teach your child to stay put if you get separated and yell loudly for you (i.e., "Mom? Where are you?") Tell him not to leave with *anyone* or go into the parking lot to look for you. If you're in a store, tell the store manager to have employees close all the exits until your child is found. Regardless of where you are, call the police right away to help you locate your child.

In advance of going out with your child, attach a contact card (pinned to his clothing, hung on a cord around his neck, or on a bracelet) that has your name, phone number, address, and your child's condition written on it. And you should always carry a recent photo of him with you in case he gets lost. If you're going to a crowded venue (e.g., a parade or fair), have your child wear distinctive clothing, like a super bright shirt or hat.

Self-Defense

Definitely teach your child the Taz moves I suggest in Chapter 17, which can be effective even if she has limited mobility or uses a wheelchair.

If You Have Concerns Your Child Has Been Victimized

I cover this topic very thoroughly in the chapters on Bullying, Digital Dangers, and Sexual Molestations and Assault, and in the Appendix on If Your Child Has Been Sexually Abused, so refer to these for detailed information on what to do if you suspect or learn your child has been victimized.

Reporting

See the Appendix for information on how to report child sexual abuse.

For Parents to Do

If you're the loving parent of a child with a disability, you are a total rock star! You face challenges most parents can't even imagine, yet every day you wake up and deal with them like a boss. Below are more ways you can positively impact your child and help her protect herself from predators.

Be an Awesome Role Model

Take advantage of the fact that your child with a disability is young enough to think you're the be-all, end-all. It doesn't matter how much you mess up or lose your cool with him, he believes you can do no wrong.

This is both a blessing and a curse. Your son desperately wants your approval and looks to you to reflect back to him who he is. If that reflection is generally positive and encouraging, he'll feel loved, valued, capable, and worthy. If it's largely negative or disapproving, he'll grow to doubt himself and his abilities, and his self-esteem and confidence will suffer. This makes him more vulnerable to predators who are looking for broken children to groom and victimize.

Set & Enforce Clear Family Rules

The family rules must be sacrosanct and consistently applied. Rules like "no one touches our private parts" and "only go on approved social media sites" should be strictly enforced and backed up by reasonable but meaningful consequences.

Speak Your Truth & Walk Your Talk

Have the crucial conversations and ask the tough questions to ensure your child knows what she needs to do in order to stay safe. When you're willing to talk openly about body safety issues, you signal to your child that it's safe for her to do so as well, and she's more likely to come to you with questions or concerns.

Your willingness to speak your truth and walk your talk gives your child permission to do the same. When you model for your child how to live from a place of integrity and authenticity, you're giving her one of the greatest gifts a child could have—a deep knowledge and acceptance of her *Self*—body, mind, and soul.

Heroic Parenting

Be Aware of What's Going on in Your Child's Life

Be present for your child. He craves your attention and it's one of the most proactive things you can do to keep him safe. Here are some ways to parent up:

- Be a visible presence in your child's life, especially at school. Rock a vibe that says you're a parent who's involved in your child's life and on alert for bad guys.

- Watch for unusual behavior in your child and check into it. Does he act anxious or sullen after he hangs out with a particular person? Is he suddenly acting withdrawn or depressed? You know him better than anyone and are in a unique position to notice concerning changes.

- Pay close attention when others seek out one-to-one access to your child. Don't allow it if you have any concerns about that person.

- Trust your gut. If someone or something doesn't feel right, it probably isn't. Remove yourself and/or your child from that situation or person immediately. It may have been nothing at all or you may have thwarted a molestation or assault. You'll never know what *might* have happened, but you *will* know you took action when your gut warned you to, which is a great thing.

- Perform a background check on anyone who will care for your child, such as sitters and other caregivers, physical and psychological therapists, coaches, and group leaders—even if they were referred by someone you trust. Don't be shy about doing this; your child's safety is more important that your embarrassment.

- Check the state and national sex offender registries on a regular basis. You'll be surprised how many sex offenders live in your neighborhood and immediate vicinity of your home and your child's school!

Provide Supervision

The amount of unsupervised play your child can enjoy is entirely up to you, based on your understanding of her maturity and developmental level and her ability to obey your family rules and handle herself if she encounters a dangerous person along the way.

If you do allow your child to walk or wheel to a friend's house, require her to call you as soon as she arrives there. Immediately. No exceptions. If you know it takes her five minutes to get there and she doesn't call within 10 minutes, go get her and bring her home. She won't be happy about it and that's the point.

Your child won't have a phone at this point, so tell her to use her friend's house phone or her mom's cell phone to call. That way, if something does happen and she doesn't make it to her friend's house, you'll only be a few minutes behind her. And, it's a good way to get her to memorize your number in case of emergency.[178]

Make it a family rule that your child has to come straight home from school and check in before going anywhere to play. Let her know that if she doesn't come straight home within X minutes, there will be a consequence; for example, she won't be able to play with her friends or use her tablet after she's done her homework. Again, if something happens and she's not home within the expected timeframe, you'll know within minutes to begin looking for her.

If your child walks to school, decide with her in advance what route she'll take and have her stick to it. Walk the route with her, pointing out safe places she can run to in an emergency until she's comfortable navigating it herself. You can make it a rule that she only walks to school with a friend or group.

If she's going to ride the bus, write down the bus number and driver's name for her to keep in her backpack to help her remember which bus to get on. Even as a kid I had terrible memory issues (due, I believe, to post-traumatic stress). I once got on the wrong bus when I was in middle school but was too scared and embarrassed to tell the driver. It wasn't until she got to the end of her very long route that she noticed me huddling at the back of the bus. She wasn't happy about having to make another 40-minute round trip to return me home!

Media Time

The Internet puts the whole world at your child's fingertips and can open avenues to social relationships that are harder to navigate in person. That's a great thing, until it's not. It's imperative that you put parental controls on any electronic device she has access to (even the ones you don't allow her to use but that she can get her tricky hands on), so you can feel fairly secure that she won't see inappropriate content.

Still, keep an eye on what she's viewing and the online chats she's having to ensure she's making good choices and not exposing herself to potentially unsafe people or conversations. Also be

---

[178] If she's unable to memorize your number, write it (and your name and address) down on a piece of paper for her to carry. Consider having it laminated so it doesn't fall apart over time.

aware of what your child is watching on the TV and gaming console. Violent and sexual situations can appear even in seemingly "childish" shows.

Support Your Child

Let your child know often that you support her. Tell her you'll always love her no matter what, even if she tells you something scary or bad. Let her know you've got her back and will always do your very best to protect her from harm. Just as importantly, tell her you'll help her learn to protect and defend *herself* so she can feel more confident and in charge of herself and her life.

PART IV

Essential Life Lessons to Keep Your Child Safe

A child's confidence and self-esteem, intuition, and solid boundaries are the very best predator repellants she has at her disposal.

In this section, I'm going to talk about how to instill confidence and self-esteem in your child, how to cultivate her three "superpowers," how to teach her to fight like a rabid Tasmanian Devil, and how to use family meetings to introduce body safety topics into your family conversations.

CHAPTER 15

Fostering Your Child's Confidence & Self-Esteem

"Everyone is a genius. But if you judge a fish by its ability to climb a tree, it will live its whole life believing that it is stupid."

Author Unknown (And no, it WASN'T Einstein)

Like Bear Repellant, Only Better

Do you know what the #1 predator repellant is? It's *confidence!* Children (and adults) who are confident and self-assured are less likely to be targeted by predators. You see, perps like to target kids who have low self-esteem because it makes them more vulnerable and less likely to resist or tell.

Kids with confidence are social magnets. Because they feel good about themselves, they assume other kids will like them and want to play with them. It's very attractive energy. Desperation, on the other hand, is a stinky cologne that other kids and predators can smell from a mile away.

I know how heart-breaking it is to worry about your child when he's shy or socially awkward. When my son was around 7, he was struggling socially after skipping a grade. I wanted him to be tough and able to roll with the punches, but I also wanted to nurture his sensitivity and compassion. Mostly I didn't want him to be a target for bullies.

I had no idea how to raise him to be a strong yet sensitive young man who fit in with his peers. It was agonizing. After many fits and starts, he eventually found his way. Now he's the father of three toddlers, including one boy, and he'll probably have to deal with the same issues.

And *that's* why I wrote this chapter. I don't want you to feel the agony of watching helplessly while your child flails socially, or for him to suffer the pain of not having friends or not being accepted by other kids. This chapter is all about how to instill confidence and self-esteem in your child, which will be life-altering for him.

What Confidence & Self-Esteem Look Like

Confidence and self-esteem go hand-in-hand; it's nearly impossible, really, to have one without the other. Confidence is a feeling of self-assurance that comes from appreciating your own qualities, abilities, and even limitations. People with a healthy sense of self-esteem project confidence and self-respect, and they expect (and generally receive) the respect of others.[179]

Confident people unconsciously ward off predators. They even carry themselves differently (head up, eyes clear) and their very energy projects power and purpose. They may be victimized in one-off incidents, but they are the least likely to be targeted by criminals.

Studies have been done in which convicted criminals were asked to pick out potential targets by looking at videos of them walking down the street. The people who were consistently chosen as potential victims were those who slouched or appeared timid while they walked.

Here's what a child who's confident and has high self-esteem looks like:

- She has a positive outlook on life.

- She doesn't wallow in negative self-talk. She's able to meet new people and quickly make friends.

- She doesn't have a victim mentality, meaning she doesn't feel like life is happening *to* her, outside of her control.

- She doesn't beat herself up over her "weaknesses," focusing more on her strengths.

- She has strong boundaries and the willingness and ability to enforce them.

- She doesn't feel compelled to go along with the crowd or popular opinion.

- She can say no to her peers and even adults when necessary.

- She can accept constructive criticism.

---

[179] And it pays off, literally—studies have proven that teenagers and young adults with high levels of confidence outearn their less confident peers later in life.

- She takes responsibility for her choices.
- She doesn't take everything personally and/or is able to quickly move past personal slights and disappointments.

Toddlers are naturally confident, and their self-esteem is off the charts. They're like puppy dogs who eagerly bounce back after every scolding—unless their spirits are warped over time by dysfunctional family dynamics or verbal, physical, or sexual abuse.

Of course, some kids are naturally shy and anxious with no discernable reason why that might be so. Know that all the above qualities can be nurtured in your child, given enough patience and loving guidance.

What a Lack of Confidence & Self-Esteem Looks Like

The cost of *not* fostering your child's confidence and self-esteem is incredibly high. Without healthy amounts of both, he's more vulnerable and likely to be targeted by bullies and other predators, and he could come to suffer from a host of negative beliefs and behaviors. For example, he might:

- Feel unworthy of respect or positive treatment.
- Engage in negative self-talk and destructive behaviors.
- Feel anxious or depressed.
- Withdraw from peers and social situations.
- Have few or no friends.
- Expect people to treat him badly and passively accept it.
- Put the needs and wants of others ahead of his own.
- Seek out negative attention (meaning he acts out to get attention because he doesn't feel he can get it through positive behavior).
- Resist positive interactions and people.
- Shy away from new experiences.
- Have poor boundaries and an inability to stand up for himself.

- Focus on the negative and believe he's a pawn in the game of life.[180]
- Feel responsible for other people's feelings and problems.
- Trust no one or, alternatively, trust everyone to the point of naiveté.
- Be acutely sensitive to criticism and slights by others.
- Not have the ability to bounce back from disappointment or trauma.

This is such a sad list! And I know way too many kids and adults who carry these tragic characteristics on their weary backs. Of course, children can—and often do—have traits from both categories. Every child is unique and special and that's okay. Just know that you have a lot of power to help your child transform his negative traits into more positive beliefs and behaviors.

Let's talk about how to do just that.

How to Raise a Confident Child with Healthy Self-Esteem

I remember one time when my younger son, then about 12, seemed really glum. When I asked him what was going on, he finally told me that he thought he was ugly. I had to bite my tongue to keep from brushing off his concerns by arguing with him and telling him he was actually quite handsome, which he was (and still is).

Here's what I said instead: "Do you remember the reason you chose Tiger (his cat)?"

My son laughed, "Yeah, he was the most wild and playful one, and he bit me."

"That's right," I said. "You picked Tiger because his personality was different from all the other cats. You didn't want just some ordinary old cat. And do you remember that you also thought his face was really funny?" My son nodded.

"Well, that cute, funny face of his and his wild personality are exactly what make you love him, right?" He nodded again thoughtfully.

I looked at my son deeply, projecting all the love I felt for him from my eyes, and said, "You're cute and funny and you're wild, and *that's* what people love about you! Don't ever change a thing."

My son smiled and said, "Thanks, Mom," and went into his room.

---

180 Like poor Mongo from the movie *Blazing Saddles*, which is one of the funniest—and most politically incorrect—films of all time.

Heroic Parenting

I tell you this story to point out that many, if not most, kids think they're ugly or stupid or socially inept. And it may be true that they're less attractive, less smart, or less socially "ept" than the average bear. If your child feels this way, it's your job, mom and dad, to help him reframe his perspective to better appreciate his uniqueness.

Your Child's Social Reinvention Plan

Reassure your ugly duckling that she'll one day be a social swan, and that you'll work with her to come with a plan to help her do just that. Here's what that plan might include:

Teach your cygnet:[181]

- To take pride in her personal appearance by helping her maintain good personal hygiene. Tell her that others like people who look and smell clean and healthy. Show her how to properly brush her teeth and fix her hair, have her bathe and wash her hair regularly (showing her how to completely shampoo and rinse!), and do your best to dress her like her peers (even thrift stores often have contemporary clothes in stock). Kids who are smelly and look different from everyone else are candidates for bullying.

- About sex and human sexuality so she becomes familiar with her body's functions and more comfortable in her own skin. Knowing what to expect in terms of physical changes as she approaches puberty will keep her from feeling shocked or ashamed when she's taken over by the invasion of the body snatchers.

- To pursue activities she really enjoys and is good at so she'll feel more confident about her abilities and what she has to offer the world.

- Help her identify areas where she could use improvement (e.g., seeing a dermatologist to control her acne or getting a tutor so she can keep up in class). If she comes up with things that can't be "fixed" (like ditching her braces), work with her to alter her attitude about them. Just about anything can be turned into a positive if you think about it the right way.

- The life-changing magic of helping others whenever she can, through both random acts of kindness and regular volunteer efforts (preferably with you by her side, modeling good behavior). I can't say enough about the power of generosity. Helping others in need reconnects your child to humanity and opens her heart to the suffering of others, which helps her develop empathy and compassion and teaches her to appreciate her own good fortune.

---

181 Cygnet = Baby swan.

CJ Scarlet

- To respect herself and to not accept disrespectful behavior from others. Teach her that respect works both ways and that to gain respect, she must first offer it.

- To stand up for the rights and protection of others. That means speaking up to express her disapproval of racist, sexist, or any other "ist" jokes or behavior by others. The offender may get his feelings hurt, but others will have greater respect for her for standing up to mean people.

- How to make friends and be a good friend. (I cover this below.)

- That she always has a choice in how she responds to the slings and arrows of life, including the words and behavior of others. Tell her that life isn't about what happens to her, but how she *deals with what happens to her*.

- That it's okay to laugh at herself. The best way to teach this is to laugh at *yourself!* Point out that often the most embarrassing things become the funniest stories she'll tell years later.

- To gain new skills and learn about responsibility by giving her chores to do around the house. Give her an allowance (however small; it could even be computer or TV time) to increase her confidence and help her develop a solid work ethic. It'll also give her a small income (or that coveted computer or gaming time), which will enhance her feeling of independence.

- To expect that when she tries a new activity or project, she's probably going to suck at it at first. Remind her that everyone's a beginner when they try something new and they feel awkward and uncomfortable and worry about looking stupid. Teach her that she'll get better with practice and perseverance.

- That it's okay to fail; in fact, it's inevitable if she's trying new things and taking healthy risks.

- To be resilient. I learned how to do this by watching my son and daughter-in-law with their children. Rather than rushing in to pick them up every time they fall or fail, Sean and Bekki reassure them that they're okay and to try again.

- To keep a positive attitude and look for the upside of every situation.

- How to sincerely apologize by looking the other person (child or adult) in the eyes and saying: "I'm really sorry." Short, sweet, and effective. Tell her that apologizing resolves most situations and makes people want to forgive her.

- That you'll love her no matter where she falls on the gender and sexual-orientation map. Let her dress like Batman for Halloween or, as my grandson did when he was 2, let him dance with abandon in his sister's Belle costume to the tune of "Let It Go."[182]

- How to make comfortable eye contact with others (not staring them down, remembering to blink, not shifting her eyes back and forth to the sides).

- How to walk (or roll) like a hero. Together, read a book on body language and talk about how she can carry herself more confidently. Have her notice the way other people carry themselves and have her guess what their body language is saying.

- To use her body to protect herself by demonstrating how to use the Taz moves I offer in Chapter 17 and having her do them until she feels comfortable with them. Just knowing that she knows how to protect herself will increase her confidence right there!

A Note about Teaching These Lessons to Children with Disabilities

I recognize that children with disabilities may have a tougher time learning or living these ideas. Especially if she has a disabling condition that leads her to be more impulsive or that affects her physical appearance, she may feel a great deal of shame about herself. Do whatever you can from the Social Reinvention Plan list above to help her find her social footing.

One idea that may help a lot is to Google and watch online videos together about kids with disabilities who are doing cool things. Some deliver speeches internationally, others are blind and climb mountains. Your kid doesn't have to conquer the world or become a daredevil, but I guarantee the perseverance and positivity of these kids will inspire her.

How to Make & Keep Friends

It never occurs to most parents that they need to teach their kids how to make and keep friends, but you'd be surprised by how many children don't have a clue how to comfortably do this. Before the age of 3, young toddlers tend to play *beside* other kids rather than *with* them, and they're likely too young to understand the instructions I'm about to share. From 3 on though, your child is probably hanging out with other kids at playdates or preschool and is becoming more interested in playing with others.

---

182 Yes, I know Let it Go is from *Frozen* and not *Beauty and the Beast*. My grandson didn't care; he just danced!

CJ Scarlet

Making New Friends

Before your child goes on his next playdate or to school, find a quiet time to talk to him about what friendship is and come up with a plan for how to make friends. If your son is new to social situations, say: "This afternoon we're going to the playground and there are going to be lots of kids there to play with. Let's talk about how you can make friends while we're there, so you have someone to play with."

Or, if your child is older but is super shy or nervous about approaching other kids, say: "We're going to Josh's birthday party on Saturday and I want it to be fun for you. I've noticed that at Maria's party you stayed at the table and didn't play with the other children. Can you tell me why?" Encourage him to share his feelings and fears or uncertainty about approaching other children.

Then say: "Why don't we come up with a plan for how you can make friends while we're there (at the playground or the party)?" Expect that your shy or nervous child may not be enthusiastic at this point.

Nevertheless, continue: "Let's talk about what to do. You can go up to one child who's playing by himself and say, 'Hi, my name is Jeremy. What's yours?'" Then you can say: "You can also go up to a group of kids and ask them if you can play with them, by saying, 'Hi, my name is Jeremy. Can I play too?'" Have Jeremy practice introducing himself until he gets the hang of it.

Then say: "After the other child tells you his name, you should ask, 'Do you want to play?' It's that simple!" Take turns asking and being the one asked. Also practice what to do if the other child says no. Say: "If he says no, you can say, 'Ok. Maybe later,' and go up to a different child or group."

Tell Jeremy that if no one wants to play with him (let's face it, kids can be such buttheads sometimes), to let you know so you can help him find a friend. You can help avoid this gut-wrenching scenario by chatting up the other moms (or dads) and working with them to get your kids to play together.

Note: If other kids refuse to play with your child, there might be a reason and you need to investigate to find out why and then address the problem. Do his clothes smell like cat pee? Is he a bully? Is he socially inept and awkward to be around? Does he have a bad reputation because he peed his pants in kindergarten class that one time?

You can do a lot to fix this. Wash his clothes, teach him how to be a kind and friendly, get help to improve his social skills, help him learn to shrug off peer criticism and teasing, implement the social reinvention plan. Parent up and help your child find his footing.

Heroic Parenting

Being a Good Friend

Next, teach your child how to have an actual conversation. Say: "When you're trying to make a new friend, it helps to ask them about themselves. You could say something like, 'I really like your shark shirt. What's your favorite kind of shark?'" Teaching your child to ask open-ended questions that can't be answered by a monosyllabic yes or no will draw the other child out.

It can be tricky teaching this, because kids this age tend to blurt out too much information, which can shock or intimidate other kids. Spend a good amount of time, on multiple occasions, roleplaying conversations with your child, taking turns being the new friend until he gets more comfortable with it.

Teach your child how to compliment others by looking for things he actually likes about the other child. (Advise him to look for neat things about their personality or abilities, rather than their appearance, and tell him not to try to fake it; kids can spot a phony).

Say: "People like it when others notice good things about them. If you like the way another boy runs super-fast or whistles, you could say, 'Wow! That's really cool! Could you teach me how to do that?'"

Teach him how to end their playtime together by thanking the other child: "When you're done playing with someone, you can say, 'That was really fun. Thanks.'" Even young kids like being appreciated and will remember your child for making them feel good.

Badass Grandma's Two Cents

You have the ability to help your child actualize her full potential in all areas of her life—social, emotional, and psychological. Your mini-me looks to you for guidance about how to be a decent and functional human being.

For those of you who were raised by loving, attentive parents who knew what they were doing, you have great role models to follow. For the rest of you who were raised by wolves, well, you have to figure it out as you go along. If you feel confident that you know how to do that, outstanding! If not, read parenting books or ask the awesome parents you know how to teach your child what you yourself weren't taught when you were a kid.

Knowing that you don't have all the answers is half the battle; the other half is being willing to keep searching until you find those answers and then apply them.

You've got this!

CHAPTER 16

Your Child's Three Superpowers

Your Kid Is a Superhero!

I'm going to teach you about three superpowers your child possesses and can summon to protect herself from emotional and physical harm by spotting danger and avoiding it before it escalates. The three superpowers are her:

1. Boundaries
2. Intuition
3. Moxie

Setting & Defending Her Boundaries

The first superpower consists of your child's boundaries, which represent the line she allows people to cross (or not) in her physical and emotional space. While intuition is an innate sense that can be cultivated to protect her from danger, establishing and defending boundaries are skills that must be learned and practiced if they are to become effective.

Healthy boundaries look like a circle, with your child in the middle (as the person she most trusts), surrounded by a slightly larger circle that she saves for you and her closest friends and loved ones, and then outer circles for acquaintances and people she doesn't know. On the outer limits, outside all the circles, are people she doesn't trust.

When talking about this with your child, actually draw these circles and have her name where people go on the drawing. It might surprise you who she chooses to put on the outer limits, which should prompt lots of questions from you to discern why she doesn't trust them.

Unhealthy boundaries are vague, and in some cases may be totally missing in action. I think of it as a watercolor painting; the edges are blurry and undefined. People with wobbly boundaries bleed into other people and others bleed into them.

This is often the case for those who've been victimized by people they should have been able to trust. When a child is abused, her boundaries become confused, leading her to either not trust anyone or to allow everyone to trample them.

You are your child's best teacher in this area. Your job is to talk to her about boundaries and help her decide what *hers* are, and then teach her how to recognize when they're being violated and how to defend them. The rest of the world will reinforce what you teach her by testing her boundaries on a regular basis. If you've done a good job with your role, these lessons from the rest of the world will be instructive rather than traumatic.

Predators WILL test a potential victim's boundaries to determine whether she'll make a good target. They may first attempt to cross her emotional boundaries by making suggestive or inappropriate comments or jokes to see how the child reacts. If she smiles nervously or freezes and doesn't react, the predator will push further in an attempt to manipulate her into a bad situation.

If someone crosses a physical or emotional boundary with your child, you want her to know how to stop the offender in his tracks—whether it's a stranger or someone she knows well. A simple, "Stop. I don't like that," may be all it takes.

How to Respond to Boundary Violations

Here are some polite but firm responses to boundary violations you can teach your child to use:

- "No thank you."
- "I don't want to sit on your lap."
- "Please don't touch me. My parents said that's not okay."
- "I don't like that. Please stop."
- "Don't do that."
- "My Mom/Dad said that's wrong, so stop it."

- "No!"
- "Stop!"

Your child can use these simple phrases to set boundaries any time someone makes her feel uncomfortable. Knowing she has permission to tell others "no," including adults and authority figures, gives her tremendous power and advantage. Often, reinforcing a boundary like that with a perp who's trying to groom her lets him know she's not going to meekly comply and is very likely to tell on him. That's the last thing he wants, so he'll most likely stop the offending behavior.

How to Teach Her about Boundaries

As you educate your baby badger about her boundaries and how to defend them, also teach her to honor other people's boundaries. This means, for example, asking others for permission before giving hugs or touching them, giving them privacy in the bathroom and bedroom, and stopping a particular behavior when asked to do so.

In Chapter 13, I talked about how to teach your child about boundaries in an age-appropriate way. Please refer to that section for more on this subject.

Teaching Your Child to Honor His Intuition

Your child's second superpower appears when he trusts his intuition—or gut. His body is a finely tuned instrument of wisdom and knowing; it's constantly giving him cues about his environment and the people in it. Some of these cues, which you can teach your child to watch for, include:

- A feeling of wariness or foreboding.
- A nagging feeling that something isn't right.
- Feelings of panic or anxiety.
- Fear or apprehension.
- A sense of doubt or hesitancy.
- A sick or sinking feeling in his stomach.
- The hair on the back of his neck and arms may stand up, just as it does in animals who sense something threatening in their environment.

- Shortened, shallow breathing.
- A pounding heart.
- A rushing sensation in his ears or head.
- Tunnel vision.
- Difficulty hearing.

Teach your child to trust that when these sensations appear, something isn't right in his environment and he needs to act IMMEDIATELY to remove himself from the situation, even if it means being rude to an adult.

That may mean excusing himself to use the bathroom and sneaking out the back door to escape, or it may mean forcefully yelling at the offender to back off. Teach him to do *whatever* it takes to honor his intuition and protect himself.

Acting on His Intuition

Emphasize to your child that he shouldn't give someone the benefit of the doubt if he feels uncomfortable around them. Teach him to challenge them in whatever way is appropriate at that moment, whether it's warning them to stop the offending behavior and running away, yelling for help, or fighting like a Tasmanian Devil (which I explain in the next chapter). Give your child free rein to do what's necessary to stop the offender and get away from him as fast as possible.

Tell your child not to be afraid of being wrong or looking silly. When he tells someone to back off and give him space, if the offender's a good guy, he'll do it and probably apologize. If he's a predator, he might get angry with your child and try to make him feel badly about setting a boundary. This is your child's cue that this person is not to be trusted and to get away from them as fast as his little legs can carry him.

Give Your Child a Fighting Chance

Let me just stop here for a moment and address those of my readers who are right now thinking, "My child is too young/nice/polite/timid/afraid/insert your own objection here."

All that may be true, but you've got to give your kid a fighting chance here. Teach him what he needs to know about how to recognize and act on his intuition and keep emphasizing how to take action if he needs to. He's more likely to repel creepy people when he knows about boundaries and intuition than if you don't teach him anything about them. At the very least, even if he is frozen and doesn't react in the moment to protect himself, he'll be more likely to tell you if something bad happens. Makes sense, right?

Teach your child that before he sits on that person's lap or obeys the command of an adult that gives him that "uh-oh" feeling in his stomach, to THINK about what he's doing. Tell him to check in with his intuition and his body to get their opinions first. He doesn't owe it to anyone to do what they want, even if they're persistent (and bad guys will be persistent).

If he feels okay about doing whatever it is he's considering and it aligns with his intuition and integrity, he should do it. If it doesn't resonate with him and he has doubts, he shouldn't do it. It's that simple.

The more in tune your little porcupine is with his inner voice, the more quickly he'll recognize and listen to it when he needs it. When it tells him to be careful, to do something different, teach him to heed that voice! It's his best friend and it won't steer him wrong.

Acting on YOUR Intuition

Your intuition is your first line of defense when protecting your child. You MUST pay attention when it tells you a particular person isn't to be trusted, even when the rest of the world insists there's nothing wrong.

When your radar or your child's indicates that a particular person is "iffy," do NOT ignore that warning! One way to handle a situation where a person creeps your child out (but hasn't done anything overtly inappropriate), is to talk to them.

By saying something as simple as: "Tommy doesn't like it when you tickle him. Please don't do that anymore," you're putting the offender on notice that he's being watched, which will almost certainly cause him to write your child off as a target. If you're not comfortable talking to the person by yourself, you can ask another adult or someone in authority to be there with you. Or, if you're really chicken, you can have that other person talk to them for you. Do whatever you need to do to deliver the message that the offender needs to back off.

A Word on the Importance of Situational Awareness

Put simply, situational awareness means your child knows what's going on around him. Not having it means he's clueless and a bullseye for predators. Predators are generally opportunistic; they tend to look for victims they consider easy marks, and many crimes are crimes of opportunity, meaning they seize the chance to molest or assault a child because the opportunity is there and there's a good chance they won't be caught.

Children are automatically considered to be vulnerable targets by perps because they're small, innocent, and trusting. Plus, they often aren't paying attention to what's going on around them. Awareness of his environment and the people around him is a necessary skill you must teach your child and have him practice so it becomes second nature. His awareness feeds his gut information it needs to decide whether he's safe or not. When his intuition is triggered, he needs to laser focus on what the problem is. If he can't discern any obvious reason for his gut reaction, tell him to trust it anyway and remove himself from the situation.

Your Child's Moxie

Your little Avenger's third superpower is her moxie, also called "nerve" or "chutzpah." It's your child's willingness to stand in her power to honor her intuition and defend her boundaries. It means summoning her inner tigress and walking her talk. It means being as rude or aggressive as necessary to someone who's setting off alarm bells in her body and pushing her boundaries past the breaking point.

Badass Grandma's Two Cents

Remember when I told you that the words you say to your child become her inner voice? It's true; you have a place of honor in her little noggin that will last throughout her lifetime—whether she likes it or not. Teach her to use that voice when she needs guidance. If she's in a tough spot where her intuition is blaring and she feels frozen with indecision about how to respond, she should ask herself the following question: "What would my mom or dad tell me to do?"

Chances are your child has a good idea of what you'd advise. The more in tune she is with her intuition, the more quickly she'll recognize and listen to it when she needs it. When it tells her to be careful, to do something different, she needs to *heed that voice*! It's her best friend and it won't steer her wrong.

Encourage her to trust her gut and her body, and then ACT! If she responds by defending herself from a threatening person—whether it's verbally or physically, or even by just removing herself from the situation—she sends a signal that it's *not* okay for the perpetrator to escalate his advances. Let her know she can be as polite or rude as needed to maintain her boundaries and safety.

CHAPTER 17

Fighting Like a Rabid Tasmanian Devil

Channeling Her Inner Tasmanian Devil

Think your child can't protect herself because she's not a martial artist? Hasn't taken formal self-defense classes? Because she's too young? Physically disabled? Too timid?

Have you ever tried to drag a resisting child to bed? When her tiny little body goes limp and she does that frustrating slinky thing, she might as well weigh a thousand pounds. Resisting kids are almost impossible to maneuver where you want them to go. Your child can use that same maneuver with a predator who's trying to pick her up or take her away.

You'd be surprised how much damage your darling can do when she's motivated by fear and anger. I like to teach kids and adults how to fight by having them channel their "inner Tasmanian Devil."

Although just the size of a small dog at around 15 pounds, the Australian Tasmanian Devil has the strongest bite of any land mammal and is so ferocious it can repel almost any predator that comes its way. If you recall the old Looney Tunes cartoons, "Taz" is a whirlwind of fists and feet, fangs, and raw power. In addition, the real Tasmanian Devil uses a pungent body odor and nerve-racking screech to ward off its enemies.

Never forget, your child always has powerful weapons at her disposal—all contained within the body she walks around in—should she need them in the event of an attack.

Using His Bodily Weapons to Protect Himself

Fear is our friend. It's your child's friend too because it tells him that he's in danger. Fear isn't to be squelched; it's to be used as rocket fuel to propel your child into action to save his little butt from harm.

Say: "If you follow our family rules, they should keep you safe. But if anyone ever tries to pick you up or take you away without my permission, or if they try to do something inappropriate to you and you can't run away, you can always try to fight them off. You know who Taz is, right?"

Explain, if necessary, that he's the Tasmanian Devil cartoon character. Go so far as to look up a YouTube video of one of the Taz cartoons on the web to show your child how he spins and wreaks havoc. Then continue, "Well, I'm going to teach you to fight just like Taz so you can get away from bad people."

After you've taught him the "Taz" techniques, make your little ninja show you how he'd fight and yell, using a pillow or couch cushion he can hit and kick. Gently correct his form or encourage him to yell more loudly as needed to help him get it down pat. Make it fun! Say: "I give you my permission to be just as wild as you can get and fight as hard as you can to get away from bad people, even if it means hurting them."

You need to let your child know that if he has to fight off an attacker or would-be kidnapper, he has your permission to do so with as much ferocity and ruthlessness as he can muster. Encourage him to fight as dirty and unfairly as he can, going for the predator's weakest spots—the groin, nose, and throat, and anywhere else on their body he can grab or twist.

By yelling at the top of his lungs and biting, clawing, kicking, gouging, and punching every vulnerable point he can reach on the perpetrator's body, your child gives himself the best chance to get away and find help.

Tell him to get angry! Tell him to get FURIOUS! After all, this person is trying to hurt him! Tell him to do whatever it takes to stop the bad man or woman. He doesn't owe it to them to be nice or polite. Again, give him permission to unleash his inner Tasmanian Devil and fight as dirty as he possibly can until he can get away or the perpetrator leaves the scene.

Predators are incredible cowards; they choose victims based on whether they think they can control them. If your child goes off like a rabid animal the minute someone starts to mess with him, he'll make predators think twice before choosing him as a target.

Martial Arts & Self-Defense Classes—Yes or No?

I highly recommend enrolling your child in martial arts or self-defense courses, *in addition to* teaching him the Taz moves below. All these will increase your child's self-confidence and help him better fight back against predators.

But I have one caveat: Don't think that having him take a few classes is going to cut it. In fact, taking just one or a handful of classes could give him a false sense of security. For the training to stick in your child's mind and muscle memory, he must master the techniques, which requires years of practice. Again, I think this training is a great idea when your eye is on long-term mastery.

It's Go Time!

Teach your child that if a predator begins to physically attack her, she should begin yelling as loudly as she can (yelling is more powerful than screaming, and it will help her breathe and make her sound more powerful). Loudly yelling "NO! Get away from me!" prepares her mind to defend her body, it can summon attention and help, and it will let the predator know she won't be an easy target.

If yelling doesn't send the perpetrator running or your child can't get away and must fight, teach her to begin fighting like Taz for all she's worth, using the techniques I share below.

Her Body's Arsenal

Teach your child the following techniques, being sure to roleplay and practice them (using a couch cushion or pillow and being careful not to actually hurt you or herself):

Voice: Remember that her voice is one of the most powerful tools in her self-defense arsenal. While she's fighting, she should screech, howl, and yell as loudly as she can to both bring attention to the situation and to scare the perp into running away.

Eyes: If she's in a furious fight for her life with the predator, tell her to go for his eyes with her fingers. She should scratch or poke him in the eyes and press as hard as she can until the perpetrator backs off, hopefully giving her time to run away.

Head: Whether she's being held from the front or behind, she can swing her head forward or backward into the predator's face or head. I don't recommend attempting to head butt him with her forehead. This may look cool in the movies, but the forehead is actually a fairly sensitive area. Tell her to use the top or back of her skull to connect with his face.

Teeth: Your child should chomp down on any body part that comes close to her face. It doesn't matter where she bites the offender, it's going to hurt so bad he'll howl with pain. With luck, the attacker will stop whatever he's doing, giving her precious distance and time to get into a better fighting position or run away, if she can.

Heroic Parenting

Palm: She should use the butt of her open palm to hit upward onto the attacker's chin or nose. A good slam with the butt of her hand can snap the perpetrator's head back and make his eyes water so she can run away. (Remember, you're showing her how to do these moves as you talk about them. I have several videos on my website that show you these techniques. You can find them on my video blog at www.cjscarlet.com/vlog.)

Fist: Her closed fist can be used to pound on the attacker like a hammer. (Show her how to keep her thumb on the outside of her fist so she doesn't break her fingers.)

Fingers: Pinching and twisting the predator's skin is *incredibly* painful. Tell her to grab the attacker's skin and twist as hard as she can and to not let go until he backs off. Again, she can use her fingers to gouge and scratch the attacker's eyes and skin.

Elbow: She can slam her elbow into the predator's chest, stomach, face, or head (anywhere, really).

Arms: Your kid can also grab onto something stable—a pole, a tree, her bike—and refuse to let go, screaming at the top of her lungs: "Stop! Help! Stranger!" the whole time until the perp gives up and runs for it.

Knees: She can use her knees to kick the perpetrator in the groin when she's in close range or smash it into his nose when he's bent over. She should keep kneeing him until he falls to the ground so she can run away.

Feet: Her feet can be dangerous when she swipes, stomps, and kicks any of the predator's body parts as violently as she can manage.

Whole body: Your child can rotate her arms really fast in a big circle, like a windmill, to keep the predator from getting close enough to grab her. Remind her to keep yelling for help while she's using her body to fight the attacker off.

Again, I go back to the image of the cartoon Taz who is literally a tornado of fury and might. Your child's battle with a predator doesn't have to win points for form or style; tell her just go completely bonkers and she'll take him by surprise and rattle him, hopefully making him flee the scene in fear of his own life!

Tell her not to stop until:

- The predator stops his attack.
- The predator flees the scene.

- She's disabled the predator enough that he can't follow her if she runs away.
- Help arrives and she's safe from the predator.

Work with your child to practice these moves over and over until she feels comfortable and able to do them. For children 4 to 9, I would advise making it a monthly routine to practice the Taz moves. The monthly family meetings I suggest in the next chapter would be the perfect time for practice sessions.

Note: When you do this, emphasize that *the Taz moves are for self-defense in actual emergencies only* and are not to be used against siblings or friends during fights or play.

Many of these moves can be done by children with disabilities too, so don't think your child is defenseless just because she's in a wheelchair or uses braces. Of course, you want to be sensitive to her maturity and developmental level when you broach this subject with her, but DO teach her how to defend herself to the best of her ability.

Remember, your child has more power than either you or she may think, and she can exercise that power to escape dangerous situations. So, encourage her to let loose her inner Taz!

CHAPTER 18

Daily Sharing & Family Meetings

I've said it several times—confidence is the #1 predator repellant. And where does a child's confidence come from? His parents, through the positive attention you provide and through ongoing communication that lets your child know he's loved and cared for.

Of course, parents are constantly paying attention to their children, but how much of that is mindful, purposeful attention versus just reacting to what their children are doing in any given moment? For "attention" to count, both parent and child must be emotionally and mentally *present* and focused on each other.

Two great ways to make this a habit are to conduct daily check-ins to ensure you're on top of the issues your child is dealing with, and family meetings, which provide prime opportunities to talk about body safety issues and make important decisions as a family.

Daily Sharing

Everyone likes to do a data dump at the end of the day. A good venting, as long as it doesn't devolve into an angry rant that contaminates the person listening, is healthy and enables you to release the cares of your day and start your family time with greater energy and patience.

The daily check-in is a conversation you have with your child as you're driving him home from daycare or school, or as you're fixing dinner. (You can do it any time at the end of the day, really, although I don't recommend doing it right before you put him to bed unless you want him lying awake for the next hour pondering his day.)

Making it a daily ritual helps you stay on top of the issues and challenges your child is dealing with. Just as importantly, it shows him that you're paying attention and are interested in his perspective on life—major confidence boosters.

CJ Scarlet

Asking Questions

If you merely ask, "How was your day, hon?" while you're thumbing through your phone, you're going to get a quiet, "Fine" and that's about it. C'mon, man! You can do better than that! And so can your kid. His day wasn't "fine;" it was filled with laughter and frustration and wonder and all kinds of epic fails.

Asking your child open-ended questions will ensure you get more than simple yes or no answers and create a stronger connection between you. Below are my favorite questions to ask kids.

Badass Grandma's "Top 10" Sharing Questions

1. Did anything really funny happen today that made you laugh?
2. Did you help someone else today? What did you do? How did that make you feel?
3. Did anyone get in trouble today? Why? What did you learn from that kid's experience?
4. Did anyone pick on other kids? What happened? Has he ever picked on you?
5. Did anything make your intuition go "uh-oh?"
6. What's the most interesting thing you learned today?
7. Did you have any epic fails today? How did you handle it? What did you learn?
8. If you could change one thing about your day, what would it be?
9. What was the highlight of your day and what was the low point?
10. What are you looking forward to tomorrow?

I think you can see how being asked these questions will lead your child to think more deeply about his day and encourage him to look for ways to help others or the environment, for example, so he can tell you about it later.

Of course, you can choose totally different questions to ask. The point is to pay attention to and connect with your child. Commit to giving him at least 15 uninterrupted minutes of your time. Admit it, you spent more time than that at the water cooler today listening to your crazy coworker rant about her ex!

Heroic Parenting

Zen & the Art of Conversation with a Kid

Speaking of paying attention, when you do the daily sharing with your child, you have to actually *listen* to him. He'll know if you're secretly ticking off the seconds until you can get back to your Instagram feed and it'll make him feel like trash. So *be present* with him.

If your brain isn't engaged because you forgot to change that oh-so-important meeting from 10:00 to 11:00 tomorrow, call your assistant and let her know so you don't have to worry about it. Then give your undivided attention to your son.

And don't just listen to him, *hear* him. Acknowledge his feelings, ask probing questions, commiserate, laugh, help him problem solve. You'll learn things that delight you and you'll learn things that scare the daylights out of you and require you to look deeper.

The point isn't just to praise the positive and resolve the negative; the point is to share his life, day by day. You won't solve all the problems of the world in 15 minutes, but you'll send the message to your child that you care about him and are on his side.

Be with your child on his journey through childhood by sharing this precious time with him. One day you'll look back and wish you had that time with him again. Don't miss a moment of it!

Validation Works

When your child is sharing, you don't want to just sit there and go "uh-huh, uh-huh." Nor do you want to jump in and tell him what he should do to stop his friend Jorge from calling him names. Below are four simple ways to respond to him that will show him you're paying attention and are on the same page:

Mirroring

This is a way to validate what your son is saying by reflecting (not parroting, which is irritating) his words back to him. For example, if he says: "Jorge called me a name and I really hate him!" You might say: "It sounds like Jorge hurt your feelings and that made you feel mad?"

The question mark at the end of your sentence leads your child to go deeper into his feelings. (Note that I didn't tell you to jump in and tell him that he shouldn't say "hate." This isn't the time to be judgmental; it's the time to draw your child's feelings out so he can explore and work through them.)

When you reflect your son's overarching emotions back to him, it invites him to continue: "Yeah! I'm *really* mad at Jorge! I wish he wouldn't call me names." This then gives you the opportunity to help him problem solve: "What could you do to let Jorge know that you don't like it when he teases you?"

Now the ball is in your son's court. Zip your pie hole[183] and let him think about it; I guarantee he'll come up with a workable solution on his own.

If he throws out a zinger: "I could punch him in his stupid face!" gently guide him to think about more constructive options: "OR... what about talking to him? What could you say?" The point is, don't TELL him what to do, help him think it through until he has a solid plan.

Clarifying

Asking clarifying questions enables you to draw your child out and dig deeper into a story or issue. Some examples include: "Can you tell me more about that?" and "I'm not sure I understand. Do you mean…?"

Paraphrasing

Paraphrasing is similar to mirroring, but rather than seeking to validate, you're looking for clarification: "It sounds like you're saying you wish Jorge wouldn't pick on you. Have I got that right?" This is really helpful for kids because it helps them identify big emotions they may not know how to express.

Summarizing

When your child has reached a conclusion in a story he's telling or a problem he's figured out, you can help him by summarizing what he said or decided: "So tomorrow you're going to talk to Jorge to let him know that it hurts your feelings when he calls you names, and that you'd like him to stop. Have I got that right?" Asking this last question gives him the chance to correct you if you heard him incorrectly or to add more to it.

If He Discloses Something

When you ask Question #4 from my Badass Grandma's Top 10 list above ("Did anyone pick on other kids? What happened? Has he ever picked on you?"), your child may drop a truth bomb in the middle of the conversation, telling you that he's being bullied. Your first reaction may be to rush in and fix everything for him.

---

183 Pie hole = Your mouth.

Heroic Parenting

Not so fast, Mom/Dad. Hear him out, try to get to the bottom of the situation to see how serious it is, and determine whether you need to step in (if it's gotten physical, DO step in) or if your child can work this out himself.

Kids disagree, they fight, they call each other names... and then they often resolve it quickly all by their little selves. Your job isn't to go into lecture mode and tell him how to fix things, it's to help him figure things out for himself by asking what *he* thinks he should do.

But if, when you ask Question #5 ("Did anything make your intuition go uh-oh?"), your child says yes and discloses any type of abuse, stay calm and ask for more information. Then, after you're done talking to him, handle that situation *tout suite*.[184] Report what you learned to the police and/or Child Protective Services, as outlined in the Appendix.

Taking Advantage of Teachable Moments

Outside of your daily check-ins, you'll have plenty of spontaneous conversations that can be turned into body safety teachable moments. This may be while you're riding in the car together or eating ice cream in the park.

You could play the "what if" game,[185] asking "what if" questions like:

- What would you do if someone tries to hurt you or your private parts?
- What if this person was someone you know?
- What if this person asks you to keep a secret?

These questions and others that I've mentioned earlier in this book offer your child the chance to talk through how to respond to tricky situations. Don't just jump into the yucky scenarios right off the bat, rather, start with more innocuous questions like: "What's the first thing you would do if I told you that you could go over to Dana's house to play?" Correct answer: "I'd call you as soon as I got to her house to tell you I made it safely."

Your response: "Good! That's right! And what if, on the way to Dana's, another kid asked you to come play with them first?" Correct answer: "I'd tell them I have to ask you for permission first. So, I'd go right to Dana's and call you to ask for permission."

---

[184] Tout suite = Right away.
[185] As described by Gary Martin Hays and Adam Weart in their book *The Authority on Child Safety: How to talk to your kids about their personal safety without scaring them.*

See how one "what if" question leads naturally to the next? You and your child will quickly get the gist of the game and have fun playing it.

Monthly Family Meetings

Daily check-ins are great and they're an important way to stay in close touch with your individual child's feelings and experiences on a day-to-day basis. Family meetings, on the other hand, are for talking through big issues that affect your whole family, like discussing family values or body safety topics, choosing where to go for an upcoming vacation, or announcing a major transition like a move to a new city.

Family meetings serve a number of purposes, including:

- **Reducing stress:** You can get everyone on the same page by syncing calendars and expectations.

- **Bringing dads into the loop:** Let's get real here; moms do the lioness' share of the work when it comes to managing the household and caring for the kids. (No offense meant, dads, but seriously, you've GOT to step it up! Props to the dads who are carrying their weight, and to single dads who are carrying it all!) Family meetings give slacker dads a chance to bond, clue them into what's going on with the rest of the fam, and make them part of the team.

- **Building a strong foundation:** Families that communicate regularly and have each other's backs are families that can weather any storm together.

- **Clearing the air:** When families create time to discuss issues affecting its members, problems don't fester and turn into crises.

- **Teaching your child valuable life skills:** During family meetings, your child will learn about cooperation and compromise, leadership, and decision-making, all of which will increase her social skills and self-esteem. Also, following the Family Meeting calendar I provide on my website[186] ensures your child is taught vital body safety lessons in a supportive, nurturing environment.

Introducing the Idea

Your 4 to 9-year-old[187] is unlikely to complain about the idea of introducing regular family meetings, especially if you tell her they'll be followed by food and fun! Associating family

---

186 www.cjscarlet.com/freebies
187 I wouldn't try to introduce children under 4 to family meetings unless they have older siblings and you want them to be included.

meetings with pizza and games will cause everyone to look forward to them and want to participate.

Make it clear to your child that while you, as the parent(s) have the final say in all matters, her input is encouraged and will be respected. Whenever possible, let her make the decisions that will impact her.

Family Meeting Guidelines

Family meetings will work best if you have clear guidelines everyone can follow. For younger kids, especially, routine is important. Here are some guidelines to consider:

- **Have a schedule and block it off on your calendar**. I recommend choosing a day and time each month that's easy to remember, say, the first or last Sunday on the month at 5 pm (if you plan on having a pizza party and games afterward) or after your usual family dinner. Weekend days are best because there's less competition from work or school projects and, thus, less stress.

- **Rotate meeting responsibilities**. Have family members take turns being the leader, secretary, and timekeeper. Playing these roles will teach your child leadership skills and responsibility and make her feel important. She'll be ready to take on each of these roles, with help from you, when she's around 6. The leader follows the agenda. The secretary takes notes of the topics that are discussed, decisions that are made, and issues that are placed in the "parking lot" (meaning they're to be discussed later in the meeting or at the next meeting). The timekeeper makes sure the meeting moves along at a brisk pace and doesn't go off on a tangent. For kids 4 to 6, try to keep the meeting to 15-20 minutes. For children 7 to 9, shoot for 20-30 minutes.[188]

- **Discuss one topic and solve just one problem at a time**. If the conversation gets off base with too many issues being batted around, the leader (or parent, if the leader is a child) should pull in the reins, remind everyone what the topic on the table is, and ask the secretary to put all other issues on the "parking lot" list.

- **Only one person talks at a time**. Teach your child how to respectfully listen to others by ensuring only one person speaks at a time. Consider using a "talking stick." This could be as simple as a stick from the back yard, but it would be more fun and special if you and your child choose something meaningful, like a cool bedazzled wand or something that you decorate together. It could also be a "talking rock" or stuffed animal. Choose something your child will respect as denoting the holder's right to speak their truth.

---

188 Your meetings may go longer, depending on what you choose to cover.

- **Create a "no judgment" zone.** At the beginning of each meeting, remind your family members that no thought, emotion, or idea is off the table (within the bounds of good behavior and decency, of course). Especially when it comes to the Q&A[189] portion of the body safety lessons, you don't want to stifle or shame your child.

- **Use "I" messages.** Saying: "When you do X, I feel angry" is more productive than if you say in a blaming voice: "You make me angry." (After all, no one can make us *feel* anything. We always have a choice in how we respond. Yes, we do. Don't argue with me on this cause I'll prove you wrong!)

- **Celebrate each other.** People, especially kids, are positively starving for validation and recognition. Many of us never got that from our families when we were growing up. Don't be that parent. Lavishly celebrate each other's accomplishments.

What to Cover in Your Family Meetings

It's really important to establish a routine with your family meetings so they're both fun and productive. Consider including the following:

- The designated leader opens with a favorite quote, story, or prayer.
- The leader goes over the agenda so everyone knows what to expect.
- The secretary reads the ground rules:
    - This is a safe, confidential space. No one will share what we talk about outside the family unless given permission to do so.
    - Speak your truth, using "I" statements.
    - Everyone is to be respectful and treated with respect in return.
    - Only one person talks at a time. Everyone else listens.
    - It's okay to disagree, but keep it kind. No yelling or finger-pointing allowed.
- A parent talks about the body safety topic of the month.[190]
- Q&A on the body safety topic.

---

189 Q&A = Questions and answers.
190 I provide you with a sample calendar on my website at www.cjscarlet.com/freebies.

Heroic Parenting

- Roleplaying on the body safety topic. Make your child repeat what you've taught her and make her show you, rather than tell you how she'd react to an inappropriate situation or person.

- Make decisions as a family about things like vacations and family activities. To reach a decision, do the following:

    - Lay out the idea for everyone to consider.

    - Let each person take a turn sharing their perspective and suggestions. (Use the talking stick to keep the conversation in control.)

    - Discuss the pros and cons of each suggestion on the table.

    - Make a decision or agree on a solution. Remember that you (and your partner) have the final say, but you want to let your child's suggestions count. (To let her down easy, say: "You have really great ideas. I don't think we're ready yet as a family for a puppy, but we can discuss it again in six months," or something like that.) Choose her ideas whenever you can.

    - Develop a plan of action, including who's responsible for each task and when they need to do them. Make sure you give your child at least one task that's her responsibility. Even if she's only 4, you can find something for her to do to help.

- Share information that will affect all family members (e.g., a change in your child's school schedule or routine, an upcoming move, deciding whether to get a new pet, etc.).

- Plan and coordinate weekly schedules.

- Always end with a "freaking lovefest." When I was the CEO of an international coaching company, my team always ended every business retreat with a freaking lovefest. It's simple: You pick one person at a time to be the object of everyone's attention. One by one, each family member tells the person who's "on the spot" something they really love about them. Once everyone else has shared something with that person, you move on to the next person who becomes the center of attention. Get creative and specific. Don't lame out and say: "I love you because you're kind." Say instead: "I love the way you share with your little brother. That's so kind of you. You're a great big sister."

- Bring it in for a hug!

CHAPTER 19

Badass Grandma's Final Thoughts

NO!

I wish I had the power to teach that word to every child in the world and give them permission to use it when they feel uncomfortable or threatened. It sure would have saved me a lot of pain and trauma. It can save your child too.

I've been a professional writer for 40 years now and I can honestly say that writing *Heroic Parenting* has been the most grueling, heart-wrenching, mind-numbing, and gratifying work I've ever done. It was a genuine labor of love; one I undertook initially to protect my own sweet grandbabies, but which grew into a larger mission to protect every child on the planet.

My goal in writing this book is to shift the current paradigm[191] in which kids are pretty much left to figure things out for themselves to one in which parents empower their kids to be safe, savvy, and confident.

I believe with all my heart that if every parent would apply what I teach in this guide, we could dramatically and perhaps even permanently alter the cycle of violence against children that has plagued our society for as long as there have been humans walking the earth.

What You (Hopefully) Learned

In *Heroic Parenting*, I taught you how to help your child learn to set and maintain strong boundaries, trust her gut, and take action to enforce those boundaries and act on her intuition. In the process, you learned a TON of new facts, stats, and probably more information than you bargained for about the dangers and dangerous people your child might encounter.

---

[191] A paradigm is a framework or "just the way things are 'round here." It's used to refer to socially accepted models that often need to be changed for people and societies to move forward.

Heroic Parenting

If some chapters made you wince or had your head spinning, I apologize. These are not pretty subjects we covered, but I hope the occasional spoonful of sugar (my humor) helped the medicine go down a bit easier.

AND you're actually much smarter now that you've read this book! Just through the footnotes alone you learned more than five dozen new words and cultural phrases you can casually drop around your mom and dad peers when you're at the next PTA[192] meeting.

My job as your guide is to make your job as a parent easier and less stressful. Hopefully you found everything you need in this book. If you were left with unanswered questions, I'd be happy to answer them for you if I can. Just ping me on the contact page of my website at www.cjscarlet.com/contact or email me directly at cj@cjscarlet.com. I'll also post your questions on the website to ensure everyone has access to my answers.

Finally, I *highly* encourage you to read my second book in this *Heroic Parenting* series (to be released in 2021) on protecting kids from 10 to 18 to see what's coming down the line for you in terms of your child's needs and development.

Thank you, from the bottom of my heart, for sticking with me and for being the parent your child deserves.

You, my dear, are a seriously heroic parent!

P.S. If your child has been the victim of sexual abuse and/or your child's case is reported to law enforcement, you'll want to be sure to read the Appendix on If Your Child Has Been Sexually Abused, which appears below the book's Acknowledgments, and check out my handout on Legal Remedies, which can be found on my website at www.cjscarlet.com/freebies.

P.P.S. *Did I ever tell you that you're my favorite? :-)*

---

192 PTA = Parent Teacher Association.

ABOUT THE AUTHOR

CJ Scarlet is a danger expert, victim advocate, and crime survivor herself. She's also the doting grandma of three precocious toddlers. She's helped thousands of crime victims, but when confronted with the simple innocence of her grandchildren, she felt utterly helpless. How to protect them? More importantly, how to teach them to protect themselves?

Heroic Parenting: An Essential Guide to Raising Safe, Savvy, Confident Kids is Scarlet's way of doing just that and, in the process, helping parents protect their loved ones too.

An expert in victims' rights and advocacy, CJ has given speeches and workshops at national and international events; and has appeared on numerous radio and television programs, including *MSNBC* and *NPR*. She's also the author of *Badass Parenting: An Irreverent Guide to Raising Safe, Savvy, Confident Kids*, *The Badass Girl's Guide: Uncommon Strategies to Outwit Predators* and *Neptune's Gift: Discovering Your Inner Ocean*.

The former roller-skating carhop, forest firefighter, and US Marine photojournalist holds an interdisciplinary master's degree in Humanities with an emphasis on human violence from Old Dominion University.

Named one of the "Happy 100" people on the planet, CJ's story of triumph over adversity is featured in two bestselling books, including *Happy for No Reason* and *Be Invincible*.

CJ Scarlet

If you enjoyed this book, please post a review on Amazon to encourage others to read it so they can protect their children too. *(I really appreciate it!)*

Sign up for CJ Scarlet's FREE parenting resources and blog at www.cjscarlet.com.

To reach CJ Scarlet for media inquiries and speaking opportunities, or to talk to her about her books, contact her at cj@cjscarlet.com.

ACKNOWLEDGEMENTS

No man is an island,

entire of itself;

every man is a piece of the continent,

a part of the main.

If a clod be washed away by the sea,

Europe is the less,

as well as if a promontory were.

as well as if a manor of thy friend's

or of thine own were.

Any man's death diminishes me,

because I am involved in mankind;

and therefore never send to know for whom the bell tolls;

it tolls for thee.

This passage is as moving and timeless today as it was when English poet John Donne wrote it nearly 400 years ago.

CJ Scarlet

This woman (*moi*) certainly is no island and this book would never have been conceived or written if not for the encouragement, love, and support of many gracious people:

- To my sweet, adorable, super-intelligent, and incredibly good-looking grandbabies for inspiring me to write this book to protect your precious little bodies, and to protect other children in the process.

- To both of my sons for tolerating my well-intentioned but often clunky care. I hope I didn't do irreparable damage. If I did, you know where to send the therapy bills.

- To Sean and Bekki for being the most amazing examples of good parenting I could hope to witness, and for encouraging me to stay true to myself and my brand.

- To my mom and dad for not smothering us all with a pillow. I get it now. I really do.

- To my sister Susan for tolerating me and for making me stop to laugh at the roses.

- To the wonderful people at Turkeyland Cove Foundation for gifting me with my magical three-week retreat at the Treehouse so I could write the first draft of this book. Thank you, Kitty, Barbara, Janice, Cindy, Suely, and Casandra for making my stay so welcome and productive!

- To Patty Aubery and all my peeps in the Big Dreamer mastermind group for your support, advice, and encouragement.

- To my intern Kenya Burton for bringing poetry and order into my life.

- To Louise Mills-Dumonceaux for offering her insight and advice, and for being an awesome therapist!

- To all my beta readers and editors who helped polish this book until it shined: Ana Joldes, Jesse Weinberger, Patty Aubery, Karen Christie, Orna Drawas, Alana Williams, Ariane de Bonvoisin, Ali Flowers, and Sam Zordich (who edited my manuscript as an act of kindness during the Coronavirus pandemic).

- And finally, to you, dear reader, for fighting the good fight every single day to keep your child safe. May you and they rest easy in the arms of the angels, knowing you are loved and protected always.

Peace.

APPENDIX

If Your Child Has Been Sexually Abused

It happened. Your precious baby has been the victim of sexual molestation or assault. I'm so sorry this happened to her and to your family. Know that it wasn't her fault or yours and that neither of you did anything to deserve it. The perpetrator deserves all the blame for choosing to commit the offense.

Now what? There are decisions to be made, and at a time when you may feel least able to make them. Your mind and body are numb, or you're completely freaked out. You may be faced with people who are peppering you and your child with questions: "Who did this?", "What happened?", "Do you want to call the police or Child Protective Services?"

Time seems to be whirring by and everything is foggy. Who do you tell? How do you handle the police? The perpetrator (if you know him or are related to him)? Your daughter's feelings? Her life? *YOUR* life?

It may feel as if the world is ending. This is seriously tough stuff to deal with... but you and your child are tougher, and you'll find your way through this by sticking together.

The purpose of this chapter is to tell you what your options are and the consequences of the choices you make in the critical period after you learn your child has been sexually abused. I'll begin by going back to the first moment you suspect or learn that she's been molested or assaulted.

If You *Suspect* Your Child Was Sexually Abused

It's estimated that only about a third of children tell an adult when they've been sexually abused. Some kids, many of whom were taught beforehand to tell if something happened, will tell their parent or another adult that they've been assaulted. The majority, however, will disclose the abuse indirectly, accidently, or not at all.

Regardless of whether or how they tell, I assure you your child desperately hopes you'll find out and protect him from the perpetrator. His secret weighs a million tons and it's wreaking havoc on his mind and crushing his spirit.

Why Kids Don't Tell

There are so many reasons children don't tell. They may:

- Feel too ashamed or embarrassed.

- Blame themselves, especially if their bodies automatically reacted and they experienced pleasure during the incident.

- Have promised not to tell.

- Fear the perpetrator because they or their family have been threatened.

- Not have the vocabulary to describe what happened.

- Not fully appreciate that what happened constitutes sexual abuse.

Hinting at Abuse

Regardless of the reason, your child may not feel comfortable telling you directly and may take a roundabout approach, dropping hints about the abuse, hoping you'll notice and ask questions so he can get it off his chest. If he says things like, "I don't like Aunt Sophia anymore," or, "My coach hugs too tight," you need to find out what's going on underneath those remarks.

He might also attribute the incident to another child in order to gauge how you might react, saying something like, "What happens if a kid tells his mom someone touched his private parts. Would his mom believe him?" Again, he's hoping you'll ask questions and get to the bottom of the situation. Assure him that the "other child's" mom *would* believe him and would never be mad. Ask what he knows about this child. With gentle questioning and your reassurances that it's safe to tell, your child might admit he's the one who has a concern.

Try saying: "I've noticed that you seem really quiet/angry/anxious lately. I hope you'll tell me why so I can help. I promise I won't get upset or angry, no matter what you tell me." You have to really mean it when you say you won't get upset or angry. (Keep reading to learn what to say and what not to say when your child discloses abuse.)

If your child denies anything's wrong but you feel certain something's up, you can add: "Sometimes bad things happen to us and we think it's our fault or we're afraid we'll get in trouble or get someone else in trouble. Sometimes we're even afraid other people may get hurt or angry if we tell. But telling is the very best thing we can do, so we can get help to make sure the bad things stop."

You can ask him to show you how he feels using dolls, stuffed animals, or other toys, or ask him to draw a picture. Children are so expressive and good at reenacting their feelings and worries, and he may feel more comfortable acting them out than talking about them.

If he still won't share, add: "I know you don't feel like talking about it right now, but I'm always here for you. I love you, honey. And remember, you can also always talk to the people you put on your 'safe people' list, like Grandpa or Ms. Randall."

Talk to Grandpa and Ms. Randall to give them a heads-up about what you've noticed and ask for their observations and support. Sometimes, just giving a child the time and attention of a safe person will create the opportunity for him to talk. It takes tremendous courage for anyone, even grown-ups, to disclose that they've been abused, so don't be surprised if your child can't tell you or another safe person right away.

Symptoms to Act on With or Without a Disclosure

Even if your child can't or won't answer your questions, you don't need the full story to get help. If you even *suspect* something has happened to him, you absolutely need to report it. And if your child is experiencing any of the symptoms below that point to abuse, don't wait for him to tell you the full story; call the police or CPS immediately. If any of the physical symptoms from the list below are present, also get him to a pediatrician for treatment.

Here are the symptoms of child sexual abuse you need to act on right away:

- Pregnancy (yes, if your child has started puberty she can get pregnant).

- Being diagnosed with a sexually transmitted disease or infection (like herpes, syphilis, gonorrhea, vaginal infection, etc.).

- Sexual promiscuity.

- Genital or rectal pain or bleeding.

- Underwear or sheets are stained with blood or other discharge.

- Urinary tract infections, or abnormal vaginal or penile discharge.
- Pain while urinating or with bowel movements.
- Obvious difficulty walking or sitting.
- Sudden fearful behavior, such as nightmares or new fears of certain people, places, or things.
- Depression or social withdrawal.
- Extreme increase or decrease in appetite, or the development of an eating disorder.
- Sudden lack of self-esteem or confidence.
- Frequent stomachaches or headaches with no medical cause.
- Bedwetting (if he's already toilet trained).
- Sudden personality changes (e.g., a normally outgoing child stops speaking, a well-behaved child develops discipline problems).
- Bullying others or being bullied.
- Extremely aggressive or passive behavior.
- Regressive behavior (meaning he reverts to behaving like a younger child).
- Sudden interest in sex or sexualized behavior that seems inappropriate for his age, including excessive touching of his own private body parts, persistent sex play with friends, toys, or pets; drawings with sexual content; or asking age-inappropriate sexual questions.
- Sudden drop in school performance.
- Secretive behavior (he seems to be hiding something).
- Attempts to run away or skip school.
- Self-mutilation or careless behaviors that result in self-harm of any kind (e.g., cutting, burning, or otherwise injuring one's self).

If Your Child Does Disclose Abuse

Be aware that when you talk to your child about the dangers I address in this book, she may very well confide that she's already been or is actively being abused.

Whether you learned of the abuse from your child or another person, your job is to take her claim seriously and to focus on what she needs in that moment. Don't be concerned about getting to the bottom of everything that occurred—leave that to the police, CPS, and the therapist who are trained to help children disclose the whole story.

Your reaction to your child's disclosure—or lack thereof—could mean the difference between her knowing deep in her bones that it wasn't her fault and healing relatively quickly, or her being further traumatized and requiring years or even decades of therapy. I can't tell you how many adult survivors have told me they were actually chastised or even punished for "lying" about the abuse they endured. Some of them said they were more traumatized by their family's reaction than by the abuse itself.

How to Respond to Your Child

If Your Child Is 0 to 3

Many babies and toddlers don't even understand that they've been abused. Others who experience severe abuse may be traumatized and fearful of everyone, including you. If your toddler tells you she's been sexually abused (or you learn that she has been), the most important thing is to reassure her that she's safe and that you'll protect her from further harm.

Say, "You're very brave for telling me this. I'm so proud of you. Everything's going to be okay." At this age, your actions more than your words will help your child feel safe. Maintain her usual routine and be with her as much as you can.

If Your Child Is 4 to 9

Say something comforting, like: "Oh, sweetie. I'm SO sorry this has happened to you! And I'm so proud of you for telling me about it. It's not your fault; you did NOTHING wrong. I promise you; it's going to be okay. *You're* going to be okay. I'm going to stop this right away. I love you and I promise we'll figure this out together."

If you think you can handle it, gently ask her to tell you what happened. Ask open-ended questions like, "Tell me more" or "What happened next?" Avoid leading questions like, "Did Miss Emily touch your private parts?"

Don't grill your child to try to get to "the bottom of it." Child Protective Services have specially-trained counselors who know exactly how to question children in a manner appropriate to their age and maturity level, and in ways that are admissible in court in the event the offender ends up being charged.

Don't be afraid to share *appropriate* emotions in front of her; just don't act hysterical or wail and beat your breast, which may cause her to shut down. This is about her, so don't make it about you. Still, showing your sadness and even tears gives her permission to do the same.

If you need time to think about what she told you and/or regain your composure, say, as calmly as you can: "Thank you so much for telling me this. I need to think about it for a bit. Can we talk again in a little while? I love you, sweetie."

When you've calmed down, go back to her and say: "Remember what you said about Mr. Holman touching your private parts? Can we talk about it now?"

Tell her what you're going to do to protect her. Say: "Here's what I'm going to do now. First, I need to make sure you're protected, so I'm going to make sure you're never alone again with XX (even if the abuser isn't in the home, your child needs to hear that she's safe). I'm also going to call Grandma/other safe person to come be with us while I make a few phone calls. It's important to tell people who can help. I need to let the police/Child Protective Services know what happened so XX doesn't hurt any other children. Do you understand?"

Allow your child to have her reaction to what you just said, but remain firm that you're going to call the police (or CPS) because you need to protect both her and other children from the abuser.

Ask what would make her feel safe and brainstorm ideas. For example, she might want a friend (or other safe person) to come over, or she may find comfort by following her usual routine of going to school, doing her homework, playing on the computer (which is okay unless the abuser contacted her online), and so on.

If the Abuser Is Someone You Love or Are in a Relationship With

Man, this one's tough. It'll be hard not to have a visceral reaction to the disclosure by your child that your spouse/partner or boyfriend/girlfriend sexually abused him.

If your child accuses someone you love, your first instinct may be to deny the claim. If you find yourself in this situation, rather than flat out calling your child a liar, be honest and tell him that his claim has surprised you and that you need time to think about what he's said.

Do NOT tell your child he's mistaken, wrong, or confused. Take him at his word. Wait to talk further until you can be supportive and really listen with an open mind to what he has to say. If you need help and support yourself to get to this point, call your local rape crisis center or one of the child abuse hotlines I reference in the Resources section of my website.[193]

If you're afraid to report the abuse of your child by someone in your home—because you don't want the offender to get in trouble or because you don't want to admit it happened under your watch—get over it! You've got a job to do, which is to protect your child from further harm and report the incident to authorities. If you don't report it, other children may be abused by this person (and may already have been).

End all contact with the abuser, even if it's a close family member or your partner. Your first responsibility is to protect your child, regardless of the consequences to the abuser. In fact, you could be at legal risk if you don't report, depending on the state you live in.

If you have concerns for your child's or family's immediate safety, call the police and then head to the home of a supportive friend or relative and contact your local domestic violence agency or the Rape, Abuse & Incest National Network's hotline at 800-656-HOPE.

If Your Child Was Abused by a Sibling

Aaaannnddd it gets tougher still. No parent wants to believe their child could be a perpetrator, but it happens—a lot.

Refer to Chapter 3 on Siblings, Peers & Older Kids for more information on this subject.

A Word about False Accusations

Some parents react to their child's disclosure with disbelief. This is especially common when he names a close relative—even your partner or a sibling—as the abuser. Here are the facts to consider:

- False reports of child sexual abuse made by children are very rare. Most of the 4 to 8 percent of fabricated reports are made by adults (who should be ridden out of town on a rail) involved in custody disputes or by adolescents 10 to 19 years of age.[clxxi]

---

193 www.cjscarlet.com/resources

- Your child *could* have misunderstood or misinterpreted the other person's comments or behavior as being inappropriate when they were not.

- The child *could* be seeking attention or revenge on the accused. Possible, but that's pretty sophisticated behavior for a child under 10.

- Some children recant their claims, but that doesn't mean they were lying. Later claiming the abuse didn't happen is fairly common among young sexual abuse victims for a variety of reasons. For example, the child may not want the offender to get in trouble, he could be in denial (which is easier than admitting the abuse occurred), or he's been pressured by others to deny anything happened.

- Small children (5 and under) may sound confused or inconsistent when they talk about the abuse, but this doesn't mean they're not telling the truth either. It's up to a trained therapist to determine whether there's any "there" there.

Getting Help for Your Child

First Things First—What NOT to Do After an Assault

If your child comes to you immediately after a sexual molestation or assault happened, her body and clothing may contain critical evidence that could help police catch the predator and take him off the street before he hurts another child. It's imperative that you carefully maintain any physical evidence of the attack.

This means you need to safeguard the clothing she was wearing during the attack, including her underwear, and not try to clean them. It means she doesn't take a bath or shower right away. It means she doesn't eat or drink anything or brush her teeth if she was orally sodomized (meaning the perp placed his penis or semen onto or into her mouth).

I know. You want to scour all evidence of that monster's presence from your child's body, but I caution you to *please* delay. Let the police and CPS collect any evidence so they can build their case against the predator.

So, please:

- No showers.

- No food or drink.

- No brushing her teeth.

- No manicures or heavy scrubbing of her nails.

- No washing of her hair.

- No disposing of items that were on her during the attack (clothing, shoes, jewelry, etc.).

- No deleting any written or digital evidence of her whereabouts during the time of the attack.

A Word about Mandatory Reporting

If your child discloses sexual abuse, you need to report it immediately to your local Child Protective Services (CPS) agency (also referred to as Social Services or Child Welfare) and/or law enforcement agency (police or sheriff's department). This is not only the right thing to do to protect your child, in most states it's the law.

In many states, parents are included on the list of "mandatory reporters," and failure to report suspected or known abuse to CPS or the police can result in criminal charges against them. They could also have their children removed from the home and placed in foster care.

In all 50 states in the US, mandatory reporters, such as healthcare professionals (e.g., nurses, doctors, psychiatrists, therapists, dentists, and staff members working for these individuals), teachers, and childcare workers are required to report child abuse if they reasonably believe the child is being subjected to maltreatment (including sexual abuse) or neglect.

Of course, anyone who's concerned that a child is being abused can report it; you don't have to be in a professional or even personal relationship with the family. Some young people have stepped forward and reported the victimization of their own siblings in order to stop the abuse.

If you're not sure whether to call CPS or the police and you need guidance, contact the National Children's Alliance (www.nca-online.org) or other national hotlines that I have listed in the Resources section of my website.[194]

Reporting to CPS

When you report suspected child sexual abuse, your case will be assigned to a caseworker who will investigate your concerns, ensure your child is safe from further harm by the abuser, and arrange medical care and counseling, if needed.

---

194 www.cjscarlet.com/resources

For a list of your local CPS agency, visit www.childwelfare.gov (see endnote for full website address).[clxxii]

Reporting to Police

These stats are from old sources, but I imagine they're still true today: Just 3 percent of all child sexual abuse cases[clxxiii] and only 12 percent of all child rapes[clxxiv] are ever reported to the police.

Holy. Cow.

Don't be that parent who doesn't report because you want to "protect your child" from all the hullabaloo that will follow (you're not, in fact, protecting her at all), or because you don't want the abuser to get in trouble (too bad, so sad), or because you don't want to deal with the fall out (suck it up). Getting justice by seeing the perp pay for his crimes not only protects other children, it shows your child that the abuser was the one who did something wrong, not her.

I'm going to say it as plainly as I can: If you don't report the abuse, *you're complicit*. AND you're responsible for any other children the perp abuses in the future. AND you're playing ostrich and putting your head in the sand (and another, darker place I won't name).

Now you know why they don't call me just plain ole' "Grandma." It's because I have no sympathy for people who knowingly perpetrate or enable others to perpetrate abuse against children.

But I'm sure *you're* not one of those people, and that you will ABSOLUTELY report sexual abuse if you learn of it, especially if it happens to a child.

I think we understand one another.

What the Police Will Do

Call or visit your local Police or Sheriff's Department (depending on where you live, and hereafter referred to simply as "law enforcement") to make a report of suspected or known child abuse.[195]

Before you go either to law enforcement or CPS, it'll be helpful to document what you know or suspect, including:

- Who the offender is (if your child knows).
- What the abuse involved.

---

[195] For a listing of your state's local law enforcement agencies, visit https://golawenforcement.com/state-law-enforcement-agencies/.

- When and where the abuse occurred.

- What events led up to the assault (e.g., efforts by the offender to groom your child).

- How the abusive incident(s) ended.

- Where the offender lives.

- Any identifying or distinguishing features the predator has (e.g., tattoos, piercings, scars, big ears, etc.).

- Any threats or statements the perpetrator made to your child.

- Whether any weapons were used to threaten or harm your child.

- What external injuries, if any, she received.

- What injuries the attacker received (e.g., scratches, bites, etc. by your child), if any.

When the police arrive, they'll first check to see if your child needs medical attention. Next, they'll want to know any details you and she can provide about the assault and the perpetrator. As her parent/guardian, you or your attorney may have the right to be present when she's questioned.

It's okay if she can't remember every detail during the first interview. If they ask her a question and she doesn't know the answer, she can just tell them she can't remember right now.

It's also okay if she can't give a statement right away because she feels dissociated, numb, hysterical, or too fearful to recall events. The police have specially trained investigators who know how to ask questions in ways that might help her remember what happened. If she's unable to give a statement immediately after the assault, they can interview her later, when her memory has become more clear.

The police will investigate the report, prepare a case to present to the prosecutor's office, if warranted, and make any arrests. If the case does move toward prosecution, it'll be assigned to a prosecutor with the District Attorney's Office.[196]

The Forensic Exam

Regardless of when the sexual abuse occurred, CPS and/or the police will want your child to have a forensic exam by a specially trained physician or nurse examiner to look for any physical

---

[196] I go into the criminal justice process in more detail in the Legal Remedies handout of the Freebies page of my website at www.cjscarlet.com/freebies.

signs of the abuse (which may not be obvious), such as internal or external scarring, tearing, evidence of sexually transmitted diseases or infections, etc.

If your community doesn't have a trained child abuse pediatrician available, consider asking for a referral to one.[197]

Here's what the pediatrician or nurse examiner will do:

- Record your child's medical history.

- Talk to your child to ask what happened, in her own words.

- Perform a thorough examination of her body from head to toe.

- Submit a full report to CPS, the police, and a multidisciplinary team (if your community has one) that includes other doctors, CPS workers, law enforcement investigators, and child therapists.

If the case goes to trial, the child abuse pediatrician will often testify in court to explain to the judge and jury any evidence of injuries that were found and medical concerns that resulted from the abuse.

Getting Counseling for Your Child

The great news is, when abuse is quickly addressed and the child is given appropriate therapy, she can heal in a surprisingly short time. Getting your child into counseling after she's been abused is a no-brainer! As I mentioned earlier, when the children who came to my child advocacy center got the counseling and support they needed, they were able to quickly process what happened and move on. When kids don't get that kind of support, they can spend years or even decades crippled by the trauma.

Counselors and licensed therapists trained to deal specifically with child sexual abuse cases can walk your child through the issues that are bothering her the most, one step at a time, which makes the incident less frightening and easier to handle. They can help you both process your

---

[197] You may be able to get compensated for this visit by your state's crime victim compensation fund. Contact your state Attorney General's Office to learn about victim compensation.

emotions about the whole ordeal. With patience and wisdom, they'll help you both recover from the trauma, find your "new normal,"[198] and move past the experience to live happy lives.

I personally could never have dealt with my traumatic past on my own. Group and individual therapy saved my life as far as I'm concerned.

For free, confidential help if your child has been abused, call the National Sexual Assault Hotline at 800-656-HOPE (4673). Their trained staff can provide:

- Support finding a local health facility trained to care for survivors of sexual assault, including services like sexual assault forensic exams.
- Someone to help you talk through what happened.
- Local resources that can help with your child's next steps toward healing and recovery.
- Referrals for long-term support in your area (e.g., counseling).
- Information about the laws in your community.

If you or your child don't like or feel totally comfortable with the first therapist you go to, keep looking until you find the right fit—meaning the person who makes your child feel comfortable and who's easy to talk to.

Ongoing Protection & Support for Your Child

When you discover or suspect your child has been sexually abused, the most important thing you *must* do is ensure he's safe from further harm from the offender. During any investigation by CPS or the police, don't let him see or ever be alone with the perpetrator. You'd be surprised how many parents fail to protect their children after abuse has clearly occurred, usually because the perp is a love interest or relative.

Continue to reassure your child that he's safe and that everything's going to be okay. He needs to hear often that you love and will protect him because he's likely terrified and feeling guilty for getting the offender in trouble, particularly if it's someone in the family.

---

198 "New normal" refers to a different way of living and thinking to the one you had before the incident occurred. No matter how much you wish things would go back to the way they were, it's just not possible. However, with support and work, life can be great again—or even better than it was before.

Especially during the investigation, keep what happened close to the vest,[199] telling only those who need to know and asking them not to share it with others. The last thing your child needs is to be the subject of rumors and speculation. You also don't want to potentially put him in the path of people who might try to intimate or discourage him from reporting or testifying because they want to protect the perp.

As much as this situation affects you and impacts your life, it's not primarily about you; it's about your child. Keep your anger, fear, guilt, and other strong feelings out of any conversation with him. Kids tend to take responsibility for the feelings of others and your son will feel badly for "making" you upset. Fake it if you have to, but show up as strong, comforting, reassuring, and confident.

That being said, you *will* have strong feelings about all this, so be sure to take care of *yourself* during this difficult time. Consider getting counseling for yourself, especially if you have your own history of abuse and are feeling triggered or guilty for not protecting your child.

If You're a Survivor Yourself

If you yourself are an abuse survivor, your child's disclosure may trigger you and dredge up painful memories and unresolved issues of your own. It's imperative that you get help for yourself so you can address these while still being there for your child.

There are a number of resources on my website you can call for help and support. Probably the best is the Rape, Abuse & Incest National Network (www.RAINN.org), which has a hotline (800-656-HOPE) and can refer you to survivor resources in your local area.

What You Can Do to Minimize Your Child's Trauma after Disclosure

- Maintain your family's routines and keep home life as normal as possible to make your child feel safer and more secure.

- Reassure and comfort your child and talk to him about ways he can soothe himself (e.g., sleeping with a favorite stuffed animal, talking to his therapist or one of his safe people, etc.).

- Let him talk about his feelings and validate them. Reassure him that his fears and anxiety will get better with time.

---

199 Don't go blabbing it to people who don't need to know.

- Don't ignore sexualized behavior or play, which indicate distress and should be stopped in a matter-of-fact, supportive way. Talk about this behavior with his therapist.

- Anticipate difficult behavior and respond gently, but consistently to rule violations.

What You Can Count On

Your child should expect to enjoy the freedom of living her life without the fear of being sexually molested or assaulted. That children can't always do that is a sad reality.

You may find you can't even count on the support of your friends and family after your child has become a "victim." They may not want to believe her, or they may even blame her and try to shame her. While it's easy to embrace the victim mentality and buy into their projections (and that's all they are, projections of their fear and ignorance onto your child), you must help her fight that urge and stand on her own two feet.

Your beautiful child was the target of a crime; that's a fact. But it doesn't say *anything* about who she is at her core or in her spirit. Still, like a major earthquake, trauma has psychological and physical aftershocks that continue to rock survivors long after the initial catastrophe. These are discussed below.

The Psychological Aftermath

There's no "right way" for your child to react after he's experienced a moral wound like sexual abuse. Some children go into shock and feel completely dissociated from the event; they may appear calm and unemotional. Others become very emotional and can't stop thinking about what happened.

Some degree of shock is common, which can impair his thinking and ability to react "appropriately" afterward. Because he may not be able to feel or recall the trauma at first, he might downplay the event or be confused about what really happened. Other children remember every detail and are completely overwhelmed by the emotions and sensations, which can be paralyzing.

It sounds counter-intuitive, but children who've been traumatized often seek balance and control, which sometimes includes self-blame and punishment in order to regain equilibrium. They don't want to accept that they were vulnerable and powerless to stop the predator; it's easier to blame themselves for "stupid" or "bad" behavior than to accept that they live in a world where such a soul-shattering thing could happen to them.

Survivors often believe that if others—especially those closest to them—could see how damaged and flawed they are, they would run from them in disgust and horror.

Post-Traumatic Stress[200]

The bad news is your abused child may experience post-traumatic stress (PTS) as the result of the abuse she suffered. The great news is, you have a lot of power to help mitigate it or even keep it from happening (depending on the duration and severity of the abuse).

I say this because one of the biggest factors that determines whether a child acquires PTS is the quality of the support she receives from her family and extended circle.

You're obviously a good, caring parent or you wouldn't be reading this book. Just by teaching her the information and techniques I share, you're giving your child the gift of self-esteem and resilience, which can help ward off long-term traumatic reactions.

AND, if anything bad does happen to her, she can count on you to support her and give her the loving care she needs to quickly recover.

Post-Traumatic Stress Defined

Most people have heard of post-traumatic stress as it relates to men and women who fought in combat, but PTS is an equal opportunity condition—it can affect survivors of any kind of trauma, from violence to natural disasters, and from car accidents to severe childhood physical and emotional neglect.

Many people go through traumatic events and may have difficulty adjusting and coping for a period of time, but they don't have PTS; with time, support, and good self-care, they usually get better. PTS is generally diagnosed when the symptoms get worse, last for months or years, and interfere with one's ability to function.

Post-traumatic stress manifests a little differently according to the age of the child involved. In babies who are pre-verbal and toddlers (particularly those with disabilities) who have very limited verbal skills, it can be difficult to know for certain whether a child is experiencing PTS, but there are clear indicators for children through age 9, babies included, such as:

- Emotional distress. Anxiety that results from being exposed to sensations (sights, sounds, smells, tastes, touches) or emotions that remind the child of the triggering event or person.

---

200 Formerly referred to as post-traumatic stress disorder.

- Hypervigilance. Being tense, watchful, and constantly on guard, even when in safe, familiar environments.

- Separation anxiety. Watch for clinginess that occurs before or far beyond 6 months to 1 year of age, when that kind of behavior is expected.

- Sleep disturbances. Children who are afraid to be left alone in their room or are terrified of falling asleep, who have excessive fear of the dark, who experience severe nightmares, or who are convinced there are monsters under their bed or in their closet.

- Fear or avoidance of places that remind them of the abusive event or person.

- Repetitive play. This includes play that repeats scenarios similar to the sexual trauma.

- Depression and/or anxiety.

- Losing interest in things they used to enjoy.

- Difficulty offering or accepting affection.

- Aggressive or even violent behavior.

- Problems in school; sudden drop in school performance.

- Dissociation. The children may mentally "check out" and lose touch with reality or feel numb.

- "Omen formation." The belief that there were warning signs that predicted the trauma, and that if they're alert enough, they'll be able to recognize and avoid future traumas.[clxxv]

- Difficulty focusing.

- Obsessive worrying about their personal safety and/or fear of dying.

- Regressive behavior, such as thumb-sucking or bedwetting.

- Physical symptoms, such as headaches or stomachaches.

Not every child who experiences sexual abuse will get PTS. A lot depends on her normal personality (confident or anxious), the strength of her social support (that's you!), other childhood experiences (positive versus negative), her natural ability to handle stress, her arsenal of coping mechanisms, and the nature of the traumatic event.

The more frequent and severe the trauma, combined with poor coping skills and low social support, the more likely it is a given child will develop PTS.

How You Can Help Your Child Heal

As I emphasized above, one of the most important factors that determines your child's ability to bounce back from a traumatic incident is your love and support, and those of his inner circle. When you combine good therapy with the suggestions I offer below, you can feel confident you're doing everything in your power to help your child.

Here's what you can do to help your child heal from and move beyond the trauma he experienced:

- Offer him your unconditional love, comfort, support, and understanding.

- Let him talk, draw, or write about what happened when he's ready.

- Tell him how proud you are of him for being so strong and brave.

- Treat him like an ordinary kid. Yes, be sensitive to his needs following the trauma, but don't coddle or baby him too much or he may begin to feel insecure about his ability to deal with what happened.

- Maintain his routine and schedule as much as possible and avoid introducing any major changes if you can.

- Find ways to give him a sense of control and rebuild his self-esteem and confidence. Trauma can make kids feel powerless, so let him make choices that affect him when possible.

- Build a strong support network around him that includes his friends, those on his "safe people" list, relatives, teachers, coaches, and other caregivers.

- Get him into individual therapy with a therapist who specializes in child sexual abuse treatment.

- Have him attend a support group for children in his age range so he'll have the support of peers. I can tell you from experience that it feels really good to have people around you who can relate to your story.

- Be patient with regressive behavior (e.g., thumb sucking, bedwetting, clingy behavior, etc.). However, if it goes on for more than a few months, do talk to a therapist about it.

- Watch for signs of self-harm and suicidal ideation. If you spot these, get him to a therapist right away.

- Remind him that the incident wasn't his fault and that he didn't deserve to have that happen to him. This is really important to do. I grew up believing there was something wrong with me that made good people do bad things. That's such a tragic way for anyone—child or adult—to feel and so unnecessary!

Badass Grandma's Two Cents

I shared a lot of information in this appendix, and you may feel overwhelmed. It's critical to recognize that there's a ton of support and so many resources in your community and around the country to help you and your child work through the aftermath of her experience.

It's so important that you know that what happened was NOT your fault and that your child possesses the strength and courage to find her new normal and move on to have a wonderful life.

ENDNOTES

i   Hillis S, Mercy J, Amobi A, and Kress H. Global prevalence of past-year violence against children: a systematic review and minimum estimates. Pediatrics 2016;137(3): e2015407.

ii   Plunkett et al, 2001, from *Body Safety Education* by Jayneen Sanders.

iii   2018 Federal Human Trafficking Report, The Human Trafficking Institute.

iv   Federal Bureau of Investigation, www.fbi.gov.

v   Finkelhor, D. (2012). Characteristics of crimes against juveniles, Crimes against Children Research Center.

vi   National Center for Missing and Exploited Children, https://www.missingkids.org/footer/media/keyfacts.

vii   Ibid.

viii   Ibid.

ix   Ibid.

x   https://reason.com/2017/03/31/kidnapping-stats/.

xi   http://www.pollyklaas.org/about/national-child-kidnapping.html.

xii   Finkelhor, D., & Jones, L. (2012). Have sexual abuse and physical abuse declined since the 1990s? Crimes against Children Research Center. http://www.unh.edu/ccrc/pdf/CV267_Have%20SA%20%20PA%20Decline_FACT%20SHEET_11-7-12.pdf.

xiii   Pinker, Steven, *The Better Angels of Our Nature: Why Violence Has Declined.*

xiv   Pew Research Center.

xv   http://www.dallasnews.com/opinion/sunday-commentary/20100326-Joe-Keohane-The-crime-wave-762.ece.

xvi   According to the Census Bureau's 2005 American Community Survey.

xvii   Bagley, 1995.

xviii   National Institute of Mental Health research by Dr. Gene Abel, 1985.

xix   www.ChildLuresPrevention.com

xx   Ibid.

xxi   http://bjs.ojp.usdoj.gov/content/homicide/children.cfm, http://www.bjs.gov/content/pub/pdf/htus8008.pdf.

xxii   FBI National Crime Information Center.

xxiii   https://reason.com/2017/03/31/kidnapping-stats/.

xxiv   http://www.pollyklaas.org/about/national-child-kidnapping.html.

xxv   Finkelhor, David; Ormrod, Richard; and Chaffin, Mark. Juveniles Who Commit Sex Offenses Against Minors. Juvenile Justice Bulletin, December 2009.

xxvi	Rennison, Callie Marie, Ph.D., Intimate Partner Violence and Age of Victim, 1993-99. http://bjs.ojp.usdoj.gov/content/pub/pdf/ipva99.pdf.
xxvii	U.S. Department of Justice, Office of Juvenile Justice and Delinquency Prevention.
xxviii	Center for Sex Offender Management, 1999.
xxix	Finkelhor, David, and Gewirtz-Meydan, Ateret, 2018. https://theconversation.com/sexual-assault-among-adolescents-6-facts-103658.
xxx	www.DarknesstoLight.org.
xxxi	Flanagan and Hayman-White, 1999.
xxxii	Ibid.
xxxiii	Finkelhor, David, and Gewirtz-Meydan, Ateret, 2018. https://theconversation.com/sexual-assault-among-adolescents-6-facts-103658.
xxxiv	https://www.verywellmind.com/facts-about-sibling-sexual-abuse-2610456.
xxxv	https://stopitnow.org/ohc-content/tip-sheet-behaviors-to-watch-for-when-adults-are-with-children-signs-that-a-child-or.
xxxvi	Sedlak AJ, Mettenburg J, Basena M, et al. Fourth National Incidence Study of Child Abuse and Neglect, Report to Congress. 2010.
xxxvii	https://web.archive.org/web/20080111204617/.
xxxviii	America After 3PM, Afterschool Alliance and JC Penney Afterschool.
xxxix	According to a 2000 report commissioned by the American Association of University Women.
xl	America After 3PM, Afterschool Alliance and JC Penney Afterschool.
xli	Ibid.
xlii	Truth Project Thematic Report: Child sexual abuse in the context of religious institutions, May 2019.
xliii	Center for Disease Control, National Center for Injury Prevention and Control (2012). Understanding bullying. http://www.cdc.gov/violenceprevention/pdf/bullyingfactsheet2012-a.pdf.
xliv	Ibid.
xlv	Ibid.
xlvi	Carpenter, Deborah, The Everything Parent's Guide to Dealing with Bullies: From playground teasing to cyberbullying, all you need to ensure your child's safety and happiness.
xlvii	Ibid.
xlviii	Ahmed, Sara. Why Aren't We Talking About This Dangerous Type of Bullying? https://www.popsugar.com/family/What-Relational-Bullying-43728079.
xlix	Carpenter, Deborah, The Everything Parent's Guide to Dealing with Bullies: From playground teasing to cyberbullying, all you need to ensure your child's safety and happiness.

l	Ibid.
li	Newport, Frank, Politics, May 22, 2018.
lii	Koplewicz, Harold S., M.D. LGBT Teens, Bullying, and Suicide: What are the causes and how can we help?
liii	Carpenter, Deborah, The Everything Parent's Guide to Dealing with Bullies: From playground teasing to cyberbullying, all you need to ensure your child's safety and happiness.
liv	Gini, G., and Espelage, D. D. (2014) Peer victimization, cyberbullying, and suicide risk in children and adolescents, JAMA Pediatrics, http://jamanetwork.com/journals/jama/article-abstract/1892227.
lv	De Becker, Gavin. *Protecting the Gift*.
lvi	Weinberger, Jesse. The Boogeyman Exists, And He's In Your Child's Back Pocket: Internet Safety Tips For Keeping Your Children Safe Online, Smartphone Safety, Social Media Safety, and Gaming Safety.
lvii	Petrosina, Guckenburg, Devoe and Hanson, 2010.
lviii	Ibid.
lix	Carpenter, Deborah, The Everything Parent's Guide to Dealing with Bullies: From playground teasing to cyberbullying, all you need to ensure your child's safety and happiness.
lx	Various Internet Crimes Against Children Task Forces.
lxi	Ibid.
lxii	Towards a Global Indicator on Unidentified Victims in Child Sexual Exploitation Material, published by ECPAT International and INTERPOL in February 2018.
lxiii	https://www.guardchild.com/statistics/.
lxiv	Various Internet Crimes Against Children Task Forces.
lxv	Ibid.
lxvi	Schlosser, Kurt, June 1, 2018.
lxvii	https://www.bitdefender.com/news/bitdefender-study-shows-95-of-parents-found-children-accessing-internet-pornography-1999.html.
lxviii	https://www.justia.com/criminal/offenses/sex-crimes/child-pornography/.
lxix	www.GuardChild.com.
lxx	https://perfectionpending.net/kids-and-pornography-the-statistics-every-parent-needs-to-know-and-how-you-can-protect-your-kids-online/.
lxxi	https://parentology.com/how-to-talk-to-your-teen-about-sexting/?utm_source=newsletter&utm_medium=email&utm_campaign=recess_reading_08_25_2019.

lxxii	Wolak, Janis, J.D.; Finkelhor, David, Ph.D.; Walsh, Wendy, Ph.D.; and Treitman, Leah. Crimes against Children Research Center, University of New Hampshire, www.wearethorn.org.
lxxiii	"Sex and tech". The National Campaign to Prevent Teen and Unplanned Pregnancy, December 10, 2008.
lxxiv	https://www.stopitnow.org/ohc-content/defining-child-sexual-abuse.
lxxv	https://www.smart.gov/SOMAPI/sec1/ch4_internet.html.
lxxvi	U.S. Department of Health and Human Services, Administration on Children, Youth and Families. (2018). Child Maltreatment 2016. https://www.acf.hhs.gov/cb/resource/child-maltreatment-2016.
lxxvii	Snyder, H. N. (2000). Sexual assault of young children as reported to law enforcement: Victim, incident, and offender characteristics. U.S. Department of Justice, Office of Justice Programs, Bureau of Justice Statistics. http://www.ojp.usdoj.gov/bjs/pub/pdf/saycrle.pdf.
lxxviii	Finkelhor, David, Characteristics of crimes against juveniles. Crimes against Children Research Center, 2012.
lxxix	https://www.d2l.org/wp-content/uploads/2017/01/all_statistics_20150619.pdf.
lxxx	Ibid.
lxxxi	Sedlak, et al. (2010). Fourth National Incidence Study of Child Abuse and Neglect: Report to Congress, U.S. Department of Health and Human Services, Administration for Children and Families.
lxxxii	Ibid.
lxxxiii	Snyder, H. N. (2000). Sexual assault of young children as reported to law enforcement: Victim, incident, and offender characteristics. U.S. Department of Justice, http://www.ojp.usdoj.gov/bjs/pub/pdf/saycrle.pdf.
lxxxiv	Ibid.
lxxxv	Finkelhor, David, Current information on the scope and nature of child sexual abuse. The Future of Children, Vol. 4, No. 2, Sexual Abuse of Children, 1994.
lxxxvi	Sedlak, et al. (2010). Fourth National Incidence Study of Child Abuse and Neglect: Report to Congress, U.S. Department of Health and Human Services, Administration for Children and Families.
lxxxvii	Ibid.
lxxxviii	Finkelhor, D.; Ormrod, R.K.; and Turner, H.A. (2010). Poly-victimization in a national sample of children & youth. American Journal of Preventive Medicine.
lxxxix	Ibid.
xc	Ibid.

xci	Putnam, F. (2003). Ten-year research update review: child sexual abuse. Journal of American Child Adolescence Psychiatry, 42(3).
xcii	https://www.d2l.org/wp-content/uploads/2017/01/all_statistics_20150619.pdf.
xciii	Ibid.
xciv	Boyer, Deborah and Fine, David. Sexual Abuse as a Factor in Adolescent Pregnancy and Child Maltreatment. Family Planning Perspectives, Vol. 24, No. 1 (Jan/Feb 1992).
xcv	Duke University. Dropping out of high school linked to child abuse. ScienceDaily. ScienceDaily, December 1, 2017. www.sciencedaily.com/releases/2017/12/171201131636.htm.
xcvi	Ibid.
xcvii	Ibid.
xcviii	Sachs-Ericsson, N., Blazer, D., Plant, E. A., & Arnow, B. (2005). Childhood sexual and physical abuse and 1-year prevalence of medical problems in the National Comorbidity Survey. Health Psychology, 24.
xcix	https://www.hg.org/child-abduction.html.
c	Sedlak, Andrea J.; Finkelhor, David; and Brick, J. Michael. US Dept of Justice, National Estimates of Missing Children: Updated Findings from a Survey of Parents and Other Primary Caretakers, 2013.
ci	Ibid.
cii	Ibid.
ciii	Ibid.
civ	National Center for Missing and Exploited Children, https://www.missingkids.org/footer/media/keyfacts.
cv	Ibid.
cvi	Ibid.
cvii	Ibid.
cviii	https://reason.com/2017/03/31/kidnapping-stats/.
cix	Ibid.
cx	https://www.nytimes.com/2002/08/27/science/who-would-abduct-a-child-previous-cases-offer-clues.html.
cxi	U.S. Department of Justice, National Incidence Studies of Missing, Abducted, Runaway, and Thrownaway Children, 2002.
cxii	http://unh.edu/ccrc/pdf/Child%20Kidnapping%20LE%20Report.pdf.
cxiii	https://www.nytimes.com/2002/08/27/science/who-would-abduct-a-child-previous-cases-offer-clues.html.

cxiv	Ibid.
cxv	Ibid.
cxvi	Ibid.
cxvii	Ibid.
cxviii	National Center for Missing and Exploited Children.
cxix	U.S. Department of Justice, National Incidence Studies of Missing, Abducted, Runaway, and Thrownaway Children, 2002.
cxx	Ibid.
cxxi	Ibid.
cxxii	Ibid.
cxxiii	National Center for Missing and Exploited Children.
cxxiv	Ibid.
cxxv	Ibid.
cxxvi	https://reason.com/2017/03/31/kidnapping-stats/.
cxxvii	Family Abduction in a National Sample of U.S. Children, published in Child Abuse & Neglect, 2017.
cxxviii	U.S. Department of Justice, National Incidence Studies of Missing, Abducted, Runaway, and Thrownaway Children, 2002.
cxxix	National Center for Missing and Exploited Children.
cxxx	National Incidence Studies of Missing, Exploited, Runaway, and Throwaway Children, US Dept of Justice, October 2002.
cxxxi	https://ojjdp.ojp.gov/sites/g/files/xyckuh176/files/pubs/249249.pdf.
cxxxii	http://unh.edu/ccrc/pdf/Nismart%203%20Household%20Bulletin.pdf.
cxxxiii	National Center for Missing and Exploited Children.
cxxxiv	https://www.ortv.org/Charter/17_lures_predators_may_use.htm. https://www.kidguard.com/prevent-child-abduction-kidnapping-and-missing-children/the-most-common-lures-used-by-kidnappers/.
cxxxv	National Center for Missing and Exploited Children, https://www.missingkids.org/footer/media/keyfacts.
cxxxvi	Ibid.
cxxxvii	Maslow, Abraham, *A Theory of Human Motivation*, 1943.
cxxxviii	The Evaluation of Sexual Behaviors in Children. Nancy D. Kellogg Committee on Child Abuse and Neglect.
cxxxix	Committee for Children, Talking with Your Child About Sexual Abuse.
cxl	https://thriveglobal.com/stories/one-skill-you-must-teach-your-kids/.

cxli	www.urbandictionary.com.
cxlii	From https://www.stopitnow.org/talking-to-children-and-teens.
cxliii	Robin F. Goodman writes on the New York University Child Study Center Web site.cxliv https://www.kidpower.org/library/article/the-uh-oh-feeling/.
cxlv	https://en.m.wikipedia.org/wiki/Puberty.
cxlvi	https://kidshealth.org/en/kids/menstruation-definition.html.
cxlvii	https://www.npr.org/2018/01/10/566608390/she-can-t-tell-us-what-s-wrong.
cxlviii	Ibid.
cxlix	Sorensen, David D. The Invisible Victims, an update of an article originally published in Prosecutor's Brief: the California District Attorneys Associations Quarterly Journal, 2002.
cl	Balderian, N. Sexual abuse of people with developmental disabilities, Sexuality and Disability, 1991.
cli	Bowman, Rachel A.; Scotti, Joseph R.; Morris, Tracy L. Sexual Abuse Prevention: A Training Program for Developmental Disabilities Service Providers, Journal of Child Sexual Abuse, 2010.
clii	Disabilities: Insights from Across Fields and Around the World; Marshall, Kendall, Banks & Gover (Eds.), 2009.
cliii	British Journal of Learning Support, 2008.
cliv	U.S. Individuals with Disabilities Education Act.
clv	https://www.understood.org/en/school-learning/special-services/special-education-basics/conditions-covered-under-idea.
clvi	https://studentaffairs.jhu.edu/disabilities/about/types-of-disabilities/.
clvii	https://www.understood.org/en/school-learning/special-services/special-education-basics/conditions-covered-under-idea.
clviii	https://studentaffairs.jhu.edu/disabilities/about/types-of-disabilities/.
clix	Ibid.
clx	Center for Disease Control and Prevention. (2013). Developmental disabilities, retrieved October 18, 2013.
clxi	https://www.t2000.com/what-is-a-developmental-disability/.
clxii	https://studentaffairs.jhu.edu/disabilities/about/types-of-disabilities/.
clxiii	U.S. Department of Education, 2000.
clxiv	Education Law Center, 2002.
clxv	https://www.equalityhumanrights.com/en/inquiries-and-investigations/inquiry-disability-related-harassment/background-disability-related-0.

clxvi	https://www.understood.org/en/school-learning/special-services/special-education-basics/conditions-covered-under-idea.
clxvii	https://www.understood.org/en/school-learning/your-childs-rights/basics-about-childs-rights/individuals-with-disabilities-education-act-idea-what-you-need-to-know.
clxviii	https://www.parentcenterhub.org/iep-overview/.
clxix	https://www.stopitnow.org/ohc-content/tip-sheet-family-safety-planning-for-parents-of-children-with-disabilities and https://www.stopitnow.org/ohc-content/tip-sheet-how-to-talk-to-your-child-to-reduce-vulnerability-to-sexual-abuse.
clxx	www.vera.org.
clxxi	Everson, M., and Boat, B. (1989). False allegations of sexual abuse by children and adolescents, Journal of the American Academy of Child and Adolescent Psychiatry. 28, 2:230-35.
clxxii	https://www.childwelfare.gov/organizations/?CWIGFunctionsaction=rols:main.dspList&rolType=Custom&RS_ID=56.
clxxiii	Finkelhor and Dziuba-Leatherman, 1994; Timnick, 1985.
clxxiv	Hanson, et al., 1999.
clxxv	https://www.ptsd.va.gov/professional/treat/specific/ptsd_child_teens.asp#one.

www.ingramcontent.com/pod-product-compliance
Lightning Source LLC
Chambersburg PA
CBHW081150290426
44108CB00018B/2503